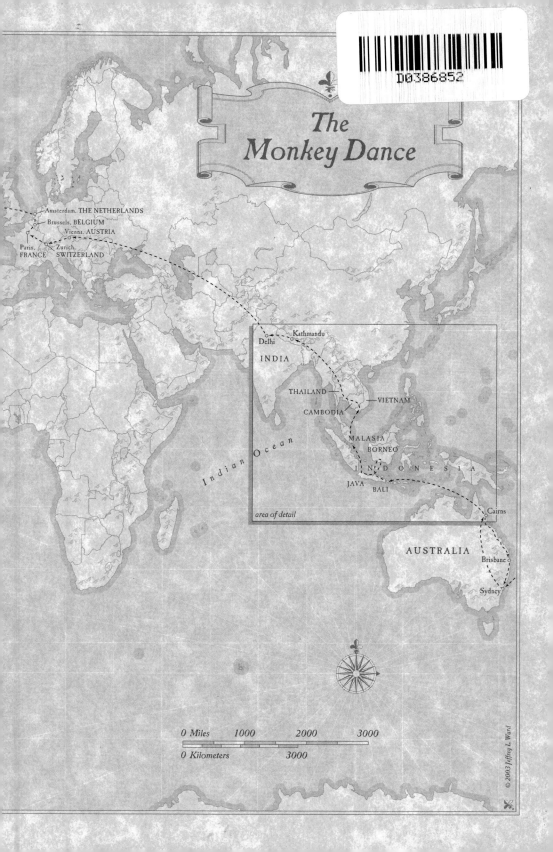

ALSO BY DANIEL GLICK

Powder Burn: Arson, Money, and Mystery on Vail Mountain

MONKEY DANCING

Kolya and Zoe taking an elephant bath
in the Rapti River, Nepal.

MONKEY DANCING

A Father, Two Kids, and a Journey

to the Ends of the Earth

DANIEL GLICK

PublicAffairs

New York

Visit the author's website at www.danielglick.net.
Portions of this book first appeared in *Outside* magazine, in slightly different form.
The author gratefully acknowledges permission to reprint lyrics from "What's the Matter with Parents Today," written by Mike Burkett, published by NOFX Music © 2000.

Published in the United States by PublicAffairs™,
a member of the Perseus Books Group.
PublicAffairs books are available at special discounts for bulk purchases in the U.S. by corporations, institutions, and other organizations. For more information, please contact the Special Markets Department at the Perseus Books Group, 11 Cambridge Center, Cambridge MA 02142, or call (617) 252–5298.

Book design and composition by Mark McGarry
Set in Scala

Library of Congress Cataloging-in-Publication Data
Glick, Daniel.
Monkey dancing: a father, two kids, and a journey to the ends of the earth/by Daniel Glick.
p.cm.
ISBN 1-58648-154-1
1. Glick, Daniel. 2. Single fathers—Colorado—Biography. 3. Divorced men—Colorado—Biography. 4. Single-parent families—Anecdotes. 5. Father child—Anecdotes. 6. Nature—Effect of human beings on. [1. Voyages and travels—Anecdotes.]
I. Title.
HQ759.915.G56 2003
306.874'2—dc21
2002037024

FIRST EDITION
10 9 8 7 6 5 4 3 2 1

To Kolya and Zoe
for teaching me how
to monkey dance

To Zoe and Kolya's mother
for the incomparable gift
of their spirit made flesh

Perhaps it's my natural pessimism, but it seems that an awfully large part of travel these days is to see things while you still can.

BILL BRYSON,
In a Sunburnt Country

———

Nel mezzo del cammin di nostra vita
Mi ritrovai per una selva oscura
Che la diritta via era smarrita

In the middle of life's journey
I found myself in a dark wood
Where the straight path was lost

DANTE,
The Divine Comedy

CONTENTS

AUTHOR'S NOTE

Out of respect for my ex-wife's privacy, I have given her a pseudonym and have remained vague about where she has moved. This is my version of the story, not hers.

With the exception of one set of characters you will meet (and immediately understand why they would not want their names to be used), all events and names in this book are real. In a literary world filled with blurring lines between fiction and nonfiction, I have tried to remain faithful to my journalism school ideals: "Facts" are presented after consulting with multiple sources, and events are recorded through the imperfect but well-intentioned eye and ear of the trained observer.

This book is, however, both a work of journalism and a personal narrative. The nature of the more personal material means that this trained observer's eye is unavoidably skewed at times. In certain cases, especially the events around my brother's illness and death, I took no notes and am relying completely on my memory and the memories of family members. Emotion and time unavoidably cloud those recollections.

PROLOGUE

A FREE TRIP AROUND
THE WORLD

*The author, Kolya, and Zoe, jumping
into the Sekonyer River, Borneo.*

IN THE MIDDLE of the night, after my daughter Zoe woke me for the third time because she was afraid of the snakes, I wondered, not for the first time, whether this trip had really been such an inspired idea. Earlier, Zoe had been complaining about leeches, and before that mosquitoes, and it dawned on me that unless you were raised in the rainforest, accustomed to strangler figs and spiders the size of gerbils, Borneo was a pretty forbidding environment. For a nine-year-old girl reared in suburban Colorado, this place looked down-right menacing. My thirteen-year-old son Kolya, also awakened by his sister, didn't help things when he authoritatively informed Zoe that, since she was the smallest mammal among us, any predator would obviously eat her first.

I shot Kolya a venomous look that temporarily silenced him and reassured Zoe that it was unlikely that snakes could board the 55-foot houseboat (called a *klotok*) where we were sleeping, moored on the banks of the Sekonyer River in southern Kalimantan. She wasn't persuaded. Zoe *knew* the serpents were lurking. Heading upriver earlier that afternoon, past suffocating green jungle crawling from riverbanks and proboscis monkeys hanging from trees like misshapen, mischievous fruit, we'd noticed a sudden movement in the water. Peering ahead, we felt certain it was a crocodile. We were wrong. The animal's head, although almost as big as a crocodile's, belonged to a 20-foot-long python with a body circumference only slightly smaller than my thigh. We gaped with disbelief as the python disappeared into the murky water, leaving deceptively minor ripples.

As the ripples receded, we became especially attentive to other motions in the silty ribbon of river that carried us deeper into the jungle. I felt acutely aware of the reassuring diesel engine chug that muted the unfamiliar and suddenly ominous chirps and creaks and rustles emanating from the overgrown banks. We moved forward from the deck, shaded by a blue plastic canopy jerry-rigged on metal poles, and positioned ourselves on the bow like sentries. Within five minutes, we spotted another serpentine motion in the river and glimpsed a much smaller bright green reptile with a classic triangular-shaped head, slithering with startling speed toward the port-side shore: a pit viper, one of the world's most poisonous snakes.

I held Zoe's hand, tried to convey my amazement rather than fear. In the space of five minutes we had seen proboscis monkeys, with their bulbous, clown-like noses, a species that didn't live anywhere else on the planet—as well as a python and a pit viper. This was what it was all about for me, heading upriver into Heart of Darkness territory with my two children—a voyage to the headwaters of grief, loss, and—who knows?—possibly even the source of healing and grace after such momentous transitions in our lives.

Dual tragedies had propelled the three of us into orbit: my older brother's sudden death from cancer, and the departure of their mother, my wife, after our wrenching divorce. The weight of those losses accompanied us as surely as our backpacks filled with shorts, underwear, Game Boys, guidebooks, traveler's checks, portable CD players, DVDs, mosquito netting, bug spray, asthma medicine, malaria pills, antibiotics, extra passport pictures, my laptop, and Kolya's skateboard.

After a treacherous passage through the past few years, a long, open-ended journey had beckoned to me like a Siren's song. Hitting the road had always served me in times of transition as an entrée into a reflective trance, as a tool of personal reinvention, as literal and metaphorical escape. For much of my life, I had sought psychic salve in the thrill of discovery amidst wild, unfamiliar places and among unpredictable traveling companions. Borneo certainly qualified as wild and unfamiliar, and my two children effortlessly supplied the unpredictability.

Still, I feared that my reflexive tendency toward flight might somehow backfire in my current circumstances. I couldn't even be sure that my trusted traveling muse would pull me from my current chasm of the soul. I certainly couldn't predict what the wild and unfamiliar might do for my two kids in their shell-shocked state. In setting out on this journey, I knew my children and I would encounter both fear and amazement, the inevitable result of exchanging quotidian sureties and the comforts of routine for bumpy bus rides and motorcycle taxi rides and elephant-back rides and the incessant buzzing of mosquitoes in gecko-squawking tropical nights.

What I didn't know was what kind of inner journey we would all take. Here on the Sekonyer River, Kolya had descended into a withdrawn, contentious teen funk. Zoe had entered her own Heart of Darkness territory, portentous and terrifying. For her, this part of the trip was an odyssey to the archetypes of fear, to a motherless land of poisonous snakes and voracious jungle animals that make little girls disappear without a burp.

Instead of liberating ourselves from the daily reminders of our losses, I wondered, would we all come unmoored completely in these unfamiliar and fearsome settings? Was I being selfish beyond all measure? Had I already pushed the kids too far?

That night, after Zoe had finally been coaxed to sleep by the houseboat's lapping lullaby, I worried about the kids' ability to cope with the stress of such an unfamiliar place. No matter how much grown-ups extol kids' adaptability when we change their routines to accommodate our jobs or our upwardly mobile dreams or our divorces, children are the most reactionary of all creatures. If I so much as cut up Kolya's French toast horizontally rather than diagonally when he was four, he would wail as if I had knocked him off his booster. Even entering his teens, he'd eat the same bowl of cereal every morning, spend every afternoon learning to kick-flip his skateboard, pass every weekend evening with as many friends as could gather in front of a Sony Playstation.

I knew this, knew that molding this routine—the Cheerios mornings, the Friday night popcorn and videos at home, the bedtimes and reading times and Saturday morning chores—was all-important as the three of us rearranged our lives. Traipsing around the world, then, where the unfamiliar became commonplace, suddenly seemed like folly rather than the dazzling idea I had imagined.

Here we were in Borneo, where we had come to see the orangutans of Tanjung Puting National Park, two months into our five-month around-the-world odyssey. I had constructed only the basic thread of an itinerary, which was to take the kids to visit a few of the planet's great ecological wonders that were in danger of disappearing as the consequence of human development. Already the three of us had completed a five-day "walkabout" on an Australian rainforest island, shooed five-foot-long lace monitor lizards away from our tent site, spotted several rare and endangered cassowary birds, scuba dived and snorkeled off the Great Barrier Reef, and climbed the highest mountain in Bali, among other adventures. There were months yet to come, however, including more jungle treks in Vietnam and Nepal, surreal border crossings into Cambodia, and, although we didn't know it yet, the even more surreal events of September 11, 2001, still two weeks away, that changed the tenor of the whole world.

*

As with any relationship that falls apart, in a marriage it's almost impossible to point to a moment where the unraveling began, which thread caught on which nail and hooked the fabric, so that the next tug and the tug after continued until the inevitable disintegration. So many marriages fail, but they all seem to fail for different reasons—a particular combination of childhood wounds, grown-up disappointments, and maybe even karmic predisposition, unique to each couple.

Rebecca and I, happily married for fifteen years with two great kids, had watched smugly as our friends struggled, separated, and split up, never dreaming we might join the ranks of the divorced. We had always enjoyed the kind of marriage that, if tested in a reality-TV show with our married peers, would have been voted "least likely to break up." The cameras would follow us into our bedroom, voyeurs would see that after seventeen years of living together, we still told stories about our day, about our kids, laughing so hard the toothpaste slush squirted on the mirror, finding passion in our familiar bodies, tenderness in each other's touch.

When the marriage did disintegrate, we at least had a slightly unusual way of cleaving apart. Yes, she fell in love with somebody else, a story as old as dirt, but that somebody else was another woman, which seemed a novel, fin de siècle, Baby Boomer, post-feminist way of going about calling it quits. Even in the face of a potential change in sexual orientation, we didn't give up easily and spent a year or more trying hard to trim the wayward threads and hold the marriage together: marriage therapy, a reconciliation after the first affair, a promise and sincere effort to break new ground. But slowly, inexorably, our marriage, our family as we knew it, came apart.

We both sensed the confusion in our kids. They had certainly seen their friends' parents in the active stages of breaking up, heard about the fights and the lawyers and the confusion. Our kids obviously felt a little like I did: How could their parents, who always appeared so happy, divorce? Didn't we start our marriage with a three-year honeymoon traveling around Asia, hadn't we just taken adventurous trips to Pakistan and Costa Rica together? Kolya and Zoe knew the creation myth of their parents' relationship like an ancient Greek child knew about Earth and Sky and Zeus and Athena: how I had met Rebecca while wearing black tights in a modern dance class when we were both undergraduates at UC Berkeley; how I had come home that day and told my younger brother Steve that I had met the mother of my children. How it came to pass that we were married and the kids were born, wanted, and loved. And they saw that it was good.

Like their dad, they wondered how it had all unraveled so fast.

And like their dad, they had to figure out how to make sense of their lives again.

Confusion or no, Rebecca pronounced the marriage dead, and when one person comes to that conclusion it's a decision for two. Or in this case, four. After we split, our lives took even more unexpected turns. When Rebecca left, I assumed that we would become another of the ubiquitous couples who, after a predictable period of being insufferable toward each other, find a modus vivendi to pass the kids back and forth to each other's houses on alternating weeks. In time, we would accommodate each other to allow for a special weekend away with the new boyfriend/girlfriend, to attend a workshop or a class reunion or a ski trip with old friends.

I was completely surprised, then, when she informed me she planned to move to the West Coast. "You know, you can't take the kids if you move there," I told her, armed with a vague notion of Colorado law that made me think that she couldn't move out of state with the kids simply in order to move in with her new lover, whatever the gender.

She surprised me again. "I know. I'm moving there anyway."

Then I panicked. Her living at that distance would preclude, among other things, the possibility of her picking the kids up from school if they fell ill in the middle of the day while I went on an assignment for *Newsweek,* where I worked as a roving Rocky Mountain correspondent. How was I supposed to make a living covering breaking news from Montana to New Mexico with a seven-year-old and an eleven-year-old at home?

And so I "got the kids." Given all the possible choices and creative alternatives that parents come up with in the divorce-crazy times we live in, I never thought that Kolya and Zoe would live with me virtually full-time. In truth, I'm not sure I would have really enjoyed the unsettling week-on, week-off arrangement that so many couples have negotiated. Each time Zoe arranges a play date these days I ask, "Am I taking you to (*fill in friend's name here*) mom's or her dad's?" Scattered around the kitchen on scraps of paper, I have written various friends' vital information: mom's home phone, her cell phone, at her boyfriend's home, the dad's home phone, cell phone, and his second wife's work phone and cell phone as well. We, too, are members of the new American family, needing a dictionary of terms that extends beyond half-brother and stepsister to include, for example, the niece of my ex-wife's live-in girlfriend, or my girlfriend Tory's brother's male partner.

Rebecca and I first separated a little more than two years before this trip, in the spring of 1998. At first we traded off weeks staying at a friend's house while the kids remained in their own rooms in our family home. Then, for six months while we sorted out the divorce, Rebecca sublet a house two doors down from me. We conducted a week-on, week-off trade, with the kids free to roam back and forth between the two houses to pick up forgotten homework and favorite sweaters. We even managed, by the end, to be civil enough for me to visit her house and watch *Monday Night Football* with Kolya on the rental house's cable, since I didn't have television reception.

Then she moved to the West Coast.

Then I subscribed to cable.

The process of becoming a single parent became an odyssey,

and it still is. During most of the marriage I had been the sole wage earner, and the Ward and June Cleaver overtones of our lives had amused us at times. Neither of us had ever imagined such a stereotypical existence when we married, a month before Rebecca's twenty-third birthday, when I was twenty-seven. After three years of Asian travels together, including a year's stint as English teachers in Japan, we arrived home, unemployed. I enrolled in a journalism master's program at Berkeley, dreaming of becoming a foreign correspondent, and Kolya was born during my first year of journalism boot camp. My postgraduate internship miraculously turned into a job in Washington, D.C., as a *Newsweek* correspondent in 1989. Suddenly, I felt like the Tom Hanks character in the movie *Big*, a kid masquerading as a grown-up, flying on Air Force One and scribbling furiously on a notepad when President Bush the First came back to chat up the captive reporters. For nearly six years I was based in D.C., wore a coat and tie, rode the train to work a block from the White House, and arrived home just in time for a late dinner.

During those years, just before and after Zoe was born and while Kolya was a toddler transforming into a kindergartner, Rebecca admirably discharged the dual duties of full-time mom and part-time student earning a master's degree in education. The division of labor generally adhered to traditional lines, although I tried to be a sensitive New Age dad. I happily played with Kolya when I came home from work, helped with dinner and dishes, and became the designated toilet cleaner. I would feel like a hero when I gave Rebecca a break and took Kolya to the park on Sunday afternoons, sitting on a bench reading the *Washington Post* while he played on the swings.

Rebecca held down the fort in every way. She researched the preschools, kept track of the doctors' appointments, the immunizations, the kids' friends' birthday party gifts, my family's birthdays and Christmas presents, and most of the sundry niceties and necessities of keeping a household of four together. Her work was especially grueling when I served the cruel master of weekly deadlines and wouldn't see the kids awake for two days at a stretch, or when I departed on open-ended assignments.

"Oh, by the way, darlin', I have to go to Haiti today with the troops. Don't know when I'll be back. I'll call when I can. Don't wait up."

Like most couples, we split the remaining chores according to inclination, disinclination, or expertise. She balanced the checkbook, I fixed the plumbing. She cooked for our potlucks on weekends with friends, I filled in health insurance forms. She took care of car repairs, I did the ironing. It seemed like we held down more than two full-time jobs between us, but we both worked hard and felt morally superior to our friends who employed nannies to raise their children or relied on electronic babysitters. We didn't even own a functioning television, preferring reading time with Mom and Dad, games, made-up stories, and big-bed wrestling matches to the one-eyed time-stealer.

How, then, did I end up here, with their formerly full-time mother a thousand miles away, me dragging Kolya out of groggy sleep for middle school in the dark, making his breakfast, filling out field trip forms, double-checking to see if the orthodontist's appointment was today or tomorrow? Coaxing him out the door just in time to awaken Zoe for the winter morning ritual of cooking hot cereal, asking her exactly what she wanted in her lunch, reminding her to ask her friend what she wanted for her birthday gift for this Saturday's party? Wondering what to make for dinner, would there be just enough milk for tomorrow's breakfast, did I really have to attend the soccer club's annual meeting, how come I just washed the dishes last night and it already looked like the kitchen had been assaulted by a Class V hurricane?

At times I worked myself into a homicidal rage, blaming every indignity of my current life on Rebecca's departure, every Kolya and Zoe meltdown on the psychological trauma of being maternally abandoned. I felt confounded by the complexities of raising a girl who would begin wearing a bra in fourth grade and overwhelmed by the challenge of shepherding a punk-rocking teenage boy through high school. I didn't see how I could learn to become a respectable single dad, earn a living, and simultaneously keep the household running. It was too much.

I had always appreciated single mothers, I reminded myself.

But never enough.

As our marriage unraveled, an even more destructive personal storm brewed elsewhere. My older brother Bob, an emergency room doctor in rural northern California, found a suspicious lump in his breast a few months after Rebecca and I separated. We could barely conceive of the worst, since breast cancer in men is so rare. The bump was surely a sports injury, we thought, another bump or bruise or break or tear from Bob's jockish insistence on playing basketball with men twenty years his junior.

Then came the biopsy and the dreadful diagnosis. He had surgery, four rounds of chemotherapy, and was told he had a 90-plus percent five-year survival rate because the cancer hadn't spread very far. Then, less than a year after the surgery, he lost weight inexplicably and learned from a bone scan that he only had a few months to live.

I spent more time with him in the last year of his life than I had collectively in the previous twenty years. Despite the fact that we considered each other to be close friends and confidants, I had to face the fact that I hadn't always been there for him. While he had suffered through a destructive first marriage and nightmare divorce, I had often been unavailable, pursuing my self-absorbed travels or, later, my career. As his breast cancer progressed and I dropped everything to be with him, another question leered at me, tearing at my personal myth of fraternal closeness: Had I even been a good enough brother?

On January 14, 2001, Bob was gone, one year to the day after a Boulder County judge formally certified the end of my marriage.

*

My two children and I were tenuously recovering from these back-to-back January shocks when I saw a news article on coral reefs proclaiming that nearly half of them would die within my lifetime. The headline underscored what I already knew: that life forms were vanishing from this planet faster than you can say "Charles Darwin." In that moment, tragedy mixed with promise, and I decided it was time to take the kids to see a few of these wonders before they were gone.

"Before they're gone" became my mantra for this trip—with a triple *entendre*. The first, literal meaning directed me to show Kolya and Zoe this planet's amazing animals and environments before overpopulation, poverty, global climate change, pollution, and development maimed or destroyed them. The global devastation of wild places during my lifetime mirrored my other losses, touching me no less profoundly. In my years of traveling to where the wild things still are, I had experienced the magic of watching moose graze at sunrise near my backcountry campsite. I had felt the frisson of danger sizzle my neck hairs while horseback riding in grizzly country. I had internalized the pure spiritual wonder of red-tinged sunrays streaming from thunderclouds like a holy writ, while an autumn breeze brushed past like a whisper of God's breath. The cumulative effect, I realized, was that I had fallen in love with my planet.

My kids, raised on flashes of music videos and DSL Internet downloads, had only the barest suburban inklings of the natural world that I clung to as my spiritual core. Perhaps I could help them make a deeper connection during this trip. After all, I had spent much of my journalism career covering national and international environmental issues; I had the background and contacts to bring global environmental issues into Kolya's and Zoe's consciousness.

The trip's second goal instructed me to seize this otherwise inglorious personal transition and use it to spend time with my children before they left my reconfigured single father's nest. In the fall Kolya would start eighth grade and Zoe fourth, and I could already tell they would become fledglings too soon. I wanted to get to know them; I wanted them to know me. I wanted to forge a new family of three using adventure as our crucible.

Lastly, the big "before they're gone" loomed especially large: after witnessing my brother's untimely death at forty-eight, I knew viscerally that I possessed no guarantees regarding how long any of us would be around. Electing to do something drastic, I nominated an epic road trip.

I broached the subject with the kids in February, as the reality of Bob's death sunk in like the winter darkness. "How would you like," I said, putting on my best game show do-you-want-what's-behind-door-number-two announcer voice, "A Free Trip Around the World!" After a bit of bafflement about what I was saying, they realized I was serious. Zoe waxed immediately enthusiastic. Kolya negotiated: Could we go surfing someplace along the way? "Why not?" I replied. Could he take his skateboard? "Sure." They'd have to miss school, of course. Not a problem, or as we would later say, "no worries." Did they want an Australia–Southeast Asia–Japan swing, or maybe go all the way around the world? Around the world won unanimously.

In mid-March, the idea sprouted wings. I investigated air tickets, researched ecological case studies, and became a walking "to do" list: rent the house, pack, clean, get immunizations, and arrange to pay all my bills online from Internet cafés in Sydney, Singapore, Phnom Penh, Kathmandu, and elsewhere. For several months I was adding two more items to the list for every one I completed. We shopped and negotiated for Game Boys (there *would* be long plane and bus rides), a laptop with DVD capabilities (there *would* be times when entertainment would be at a premium), electrical connectors and adapters, and beneath-the-shorts passport holders, and argued over essential items (no, Zoe, you will not need high-heeled boots on this trip). I arranged for insurance of all sorts to be shifted or canceled or altered or prepaid (I'll need travel insurance—and if I change our health insurance policy, will Zoe's asthma be considered a preexisting condition?). At the last minute, I was still packing and cleaning while friends dropped by to run a vacuum or take out trash or just lend moral support.

Along the way, I collected little aphorisms that bolstered my decision to do something so rash. Like treasures found at each stop in a scavenger hunt, people offered them unsolicited. A friend who had been in the car as a child when his father had crashed it and died said, "When you come face to face with death, you realize that life isn't endless." While waiting in the dentist's office for Kolya's teeth cleaning, I found a book quoting Mark Twain, that wry wanderer: "Twenty years from now you will be more disappointed by the things you didn't do than by the ones you did do. So throw off the bowlines. Sail away from the safe harbor. Catch the trade winds in your sails. Explore. Dream. Discover." In another place, Goethe weighed in on the subject: "Whatever you can do, or believe you can, begin it. Boldness has genius, power and magic in it."

The words resonated like a coach's pep talk, countering the voices (some of them mine) asking what the kids would do about school, what I would do about work, why I was being so damned irresponsible, and whether I really planned to take the kids to Borneo, for Chrissakes? What would I do if they were lost, or if somebody stole Zoe from a toilet stall in the Ho Chi Minh airport, surgically altered her face, and sold her to a wealthy Bedouin on the black market? What if we all contracted dengue fever and yellow fever and rheumatic fever and malaria and dysentery and cholera and hepatitis A and B? How could I break the news to Rebecca?

Uh, Rebecca, hi, this is Dan. I'm calling from Saigon.
How are the kids?
Uh, well, Kolya's doing fine. He's growing like a weed. He likes the food here.
And Zoe?
That's sort of what I'm calling about. Interpol's on the case . . .

We threw a going-away party for ourselves with all our friends, a wild, tequila-laced bacchanalia, letting rip for the grown-ups, a group catharsis. "As soon as you leave, you know you'll be a folk hero to all of us," a musician friend told me, leaning on a margarita as the sun set over the Rockies from our back deck. I thought, yes, why not, we'll become folk heroes! Let people tell tales of our exploits (posted on the Web, of course). Let them say they'd like to do the same thing someday, knowing they never will themselves. A friend approached me, serious. "I've been doing genealogical research, Dan," he said, and I wonder why. "I found out you're my father." I looked at him blankly, not getting it. He helped me out. "You have to take me with you."

Shortly after Rebecca and I separated, I began dating Tory. She and I had met through mutual friends on a backcountry ski trip, and after Tory heard that my wife and I had separated, she offered condolences as a veteran of an eleven-year marriage that went south. With alluring blue-green eyes and a knowledgeable guide's compassion (Tory had divorced three years ahead of me), she offered a tantalizing diversion. After a single date, she told me she was moving to Idaho to become a wilderness ranger for the summer and invited me to come up and hike.

I smiled wanly and told her that wouldn't be likely, given my single-dad status.

Three months after Rebecca and I separated, she and the kids visited her family in Maine for ten days. I had made plans to go backpacking with a buddy, but he canceled at the last minute because of an injury. I remembered Tory's offer, called, and asked if I could still meet her. We backpacked in the Sawtooths and the White Clouds, then met on her days off in Jackson Hole to climb and frolick in the Tetons, where she had once been a rock-climbing search-and-rescue ranger. It felt fabulous to sense such a strong attraction to her athletic body, to the smell of her thick, shoulder-length brown hair, to her grace and sleekness as we dove naked into mountain lakes. I wondered: Could there be life after Rebecca?

Maybe, but not so fast. Tory moved back to Colorado, and we continued to see each other. Over the next two years, I felt like an emotional cripple trying to limp up a rocky, tortuous path to a new relationship. I read books about rebound relationships (warning women never to date a man until he's been divorced for a year) and concluded that I couldn't move seamlessly from marriage to new relationship. A friend offered sage advice when I told him that Tory and I were having trouble getting on the same relationship page. "Of course you are," he said. "You guys are in different time zones."

So we struggled. Rebecca went AWOL, moving to the coast and calling the kids only infrequently that first year. I rarely wanted to leave the kids to go on dates with Tory, revolving my life around their schedules and not exactly being the most spontaneous and open partner. Bob's sickness and death consumed whatever heart I had left.

Finally, when I started planning this trip with the kids, I told Tory that I would need to head off as a single dad, as a single man.

Then I wanted her to come along.

Then I didn't.

Then I wanted her to come along for part of the time.

I was maddening.

Just weeks before leaving, I proposed a thoroughly uncomfortable compromise: I would leave with the freedom of a single man, but she would join us in Bali six weeks into the trip. We were both free in the meantime, but we held hopes that we could be together during the trip and beyond.

It was wildly unrealistic and, from my point of view, completely necessary.

From Tory's point of view, it was simply unrealistic and painful.

What I needed more than anything was this: the illusion that I was single, carefree, flirtatious, and available. My relationship with Rebecca had lasted seventeen years, and I had moved almost immediately into another monogamous relationship with Tory. I didn't trust it, couldn't discern if I was turning to Tory out of loneliness and fear or had truly found a too-lucky-to-believe new love. I needed to rediscover who I was again, not who I was in relationship with a woman. I wasn't at all sure whether, or when, I'd be ready to enter into another pairing.

The day before we left, I gathered the kids into a circle with me in my bedroom with a picture of Bob in the center. It is a difficult picture to look at, taken months before he died. He is braced on a walking stick, his hair and beard grown back thick but his legs skinny, his face thin but not yet gaunt. But he is dying in the picture, I can see that now. I reminded Kolya and Zoe of what I had said at Uncle Bob's memorial service: People who die live on in the memories of those who loved them. In many ways, Bob's death had inspired this trip, and I wanted to take a moment with the kids to dedicate our trip to his memory. Kolya, teen and rebellious about anything that seemed New Age (he called it "ooga-chucka"), still grasped my offered hand and took Zoe's when I offered it with a nod. Zoe held my hand and her brother's, looking solemnly at each of us in turn.

We stood for a moment, spontaneous tears welling together, our circle of three, and lit some candles.

To Bob, then.

To us.

I arranged with the kids' schools to bring math homework, to make sure they read, and to have them write regularly in trip diaries. In an attempt to habituate them to journaling, I compelled them to write a pre-trip entry at my parents' house in California a few days before we left for Australia.

Kolya's enthusiastic first entry:

This is making me pretty pissed off, I hate writing for no reason, and my dad is being such a dick about it, god. I know I'll love looking back on this, but I just don't want to right now. I am ok with writing in this journal, I even want to, because I'll love it when I'm older, but it might be a problem for me to write in it on a day to day basis. This is a pretty important entry in my dad's opinion, so I'm gonna simmer down and write how I am feeling about leaving.

Right now, we are with the whole family up in Tahoe. We only have a few more days up here until we go down to San Francisco. From there, we head off in to the wild blue yonder, never to set foot on American soil for another five months. As of right now, I am nothing but excited to get going. We travel a lot, and its not a big deal to be away for a week, so I am fine right now, but I know I'll start missing home soon enough.

Australia is a place that I have always wanted to go, so this makes me even more excited right now. When my dad very first mentioned that we could go on a trip all of us, around the world, I was super psyched, I had heard all kinds of stories from my mom and dad's travels, as well as the travels of my dad in Africa with grandma and grandpa. But I had no idea that we would actually go, so when he asked I just decided to say yes for the time being, thinking that my dad was just blowing off steam.

Somewhere around one month after he had originally mentioned it, he brought it up again. Zoe and I were so surprised that he still had the idea, so we actually took him a little more seriously than the last time. This time, I had just come in from a fun day skating with Sam, Ben, and Michael, so the thought of going away for an extended period of time seemed out of the question. My overall message to him from this discussion was that I didn't want to go, but if we had to, only for the last 2 months of summer. That way I got some fun and I also got to play football that next season. I was still fairly confident that this was still one of those things that he would "grow out of," so I still wasn't too worried.

By April or so, my dad had talked enough about this that I realized this was a big enough mid-life crisis that he might actually follow through. At this point, I said forget it to football and set another limit of being home for Christmas. I tried as hard as I could to sound like there was no budging on this part for me, but then again, I had tried to do it for the football thing too and maybe I would change my mind again.

To skip forward in time a little bit, when the school year was over, my dad had bought the tickets, so we were going for sure. I had the best month of my life in that little lapse of time between school being out, and us leaving on the trip, which made it about ten times harder to leave. I was pretty pissed, and if I had had the power I might have cancelled, but I didn't, so I couldn't.

The goodbye between me and most of my friends was pretty awkward, it consisted of a "see ya later man", and a hi-five. I was still pretty excited at this time, but whenever I thought about how long I was gonna be gone, I was a little nervous.

The day before I left, I was talking with Sam. We were talking about the trip, and Sam said "Dude, there is no way that you are going to last the whole five. Either your dad is gonna get too fucking fed up with you and Zoe, or one of you is gonna get some kind of nasty ass disease, and you'll have to come home. I would bet money on it." This had never occurred to me before, and I thought about betting him, but it made too much sense at the time.

I wonder if we will make it the whole five months, that's a long time.

Zoe, a few days later:

My Around the World Trip

My uncle was sick, he had breast cancer. Everyone in my family was sad. We visited him now and then, but mostly we stayed home. After a cople of months we thought he was better, but it was spreading worse and worse into his bones. We didn't know until it was too late. He took some medicine, but a few months later he died. One day my dad had a strange feeling, he came up to us and said "hey kids wanna take a trip around the world?" Next thing I knew I was on the plane to Australlia.

PART 1

THE FIRST MONKEY DANCE

Kolya swinging from a lawyer vine,
Hinchinbrook Island, Australia.

Something Unpredictable

We winged our way west and south, San Francisco to Sydney, thirteen hours in a flying aluminum can, the kids playing Game Boys and waiting for their chicken Caesar salads to arrive in our business-class accommodations. To start the trip with pure frivolousness, I posted 13,000 hard-earned miles as bond (we *did* earn them flying back and forth to California to be with Bob, after all) and upgraded the first leg of our round-the-world coach tickets. At the airport, in our first small-world experience, we met the counselor at Zoe's school, who worked with kids like Zoe whose parents were getting divorced. Zoe proclaimed her amazement, we all felt a little excited by seeing a familiar face, the kids so jazzed and nervous, geared up for the adventure and struck by the magic of such a chance meeting.

I needed a little more frivolity again, even as I undertook this enormous responsibility of wrestling these two children around the planet. I realized I'd been overcompensating for being the only parent, going on overdrive to keep a semblance of order in the house, burned out trying to keep Rules and Boundaries and Routine for the kids, and for myself. By the time I was into the second Bloody Mary proffered by the solicitous steward, I already didn't care that Kolya began his meal by eating the cookie. Zoe fed me bites of chicken salad as she swayed to her headphones, and I stared out the window noticing that the plane couldn't quite catch up with the sun. She dove giddily into a way-above-average fruit bowl, sprinkled with chunks of mango or papaya and pineapple. "We're going to be plucking this stuff off the trees!" she exclaimed. I kissed her forehead, snuggled her into an embrace, felt smug embarking on such an amazing adventure.

Later, the foie gras consumed, the Côtes du Rhône imbibed, the filet mignon digesting, the port downed, I allowed myself a self-congratulatory pause. What a coup to begin this trip in the lap of luxury: Red Carpet waiting room, airline chairs reclining seven ways to heaven, video choices throughout the evening and night. We departed at just past 11 P.M., which, as we figured out, was sometime in the very early afternoon tomorrow in Australia. "This is as good as it gets," the kids enthused to each other, even amidst the tension and fear of leaving friends, stuffed animals, and poster-plastered rooms behind. Zoe, with her travel pillow around her neck and earphones on, leaned over, kissed me, and enthused, "This is the life, eh?" Kolya nodded and offered a gang-like hand-wagging sign of approval.

I countered that they should remember this scene when we were stuck in some mosquito-infested swamp in Borneo.

They laughed.

We didn't have to wait even until the plane landed for their exuberance to turn into vile, Jekyll and Hyde brother-sister torment. Somewhere in there, when the quarter of a Halcion I'd fed each of the kids wore off and they emerged, still before the sun, their anxiety took form not with simple fidgeting but in downright nastiness. "Dad, how come she's soooooo stupid?" Kolya whined, when Zoe couldn't figure out how to switch from video mode to video game mode on the personalized seat-back machines. "Just help her,

Kolya," I replied, sighing, since I couldn't figure it out, either. Zoe, understandably, doesn't like being called stupid, and she exacted her piercing revenge at decibel levels that could have possibly interfered with the captain's navigational instruments. Fellow travelers looked askance at me as if to ask, "Isn't their *mother* around here somewhere?"

Now mothers, I've noticed, don't have the corner on the market on eliciting good plane behavior from children of any age, but still I felt the onus of my single fatherhood prominently challenged by wayward glances—especially in our upgraded business-class seats. Ironically, the front page of *USA Today* distributed free in our class of service cataloged how business-class service wasn't what it used to be, how the hoi polloi with too many frequent flier miles on their hands cashed them in and—God forbid—took their children with them. These first-class wannabes even had the temerity to wear shorts on the plane, confirmed by the fact that both Kolya and I were (apparently inappropriately) exposing our knees.

Kolya again questioned Zoe's IQ in vicious tones, my bubble of self-satisfaction burst spectacularly, and we hadn't even crossed the equator. Why, again, was I doing this? I thought about my own travel experiences, how important it had been in my life to see the incredible disparity between privilege and poverty and the relativity of everything. How much those trips had forged my connection to the natural world—during safaris to Tanzanian game parks to see cheetahs, while witnessing erupting volcanoes and howler monkeys in Costa Rica, by listening to the nocturnal scampering of reptiles in Death Valley's sand washes in my native California.

My own wanderings, youthful and otherwise, had produced formative experiences of both hiding and seeking. I'd spent a year in East Africa as a kid, when, feeling both liberated and abandoned by my mother's frequent work trips, Bob and I had pursued precocious exploits. In my teens, I headed off on hitchhiking forays into wilderness areas throughout the United States and Canada, beginning a lifetime of backcountry wanderings. Europe beckoned in my early twenties, and I spent two years, on and off, kicking around the Old Country while I dropped out of college four times and postponed my career choice. Rebecca and I traveled for three years in Asia as newlyweds on a voyage of marital discovery and ongoing vocational uncertainty. Later, as a journalist, I had been on various reporting trips to Haiti, Pakistan, Siberia, France, Australia, and Mexico.

With this trip, I wanted my children to see and understand how they are blessed and favored by the luck of the cosmic draw, as I've been. I don't know what effect these travels will have on them, but I am certain it will be profound.

It is 1967. I am eleven, Bob is just about to turn fifteen, and our youngest brother Stevie is nine. We are flying, first class, from California to New York to Frankfort to Tel Aviv to Rome to Cairo to Khartoum to Kampala, Uganda. Mom was hired by the Ford Foundation, part of her graduate-school dissertation research in education and linguistics, and she is taking all of us to Africa for a year. Dad takes a sabbatical from his medical practice, they pull us out of school before Christmas, we stop to see cousins in New York who think we're developmentally disabled because we've never had gloves on before and can't put the fingers in the right places. But we're from California, we don't know from cold in New York in December. They live in huge brick apartment complexes, thousands of people in each of them, nobody even glancing at each other in the elevator. I look around, incredulous, feeling like I want to wave my hand in front of some dour woman's face and see if she's alive. It is all so new. I feel already like I am in a foreign country.

We stop to see family in Israel. My dad's first cousin married an Israeli man who owns an Alpha Romeo. We are driving very fast to go to a place, the Golan Heights, where there had just been a war or something. We see overturned Russian tanks, bunkers, barbed wire. When we stop to pee we are told not to wander, there are still live mines everywhere. We look over into Syria, those bastards, my uncle says. Bombing poor kids in the kibbutzes, they all have to play in little tunnels, which sounds a little like fun to me. On the way home, we eat spicy sandwiches in pocket bread, and all around teeming marketplaces and people shouting in Hebrew and Arabic and wearing clothes with so many colors, scarves, headdresses.

We are traveling forever. I trace our path southward over the earth in an imaginary movie montage, can't believe that I am now in Cairo, now in Khartoum, what evocative names, what exotic places! At home I have been looking at my globe, the countries with different colors and the oceans so big in between the continents. We arrive in Entebbe, drive the 60 miles to the capital, passing the equator—the equator!—on the way, marked by what seem to be pairs of enormous elephant tusks, and the mud huts and thatched roofs and children running naked and women with babies on their backs wrapped like papooses just staring at our car and us.

My brothers and I fight in the back seat.

We landed in Sydney, changed planes in a daze, and caught another plane to Cairns, in northeast Queensland. By the time we landed, hailed a cab to our hotel, and settled in, we had been traveling for twenty hours. While the clocks read mid-afternoon in Australia, our whacked-out bodies told us it was still yesterday in San Francisco. The kids really wanted to sleep, but I forced them to stay up, like a torture, until seven o'clock, resetting their circadian rhythms to our new time zone. I forcibly marched Kolya around the room at one point, and we managed somehow by playing cards and watching TV to make it past sunset, which, thankfully, came early because of the Southern Hemisphere winter. Zoe, too tired to understand my chipper explanation for the backward seasons Down Under, merely whimpered. Besides, it was warm outside, with palm trees. The collective assault was too much to take in.

As the sunset brought the kids blessed sleep, I replayed our first bipolar day, wild highs and crushing lows, the kind of day I knew would happen and yet so hard. Fatigue, transition, boredom, fear— all rolled up into one fight or another, the three of us going at it in every conceivable mathematical combination: me vs. Kolya; me vs. Zoe; Zoe vs. Kolya; Kolya and Zoe vs. Dad; Kolya and Dad vs. Zoe; Zoe and Dad vs. Kolya. Zoe screamed and yelled and behaved inappropriately in public places. Even in the hotel room, she howled at Kolya's tortures as if we were at home rather than on the eleventh floor of a resort hotel. Worried about being evicted, I lost it and screamed back.

I realized with almost adrenal fear that I no longer possessed my main parental disciplinary tools, the threats of "consequences": no television or no sleepovers or no playing after school. I felt the way prison guards must feel when their charges are in for the duration, life without parole, maybe even death row. These kids had nothing to lose but their Game Boys, and removing that source of self-directed entertainment would inflict more hardship on me than it would on them. And they knew it.

I would need to be clever, patient, wise, forbearing.

I would yell a lot.

At that moment, I plunged once again into that great universal reservoir of parental patience, the magical pond that has allowed most of us to squirm through childhood and teenagerhood into adulthood without being strangled by our parents. I reminded myself that Kolya and Zoe were just thirteen and nine, and as different as two kids can be.

Kolya, fully engaged in puberty, now grows as he sleeps. Our shoes are the same size already, and by the end of the trip he will complain that mine, size eleven and a half, are too small for him. He is all about punk bands and skateboard videos, surreptitious Britney Spears sexual fantasies and budding rebellion, exacting about the food he will eat, opinionated about any subject he opines upon, and dismissive of any subject that doesn't interest him. His blue eyes already draw adoring glances from teenage girls, but he doesn't yet realize he's going to be a looker. He wears his dirty blond hair short, buzzed tight on the sides, invariably covered by a backwards baseball cap.

Zoe, four full years his junior, with shoulder-length brown hair and brown eyes like her mother, exudes an energy so exuberant and expressive that people are drawn to her like a magnet. Her aunt once gave her a pink tutu Cinderella ball costume for Christmas, and Zoe wore it to school for most of the year, until she looked like the pre-ball Cinderella who still scrubbed fireplaces. Zoe will try most anything that is beyond her ken and pushing her capabilities. As a kid at the playground, Kolya would never try anything he couldn't do, which is why I could read the paper while he played. Taking Zoe to the park, on the other hand, resembled a suicide watch: If she could climb up something, she was equally capable of jumping off. Now that she is a prepubescent with a penchant for cuss words and cosmopolitan pronouncements on fashion and style, I sometimes forget she has not yet hit ten years old.

After a rest day to let our bodies catch up a little, we picked up our new roving home: a rental Toyota Hiace camper van from a business with the cryptic Aussie name of *Travellers Auto Barn,* two "l's" and no apostrophe. It's a basic model, smaller than a VW van, with just enough room in the front seat for Zoe to squeeze in between Kolya and me, now driving on the right side of the car and the left side of the road.

> We just got our camper van in Cairns. It's decent, but certainly not great. It has everything that we need: a fridge, beds to sleep three people, an oven, a stove, and a table. The bad parts of this is that the van is from like 1986 or something, and it's pretty rickety, also, we have to sit three people up front all squished together, and there is no stereo besides a crappy FM radio, not even a tape player. All in all, it's not too bad, and I'm sure I will live, as soon as Zoe stops crying so much.

We soon filled the cupboard with unfamiliar brand food we purchased at Woolworth's, which we quickly learned to call "Woolies," and began unearthing the van's minor eccentricities. A hard right turn overpowered the cupboard door catch, until we learned to wedge a backpack between the sink and the door. If we didn't crank the refrigerator power to high while we drove, we would drain the battery that kept things cool overnight.

I had planned for our first leg to be a gentle introduction to the traveler's way—nothing too challenging. We had our tortoise shell on wheels, people spoke English, okay Australian, and we would see kangaroo road kill and wallabies by our campsite and eat sausage rolls and fish and chips. Our first environmental stop on the itinerary would be to explore issues of the Great Barrier Reef region: where, as the tourist brochures promised, "the rainforest meets the reef."

We began by heading toward Daintree National Park, the "tropical north" in mind-bending antipodal fashion. Zoe temporarily complained about being relegated to the middle seat, but Kolya really couldn't fit there and even Zoe could see that. We settled in and drove up the coast on a beautiful July day, tropical green everywhere and a coastline that ends somewhere just south of Papua New Guinea. Suddenly a perfect song comes on the radio and we experience a sound-track-to-a-movie moment, with Green Day blaring "Good Riddance (Time of Your Life)" through the van's cheap speakers at high volume—a song, remarkably, that we all know. We sang in unison, making our own road movie, passing through fields of sugarcane and coastal vistas, windows rolled down, warm Australian air infiltrating our nostrils and lungs and brain cells. I could imagine the camera panning, following the van down the highway, the cinematographer pulling back until we were a white speck in a vast sea of green, music filling the theater. We grinned wildly at the perfect, exhilarating sequence. Five months won't be enough time, I thought. We could, we should, do this forever.

"Tell us an Uncle Bob story," they begged, when the song ended and we cruised further north, sated with snacks and drinks and not needing to go to the bathroom or really end up anywhere at all except for wherever we would sleep tonight. Somehow they knew how much Bob occupied my thoughts; they had witnessed how I had dropped everything to be with their uncle as he was dying. They didn't know, couldn't know, how much I struggled as I replayed scenes from our lives.

Kolya and Zoe want a Bob story, of course they do. We thrive on stories. Stories we tell, stories we hear.

After their mom and I separated, my family came through the way families are supposed to, and Uncle Bob in particular really rose to the occasion, calling up from California to talk, especially to Kolya. A few months before Rebecca pronounced our marriage irreconcilable, Bob had sent me a ticket to visit him on Super Bowl weekend, a fraternal attempt to use televised sports as communion during a time of crisis. Over that weekend he commiserated with me, having already been there: a classic California divorce, messy and tortuous and interminably expensive. I was so wrapped up in my marital trauma that it wasn't until later that I realized that I had never sent *him* a ticket to watch a Super Bowl together after he and his wife parted ways. I wondered if he ever felt like I had abandoned him as he struggled to leave his unlovely marriage.

More than seven years had passed since his divorce, but he remained virtually estranged from his daughter and struggled painfully with his son. He wished he had good advice for me, he said, shaking his head at his own abject failure with his first family. In a miserable attempt to cheer me up, he told me that his second marriage was a godsend—which wasn't exactly what I wanted to hear.

We watched the game in a tribal gathering, Bob and Steve and Dad and my nephews, but my heart wasn't in the game even though my Broncos beat the hell out of the Falcons. Then, a few months after Super Bowl XXXIII, my wife of XV years moved out of the house. Before summer was over, she would relocate a thousand miles away, begin cohabiting with her new lover, and suddenly transform me into an ill-prepared full-time single dad of two decidedly spirited children.

Two months after Rebecca and I separated, Bob found the lump.

Even after he had been diagnosed with breast cancer and had undergone surgery and chemo, starting a few months after Rebecca and I split, Bob would check in with Kolya regularly, having long conversations even when I wasn't around. With me, Kolya had fallen into his natural, reserved and relatively expressionless state when it came to talking about Momma leaving or her becoming a lesbian or the divorce. Bob could joke with Kolya in a way nobody else could. The resemblance between the two of them was uncanny at times; both oldest sons, both athletic, both charismatic, both a little awkward in new situations, both gagging at the slightest hint of gristle on their meat.

When we first heard the news about Bob's cancer being terminal, Kolya and I cried together in the living room, hugging without any hint of embarrassment from him, just devastation. When we visited for the last time, Bob could barely stand. I watched Kolya and his uncle embrace, both knowing they were saying goodbye, both unfathomably sad about what they would never be able to do together—all the games of catch and learning to drive and, eventually, the beers they might have shared watching the playoffs and holiday bowl games and SportsCenter.

An Uncle Bob story:

Bob and I are playing tennis on a clay court at Paraa Safari Lodge in northern Uganda. He can beat me of course, since he beats me at any sport that involves a ball, or running, or hand-eye coordination. But although I am three and a half years his junior, I am also tenacious, and he has fun toying with me as I run and dive and occasionally hit a shot that whizzes past him. He spots me a lead, usually I start serving at 30-love, but he still wins nearly every point, most every game, and certainly every set. The day is warm, sultry. We are in Uganda but we are just playing together, two brothers passing the interminable hours of childhood engaged in a game whose conclusion is foreordained.

Suddenly, we spot about half a dozen baboons approaching the chicken wire fence surrounding the court. We are amazed, amused, put our rackets down to our sides and stare. The baboons stare back. We start to think about aping them, scratching ourselves, and involuntarily we each approach closer to the net, closer to each other. The baboons are bigger the closer they get, and we are amazed and a little afraid. We drop the monkey act. The baboons, their arms are so long and nostrils so big, start climbing the fence. Bob jokes that they don't have the court yet, we've reserved it for another half-hour. We think the baboons are funny, that they want to play with us. We are thinking that it might be fun to play with them, too, but they are getting bigger and wilder looking as they scale the chicken wire.

"I think we'd better get out of here," Bob says.

I'm already heading for the gate.

"Do you think the baboons would have hurt you?" Zoe asked.

"I don't think they wanted to play tennis, Zoe," Kolya countered.

"I don't know, Zoe," I said, ignoring him. "I think they were curious. They were pretty big, wild animals, and Uncle Bob and I didn't want to find out what they'd have done to us."

We fell silent, rollicking along in the van. The radio stations became scratchy or intolerable. We listened to individual tunes through our personal music machines, which thankfully escaped the last minute paring-down during packing. Kolya has downloaded three gigabytes of music onto my laptop, which he loads and reloads onto his mini-disc player. Zoe and I make do with our judicious CD choices. We listened, respectively, to Screeching Weasel, Britney Spears, the Crash Test Dummies; Less Than Jake, Aqua, John Gorka; Sublime, Christina Aguilera, Chick Corea. We traded earphones every now and again to share favorite tunes; Zoe offered her Bare Naked Ladies CD, which I like, and Kolya handed me his headphones to share lyrics by a band called NOFX (No Effects) about a kid bemoaning his impossibly hip parents:

> *Mom and dad*
> *How'd ya get so rad*

When exactly did you get so hip?
Wearing teenage clothes
You're always coming to my shows
And telling me that I should mellow out

The three of us headed north, exchanging intergenerational information, intermittently engaging with each other, blissfully on the road.

We pulled into a shady camper van park around midday in a place with an irresistible Australian name, Wonga Beach, for what I hoped would be a seaside picnic. Within ten minutes, Kolya virtually accosted a seven-year-old boy who was running around the campsite with a plastic rugby ball and initiated play with him, already starved for companionship that wasn't me or Zoe. Soon Zoe joined in and the three of them played on the beach burying Zoe in the sand. They implored me not to take us anywhere else that day. I asked the newfound friend, James, if, when Australian kids dug deep holes, they said they were digging to China the way American kids did. He didn't rightly know, but his dad, Mark, said that the geographical unlikelihood of it notwithstanding, Australian boys did in fact still dig, or perhaps tunnel, to "Chiner."

We buried each other and watched the tide change for hours, an inadvertent lesson in maritime ecology. I subversively prepped them for our upcoming educational adventures on the Great Barrier Reef, where we would soon dive and snorkel. The line between the land and the sea seems so clear-cut, but I showed them how a small stream emerging from the jungle merely trickles into the ocean at low tide, but turns into a brackish lagoon at high tide. We have discovered a classic transition zone between freshwater and saltwater, where amazingly adaptable creatures such as estuarine crocodiles have learned to live (the signs to "Beware of the Crocs" are eye-catching), like salmon in our own country, making mind-boggling journeys from the ocean into freshwater rivers to spawn. What comes from the land flows into the ocean. It's a simple lesson, especially as we delve deeper into the environmental problems growing along the Great Barrier Reef, but I don't think they've ever really thought about it before.

I had more or less planned to drive farther north that afternoon, but it wasn't hard to adjust and let the kids have a day of beaching and hanging. We swam and frolicked waist-deep in the ocean during the early sunset, water warm and soothing, a kid hanging on each of my arms, all of us thankful that the killer jellyfish, called stingers, had gone someplace else for the Australian winter.

At dusk, Zoe and I strolled down the beach and sought out James, whom Zoe announced earlier with worldly pride was from Wales. (Wales, New South Wales, it's a big world out there.) We found James with his dad and mom, who have five kids between them from three different family units. We lounged on lawn chairs sipping cold ones ("stubbies") as the tropical sunset concluded with predictable suddenness, said good night, and headed for bed sated and happy.

And then something happened and the kids snarled at each other. An offense, real or perceived. An insult. Low blood sugar. Boredom. A tap is a bop is a slug is a slugfest. Calm discussion transformed into a screaming fit.

We entered into difficult and prolonged negotiations about the bedtime ritual—who would sleep in which bed for the rest of the trip. It's unclear which was considered better, to sleep with me on the queen-ish sized bed over the reconfigured kitchen table, or on the private but cramped upper bunk, which made midnight pees a little more challenging. I'd figured that Kolya would prefer to sleep alone, the pee handicap notwithstanding, but it's more fun wanting whatever the other one wants.

If sibling bickering were an art form, these two would be Old Masters. Before the trip was through, Kolya and Zoe would have bickered in Ubud and in Dalat, in Pangkalan Bun and in Kathmandu. They would bicker in hotels and customs lines, on buses and trains, at friends' houses and tourist attractions. Sometimes I found creative ways to pull us out of it. Sometimes I just broke down and cried.

Here, I ineffectually tried a coin toss, and it was decided: Zoe would sleep with me, Kolya up above—but either of them had the right to ask to switch two times, no questions asked. Fine, shake, agreed.

Soon it became apparent that the victory was short-lived. Zoe suddenly changed her mind and insisted she had been coerced in the first place. I think she knew in her heart that whatever the decision was, she would not be able to live with it down the road. She fretted already with the knowledge that she couldn't stick with the decision, whatever it was. She also knew that Kolya and I would become enraged when she eventually reneged on her agreement. Choices have always been paralyzing for her.

For the moment, I read a bedtime story on the kitchen table bed, the kids on either side of me begging for "one more chapter" after each chapter, until I was so sleepy that I sought the solace of my own dream time. Sensing that Zoe needed a little extra attention, I asked, gently and discreetly, that Kolya not exercise his option to switch beds tonight, so I could snuggle with Zoe.

No way.

I insist.

Zoe wasn't sure she wanted to accept the offer, anyway.

"Fine," I said. "Whatever. Zoe, do you want to sleep up there?"

"I don't know."

Stock reply from both Kolya and me in unison (bad idea). "It's a yes-or-no question."

"I don't know."

She knows. I know.

"Kolya, get your ass up there and don't say a word."

"But ... "

"That's a word."

"I don't know," chimed in Zoe.

I was about to go crazy. I pushed Kolya out of the bed and upward. He was already getting harder to push anywhere.

He went up, reluctantly and petulantly. Zoe started to pester me further.

Suddenly, I began crying, frustrated beyond words and at the end of the day's allotment of patience. Zoe doesn't really like to hear me cry, I know, but I had nothing left to give her.

"Why are you crying?"

You know full well, I wanted to say to her.

"That's enough now," I seethed, dredging up the Parental Voice of Finality. "Good night."

"But ... "

"Good. Night."

SATORI AT WONGA BEACH

THE NEXT MORNING I stumbled onto what I'll call my *satori* at Wonga Beach, a slim glimmer of revelation in the tropical dawn. Still a little jet-lagged, I awakened easily about an hour before the sun, crawled out of the van in order to claim a small bit of day to myself, and stretched creakily on my yoga mat on the hard-packed low-tide sand as the dawn light slowly trumped the three-quarter moonlight.

I decided, simply, that I had to lighten up. Sifting my thoughts through an offshore breeze during a long, post-yoga beach walk (the kids were having no trouble sleeping in), it occurred to me that the past few years had really been hellish. It wasn't as if I could claim compensation for psychological loss and damage from some spiritual insurance company. But even if *I* didn't deserve anything special, the kids sure did, after losing their uncle and, at least for awhile, their mother.

And, okay, come to think of it, I could use a little pampering, too. Even if it was just from me.

In that moment, standing shirtless on a spit of sand peering across the Coral Sea about 10,000 miles to nowhere, I felt like something was coming together, as if pages of a life swept along by the wind could be recovered and at least partially sorted. One of our more subtle activities here on this trip, I hoped, was to lick our substantial and collective wounds. It is *huge*, I reminded myself, that their mother, my wife, had left us, moved away. The kids could at least comprehend divorce; half their friends were from broken homes. They even knew kids whose mothers were formerly married lesbians. But the moving away part—that's the nightmare of epic proportions: to be abandoned, by their *mother*.

They wouldn't talk about it much. After the divorce I had cajoled Zoe and bribed Kolya to see a family therapist with me. Kolya tried to make it sound like it was *no big deal*—hey, Mom did what she had to do. But I worried about him, saw his rage eke out at times aimed at his sister. I never knew—and still don't—if it was just sibling stuff or if Zoe had taken over as his surrogate target. Zoe could express how much she missed her mother, how baffling it was. "You love your work more than you love me," I have heard her scream to Rebecca on the phone.

In my better moments I could rationalize Rebecca's departure: a thoroughly epic midlife crisis, a combination of ancient wounds of her own, an exigency of sexual awakening, a need to establish her identity not as a mother, a daughter, or a wife, and a marriage that, for various reasons, didn't make sense for her anymore. She had exemplified the consummate full-time mom until then, performing household chores with Zoe attached to her like a marsupial and entertaining Kolya with craft projects found in books at the local library. Somehow she had burned out completely and needed to escape, whatever the cost.

I can't, though, and probably won't ever be able to fully understand Rebecca's choice. I felt like such a *victim*, and I wondered how to find my way out of that barren emotional wilderness of blame. *She did this to me. She screwed up my life.* I pulled off my shorts, stood on the soft Australian sand, and faced the surf. I also knew it was too easy to blame her for everything, for leaving me, for leaving the kids. I wrestled with a nagging feeling that maybe I had driven her away through inattentiveness or careless cruelty. I could be so exacting, so demanding. I remembered with shame the time I berated her when she had forgotten to buy hot sauce even though I'd written it on the shopping list. I felt sadness as limitless as the ocean vista in front of me.

And then, like a second blow to the solar plexus, the memory of Bob's death hit me again, striking with the adrenal force of a cold-sweat telephone call in the middle of the night. I wondered about the kids, how much they must fear death. Sure, Bob wasn't Rebecca or me, but obviously for Kolya and Zoe it meant that if an uncle could die, a father could die, a mother could die.

My mind scampered like the sand crabs surrounding me and I muttered to myself. *Stop hiding behind the kids,* I reprimanded. Sure, Rebecca's departure was hard on them. But you're never going to move on with Tory or anybody until *you* make sense of your failed marriage. Sure, the kids feel sad about their uncle. But Bob's death also lifted a veil of immortality you had thrown over your head like a child's magic cloak. It's about time you figured it out, buddy. *You* could die. You will die.

Naked on that beach, everything that had once seemed so certain suddenly felt so precarious.

So there at Wonga Beach, it struck me that we should have chocolate for breakfast if we wanted it, and sodas before noon, and maybe even an occasional beer (for me) to watch the sunrise. We'd been reading *Harris and Me* aloud (a classic 1950s-era city-boy-meets-country-boy tale), and the irascible Harris (the country boy) declares during a make-believe cowboys-and-Indians game that Red Indians don't have to obey a bunch of *rules,* and by God why should he? The fact that Harris's disdain for rules leads him to pee on an electric fence with disastrous results doesn't detract from the appeal of a certain anarchy.

Yeah, I was thinking. Why should we pay attention to a bunch of stupid *rules*, anyway? Why don't we just become a sort of modern-day *Paper Moon*, that 1973 flick with Ryan O'Neal and his daughter Tatum, the two of them picaresque swindlers relying on their wits to survive, and damn the truant officers? I could set up my guitar case wherever we went; Kolya and Zoe could work the crowds, stealing watches and picking pockets. We could revive Oliver Twist in our own road show, surviving forever on purloined booty and tragically misplaced sympathy, living like gypsies in our little caravan. We'd frighten suburban mothers with our fierce, undomesticated appearance, washing ourselves in public parks, eating grapes and doughnuts from the grocery market before paying, and helping ourselves to whatever we could abscond with.

But of course we couldn't do that, I was also thinking. Parenting requires imparting important ideals, moral truths, a voice chimes in like a bad headache. *Take what you need, eat what you take. Save some water for the next person.* Do unto others even if they won't necessarily do so well unto you. Kindness is contagious, or at least karmically defensible.

I started to laugh. From whom did I inherit this streak of moral rectitude—keep your voice down, don't take too long in the shower, eat everything on your plate, keep your room neat, hang the clothes on the clothesline rather than using the dryer because it saves electricity? Did somebody inject me with a microchip when I took Kolya home from the hospital, the one that programmed me to say "you have to eat your vegetables" (I've actually said this) and "no, you can't, it's not sugarless" (ditto)?

Shoot, though. It's not a lot of fun saying "no" and "absolutely not" all the time. It's no wonder Calvinism never managed to take hold as a world religion. Maybe there's middle ground here somewhere. Maybe I've stumbled onto it here at Wonga Beach.

We stayed at Wonga Beach that whole day, swimming and relaxing with James and his family. At dusk I gathered the kids by the camper van and shared my revelation without giving away all parental prerogative. "I was thinking," I tried on Kolya first, "that we've sure been through a lot recently." Kolya looked at me warily, wondering what kind of surprise his dad would spring on him. "I just decided we should lighten up a little," I told him.

He got the drift but wasn't sure about whether I was talking about letting him have a whole Coopers Ale to himself (as I was, a big bottle) or maybe just a Mountain Dew for breakfast every now and again. "How about a free trip around the world?" he countered, evoking what had already become our standard refrain.

We took a short walk, me pushing him on his skateboard since he almost categorically refused to walk anywhere he could ride, and I made the first offering: a Cadbury's white-topped chocolate bar, which he consumed just before dinner. How's that for being a wild and crazy dad?

Then Zoe and I walked along a stretch of deserted white sand, holding hands and meandering as the day turned dark and then darker. We stopped, looked to the sky, and listened to the waves, and I explained why the sky was different here, Down Under. I pointed out the Milky Way, a vivid dusting across the southern sky, and tried to explain Earth's place in the whole spiraling morass. The universe, galaxies, solar systems, planets, black holes, quasars, the way gravity bends light over time and space (okay, so I simplified it a little). She allowed that she had never actually been able to see the Big Dipper when people pointed it out (she just pretended), and quickly moved the conversation into the deepest places, as I suppose the night sky has inspired since there were humans and a night sky. How did we get here? I try explaining the Big Bang theory, elemental chemicals supercharged in a pre-biotic stew, the long, primordial slow dance from single cell to cell phone.

But, but, but, she counters, how about that first impossibly dense ... thing ... that everything burst out of? she wondered, her nine-year-old mind wrapping around the next closest thing to infinity. I told her I didn't know—who can really know these things? Too much faith I probably have in those scientific minds that think they have pieced these theories together. So much easier for the mind to grasp, perhaps, a Creator and all things following suit in a perfect Divine plan.

She shifted the conversation abruptly, back to my epiphany about lightening up, about how hard I am on her sometimes, how my expectations are too high. She'd been having a tougher time here than Kolya, and the two of them had been at each other constantly, even by siblings' high standards of disharmony and strife.

As she can so well, she nailed what had been bothering her: Although Kolya acts real grown-up and doesn't need me to take care of him so much (if I would let him survive on Top Ramen, Cocoa Puffs, Jolt, and Otter Pops he would need only a bimonthly stocking of these essentials), she, Zoe, still needed me to take care of her. "I'm only nine, you know?"

She was right. I'd been expecting too much from her, mistaking her sophistication and attempts to act grown-up to garner her brother's attention for needing less from me in the day to day. I needed to keep dialing back, slowing down my expectations all around. For asking her to do her homework by herself while I wrote in my journal, for her fears in the dark, for the agitation before every transition, for her paralysis at seeing too many choices on a breakfast menu. For her behavior, for their behavior, for keeping the van neat or helping with dinner. For everything.

The next day, we stayed put at Wonga Beach, ate ice cream before lunch, and the kids buried *me* in the sand. We watched an episode of South Park on the laptop DVD *(Oh, my God, they killed Kenny! Those bastards!)* and finished *Harris and Me,* which gave us a new vocabulary word for the rest of the trip: *gooner,* which is a cross between an idiot and an even bigger idiot. Usage: "You are such a *gooner.*"

We stayed at Wonga Beach for one last relaxing day before ambling north into Daintree National Park, a relatively intact rainforest ecosystem. We pulled up to a campsite and had to shoo away a five-foot-long lace monitor lizard, called a goanna, sunning itself right where our camper van wanted to rest. We won the territorial battle, and the lizard seemed resigned to the fact—so he went to raid the neighbor's garbage bag.

The neighbor—one of an odd breed of retired south Australian bachelors who customize 4×4 pickup trucks called "utes" for outback travel, then head off to warmer climes for four months a year with fishing rods and pictures of their grand-nephews—whacked the lizard with a rolled-up magazine.

Kolya and Zoe couldn't believe they'd just witnessed a man swat a five-foot-long lizard the way we'd swat a fly at home. They looked at each other, eyes wide, and ran to the beach to scour for low-tide treasures while I grilled their new favorite dinner, Australian lamb chops, over the camper van park's "barbie," or gas grill. I pulled out one of our camp chairs, stared at the bewildered lizard waddling off to the next campsite, and contemplated my morning satori, searching for ways to lighten up in the brown glass beer bottle and the receding tracks of the goanna's tail.

A Cassowary Totem

I DECIDED to play ecological tour guide the next day and dragged the kids to a local tourist attraction, a one-hour jungle riverboat ride advertised as the only one actually *inside* Daintree park. Despite Kolya's I'm-thirteen-and-I-can't-believe-I'm-going-on-a-tourist-boat-with-a-bunch-of-old-people-and-Dutch-tourists-with-toddlers-and-worst-of-all-my-Dad-with-a-camcorder attitude, we saw three crocodiles, a blue heron, and a kingfisher as we skimmed through the mangroves with a pithy Aussie guide at the helm. Even Kolya allowed that it's not every day one sees crocodiles in the wild in Colorado, so I counted the trip a success.

Earlier, we had noticed a sign for a tropical ice cream parlor and headed up the road to check it out. On the way I made the kids peel their earphones away from the CD/mini-disk players and listen to an Ecosystem 101 harangue about endangered species, habitat loss, human effects on wildlife, and why species were disappearing so fast. They had already heard me droning on about how all the sugarcane fields we had passed caused problems for marine life because of fertilizer runoff, how more nutrients in the water could give certain plants or animals a competitive advantage and lead to a whole cascade of unnatural ecological events. Not to mention all the rainforest that had been cleared to make way for the cane in the first place, and the animals that had to find other homes or simply disappear. I ignored Kolya's under-the-breath "hippie tree-hugger" epithet (what generational leap occurred to make "hippie" an epithet?) and tried to make this interesting to them.

We arrived at the ice cream place, and what a find. All the fruit grows on the premises, exotic stuff we'd never seen or heard of: star fruit, chocolate pudding fruit, wattleseed fruit. A young single mother named Shakti served us, all piercings and tie-died fabric, and noticed that we were a different breed from the vans full of European tourists on day trips up from Cairns. We hung out, chatted, and she told us of a secret swimming hole on a river, no crocs, up a dirt road past the Heritage Rainforest Lodge and to the "Y," take the left fork, and go to the causeway.

Among the things I promised Kolya before the trip was a driving lesson somewhere in the Australian outback. The wide dirt road to the swimming hole, while hardly the outback, presented itself as a perfect place to let Kolya try. He took the wheel with aplomb, only stalling a few times, and got the hang of most everything except for steering between first and second gear and recalling that the clutch needed to be depressed while stopping.

I watched him in the driver's seat, observed his face changing, pimples forming, his focus intent. Unbidden tears came to my eyes. Seeing Kolya was like watching Bob sometimes, and memories flooded over me: Bob teaching me to drive down Calvert Street in his 1961 robin's-egg blue VW minivan named "Mukirda," which he told everyone meant "penis" in Swahili; Bob learning to negotiate a right-hand-drive Ford Taurus in Africa.

Kolya glanced over, I actually thought he knew why I was crying, and he proceeded to grind the gears. It felt like an appropriate sound. He already knew the story.

Somehow we take a wrong turn at a roundabout leaving Kampala. As soon as we leave the city, Mom and Dad let Bob take the wheel. He's only fifteen, but he's already a pretty good driver. The road quickly becomes unpaved and washboard bumpy and the dust is red when another car, stuffed with about a hundred Africans, passes in the other direction.

We drive and drive, stopping to pee and looking for snakes before we unzip. With each mile the scenery becomes more rural and then just plain uninhabited and swampy. The road narrows. Somewhere in there we all begin wondering, we know this is Africa and everything, but on the map this is supposed to be a pretty main road up toward Murchison Falls, the Nile River, a national park. We're going to see hippopotamuses and crocodiles.

The road turns into a dirt track, finally emptying into a village, thatched roofs and dirt floors and little stores that only sell matches and rice and Fanta orange. The little kids wear holey T-shirts but nothing else, and the whole village gathers around our car. Mom speaks a little Swahili, but they don't even speak Swahili up here. We notice the crowd shifts aside as a bunch of the half-naked kids pull a young man toward us. He is shy, but Mom says he's the English teacher, which is pretty amazing to me because he really doesn't speak much English.

The next thing I remember is everybody laughing—their skin is so dark but their teeth so white—laughing at something the English teacher says to them in their tribal language that none of us understand. But even I understand that they're laughing because we've taken the wrong road, we're probably halfway to Burundi or something, and that we have to go all the way back to Kampala and take a different road.

Bob doesn't really mind, he just gets to drive more.

The next day, after heavy lobbying (this time from Zoe, too), we drove from our campsite to the Bob Bondurant School of Outback Driving course (and swimming hole), en route to the ice cream store. After stalling the van a few more times and forgetting to steer and shift (Zoe, laughing, "What a *gooner!*"), Kolya relinquished the wheel and we visited Shakti and the mango/papaya/macadamia nut treats.

On the road we observed a series of curious signs to watch out for cassowaries. These flightless, enormous, endangered birds are cousin to the ostrich, rhea, kiwi, and emu—and are the second largest bird in the world (after the ostrich). One sign depicted a silhouette of a cassowary. Next to that stood a sign for a speed bump. The signs were modified, revealing an artist's macabre sense of humor. On the road sign icon of the cassowary was written the word "Before." On the sign with the speed bump icon, which resembles a squashed big bird, was the word "After."

In pictures we'd seen, the cassowary appeared wild looking, with a pale blue crest on the top of its head and a pair of crimson wattles at the base of its neck like a turkey gobbler. But cassowaries possess three deadly dagger-like toes, which they use to defend themselves and also to help them swim. They grow as tall as I am (almost six feet), live longer than I have (forty-four years), weigh more than I do (165 pounds), and win the prize as the largest land animal in Australia—they're bigger than kangaroos. Unfortunately, only about fifty cassowaries remain in the Daintree region.

The huge birds are critically important to this tropical ecosystem because they eat so many different kinds of fruit, then spread the seeds around through their poop as they wander around. Because of the cassowary's eating and roaming and pooping all over the place, seeds from more than seventy species of trees spread all over the rainforest instead of just growing in concentrated pockets. The cassowary also spreads seeds of about eighty other plant species, including a number of plants that are poisonous to other animals but that the cassowary can digest without killing itself.

"Do you know what a keystone is?" I asked.

Silence. Shrugs.

"On a stone arch, it's the one at the center that holds the whole thing together." I drew a little picture.

"Your point being?" Kolya prodded.

"They call animals like cassowaries 'keystone species' because they hold up so many other species in the rainforest. Not just the plants and trees, but other animals that need all those fruit trees to survive."

"Because they poop all over the place?" Zoe wondered.

"Yeah, pretty much."

I lectured a few minutes about genetic bottlenecks, how if enough members of one species are killed off, it's hard for the population to recover because the reservoir of genetic diversity is so small. Cassowaries face another, related problem: The fifty or so cassowaries around the Daintree region represent an island population, cut off from other cassowaries who live much further north, on Cape York. That means the Daintree cassowaries can't mate with the Cape York cassowaries because they live too far away.

We stopped at a roadside information center, which helps illustrate another evolutionary phenomenon the children had been wondering about: how different animals arrived on different continents, and why there weren't, say, kangaroos in Colorado. Australia (so the theory goes) once belonged to a supercontinent called Gondwanaland, which included South America, Africa, peninsular India, Australia, and Antarctica. Animals that evolved to survive in a specific region simply couldn't cross from one supercontinent to another and over time grew more and more adapted to specific climates and more and more isolated. Kangaroos, no matter how far they can jump, just couldn't make it over to North America. And if they did, chances are we would've wiped them out like we did the bison.

Kolya asked, "Dad, have many things gone extinct in your lifetime?" and I said, yeah, sure, you betcha. More than anybody can count. I wondered if he'd even heard of the dodo, anyway, metaphor for all things extinct, and he hadn't. I told him that species have always gone extinct, but ever since humans have been around the rate of extinction has increased geometrically. I read that Pulitzer Prize–winning scientist E. O. Wilson once estimated that if we don't radically change the way humans keep wiping out habitat on the planet, we're likely to kill off 20 percent of existing species by the time Kolya is my age. By the time Zoe's grandchildren celebrate the end of the twenty-first century, we could easily commit to extinction half of all the species alive today.

Suddenly, we all caught sight of an enormous bird 200 yards ahead, crossing the road at a gangly, measured pace.

A cassowary!

The kids perceptively perked up, and Zoe took a good bead on it: brown or black body at least four or five feet long and three feet high, sitting on top of legs that seemed almost that height. The signature crest looked like a Mohawk haircut atop its head, and colorful plumage surrounded its neck area. We stopped the van, grabbed various cameras, and stalked the bird, which disappeared into the rainforest.

Back in the car, Kolya ventured (bless his soul), "That's what you were talking about, Pop, taking us to see things like that before they're gone?" Sadly, sadly, that is part of the trip. We arrived at the ice cream store and told our newfound friend Shakti about the cassowary sighting. She was ecstatic, adding to our excitement, and grilled us for details. Where exactly had we seen it? Was it male or female?

How could we tell, we wondered?

The females are bigger, she informed us.

"Bigger than what?" Kolya asked. "We only saw one."

"Do you know how lucky you are?" she asked. Zoe nodded, and informed Shakti authoritatively that there were only about fifty cassowaries left in the *whole world*, and although this wasn't quite true (the estimate is about 1,500 left in the wild, and only fifty or so in the region where we were), I was touched by Zoe's wonder and concern.

Shakti then told us a fact about cassowaries that she had no idea would be so amazing, given our circumstances. The cassowary female lays its eggs and departs; it is the *male* cassowary that incubates the eggs (alone for about fifty days, often forsaking food and water) and raises the chicks for a year, teaching them what they need to know.

I took it as a totemic tale, a cosmic clue, an auspicious analogy.

We rode in marvelous silence until we arrived back at our campsite, this time lizard-free, just before nightfall.

SWIMMING WITH CROCODILES

WE'D COME TO the Great Barrier Reef to begin our "before they're gone" case studies of extraordinary ecosystems that are threatened by human development. When coral reefs are healthy, they are among the most fecund ecosystems on earth, known as "rainforests of the ocean." Where they have become unhealthy, as many of them have, these underwater rainforests are disappearing as fast as the more publicized equatorial rainforests of the Amazon and Indonesia are being decimated by land clearing.

By the time we visited this aquatic realm, the kids had already been primed by our mainland cassowary encounter and our ocean-meets-the-sea tutorial at Wonga Beach, not to mention a few of Dad's mini-lectures. They'd heard about the diversity of life contained in the planet's rainforests—all the unnamed bugs and microbes and plants and animals of the disappearing Amazon. But their textbooks told them precious little about biodiversity in the oceans.

To prepare further for our exploration, I had armed myself with books, articles, and research papers about the Great Barrier Reef, or

GBR, as it's known in all the literature. I had pored over the material at shady caravan parks each night while the kids perfunctorily whipped through their math and journaling before hitting the Super Mario. I peered up every now and then from my papers, lowered my reading glasses, and shared some arcane fact I hoped they'd find interesting:

"Hey, you two. Did you know that humpback whales come from the Antarctic to give birth to their young in reef waters? That six of the world's seven species of sea turtle breed on the reef?"

Occasionally, they'd glance up from their Game Boys and humor me. "That's really interesting, Dad. Gee, thanks." And then, back to Super Mario. More often, they'd treat me the way I'd imagine a group of East L.A. gangbangers might react to the congenitally perky science teacher Ms. Frizzle in *The Magic School Bus* series. "Dad, you hippie, you don't *get* it," Kolya would snap. "We don't want to hear it right now."

So mostly I shared interesting coral reef facts with myself:

- Coral reefs are among the world's oldest continuously extant life forms, thought to have originated 225 million years ago in the early Mesozoic era, when the rest of the earth was still dominated by ferns and cycads and dinosaurs were beginning their (relatively) brief and tumultuous terrestrial reign.
- The GBR is the earth's largest natural structure. It runs more or less parallel to Australia's northeast coast for more than 1,200 miles, an amalgamation of 2,600 separate coral reefs that together form one of the most diverse ecosystems in the world.
- Debate rages about the GBR's age. Once thought to be about 20 million years old, current research indicates that it has probably been around just half a million years, give or take. During that time, sea levels have risen and fallen, killing off the coral several times. In its current incarnation, the reef may only be about 6,000 years old, having had to start rebuilding after sea levels stabilized after the last ice age.

- Coral polyps, the basic building block of coral colonies, aided by algae and sponges, convert dissolved limestone into architecturally improbable undersea structures over thousands of years. The polyps need warm water to grow, as do the algae and sponges, which act as cement to hold the coral together. They also need light—especially the *zooxanthellae*, the single-celled algae that produce important nutrients for the coral. As the coral grows, it leaves behind calcium carbonate, which forms the skeletal structure that the living coral covers like skin.
- Coral forests provide habitat for about 4,000 species of fish and 800 species of corals. Reefs also host innumerable invertebrates, algaes, mollusks, and at least one creature from each of the thirty-six phyla, the basic organizing blocks of the Linnaean system to categorize life on earth. By comparison, only ten phyla are found on land.

The news articles about the worldwide devastation of coral reefs that helped inspire this trip did not single out the GBR as one of the world's most endangered. Indeed, although Australia contains the most reef in the world—nearly 50,000 square kilometers (followed by Indonesia, Philippines, Papua New Guinea, and Fiji), its reef systems are by no means the most threatened. That dubious honor belongs to coral reefs in Indonesia, the Philippines, Africa, the Indian subcontinent, and the Caribbean.

Nevertheless, the Great Barrier Reef provided a perfect place to begin our ecological tour. Here, the kids and I could comfortably check out some of the forces bearing down on the world's coral reefs without having to brave pirates on the Sulu Sea near Sulawesi, Muslim insurgents in the Philippines, or malaria in Papua New Guinea.

Our quest would, however, take us to one of Australia's most reactionary states. The GBR extends offshore parallel to the middle and northern coast of Queensland, a remote and sparsely populated area of Australia forming the northeastern quadrant of the continent.

In many ways, Queensland has attracted inhabitants with politically conservative mindsets and libertarian penchants that closely resemble the prevailing worldview of the American West, where I live. The politicians in the two places mirror each other. We have James Hansen, a recently retired congressman from Utah, whose idea of wilderness is a place where there's likely to be undiscovered oil, and they have Pauline Hansen, leader of Australia's One Nation Party, whose right-wing anti-immigrant tirades have made her an embarrassment even to some Queenslanders.

Like the American West, the Queensland landscape itself acts like a Siren's call to tourists (and increasingly, to tourism operators, developers, and curio shop owners, who thrive on the assumption that nobody ever has enough engraved shot glasses or T-shirts emblazoned with the logo of a local beer). Both regions, in past decades, have become a magnet for mass tourism, rapid population growth, second home-ownership, and the proliferation of real-estate offices. An uncomfortable collection of tourism-centered boom towns has emerged, overrun by recent lifestyle refugees. These newcomers clash loudly with the locals, iconoclasts who moved away from the populated urban areas to follow their own unmistakably eccentric ways.

Unlike the American West, though, which is marked most distinctly by its aridity, Queensland lies in the tropical north, with a rainy season that makes it among the wettest places on earth. The township of Tully, on the coast, averages more than 167 inches of rain annually, compared to, say, 36 inches in Pittsburgh. And while parts of the Rocky Mountains rightly claim their share of international cachet, the Great Barrier Reef indisputably ranks high on anybody's short list of the world's great natural wonders.

*

On a geologic timeframe, coral reefs are fairly frequent victims of natural cataclysm. Cyclones, hurricanes and other storms, volcanic eruptions, the ebb and flow of ice ages, El Niños (which increase sea surface temperatures and result in extensive coral die-offs), and extraterrestrial detritus such as meteors and comets all affect their life cycle. Infestations of coral-eating predators as well as global climate variations have forced entire coral systems to crash, bleach, and then start over the grindingly slow process of rejuvenation.

Now add to coral reefs' impressive list of natural enemies the consequences of human activity: nearby cities, airports, military bases, mines, tourist resorts, ports, oil tanks and wells, shipping routes, erosion, coastal development, marine-based pollution, land-based pollution, dynamite fishing, cyanide fishing, and your basic commercial trawlers. All of these help to stress and kill coral reefs.

The GBR, in fact, may be one of the most protected of the world's signature coral reef systems, which is a sobering thought considering its problems. In 1975, the Australian government established the Great Barrier Reef Marine Park Authority, GBRMPA (known as GaBrumpa among marine cognoscenti) to monitor the reef's health and well-being. In an attempt to circumvent problems facing coral reef systems elsewhere, GaBrumpa began imposing a number of restrictions on human activities, including fishing quotas, permit systems for tourist operators, and water-quality regulations for industry.

Still, unmistakable signs point to the fact that all is not well down under Down Under.

Although GaBrumpa arguably does a good job controlling what happens on the reef itself by limiting tourist operations, it has had less luck convincing the government to take a harsher stand on other industries. Land clearing—whether to create dive shops, fast-food restaurants, sugarcane fields, or grazing pastures for Australian beef production—presents a formidable problem. Australia recently passed Congo, Myanmar, Nigeria, Zimbabwe, and Malaysia as having one of the fastest deforestation rates in the world—and most of that is taking place in Queensland.

As we discovered, accelerated land clearing is just one force that places the GBR at incredible risk from an unlikely source: a voracious, coral-eating, twenty-six-armed starfish.

Before exploring the reef, we drove as far north as we were allowed in our rental van, to where the coastal paved road stops and the land of tricked-out utes and benighted Australian bachelors begins. Flush with our success spotting cassowaries, I splurged on a night in one of the ubiquitous lodges that cater to the world traveler circuit: PK's Jungle Retreat.

I suppose that people of every generation must marvel at the changes that have occurred in their lifetime, but it feels like so much has accelerated at a space-warp clip since my birth in 1956. Just about the time I was religiously watching *Leave It to Beaver* with one hand in my mouth and the other clutching my blanket, the commercial aviation industry was taking off, and along with it the ability for the masses to travel long distances fast—and without getting seasick. President Dwight D. Eisenhower hatched his idea for an interstate highway system that would make my generation the most mobile in history. At the time, the phenomenon we now know as globalization confined itself to concerns that the Soviet Union, having just taken Czechoslovakia, would continue west until the Brits drank vodka rather than warm stout. The Internet remained in Jules Verne–land, Nepal didn't yet admit foreigners, and McDonald's had yet to open its first franchise.

In the 1960s, wayfaring hippies made their way to exotic places such as India and Afghanistan. But for a variety of reasons, it took until perhaps the late 1970s for independent world travelers to migrate en masse around the world and be assured of having menus in English wherever they arrived. Since an Australian couple, Tony and Maureen Wheeler, wrote the seminal low-budget travel guide, *Southeast Asia on a Shoestring*, more than twenty-five years ago, initiating the wildly successful Lonely Planet empire of travel books, the world has become more accessible, even in its remotest corners. As a result, entrepreneurs in every culture have sprouted businesses to accommodate the hordes of tourists. From the college student taking a month or a year off to the yuppie couple cashing in their BMW for backpacks and a ticket to Ulan Bator, the world filled with a globe-trotting subculture I like to call Lonely Planeteers. Wherever Lonely Planeteers go in the world, they find a version of pizza, Coca Cola, and menus featuring yogurt shakes and truly atrocious approximations of Mexican food.

For three years in the mid-1980s, Rebecca and I lived a Lonely Planeteers' existence. Five days after our wedding, we took off for our honeymoon to Japan, beginning a three-year odyssey of discovery for the two of us. In 1984, I had just built my parents' house and she had just finished college, and neither one of us had anything particularly pressing to accomplish in the real world or otherwise. I had a friend who had already spent a year in Japan, and she invited us to join her on a bicycle tour. We rode northward at the same pace as the cherry blossoms, stumbling upon festivals and parades along the Japan Sea coast. In fluent Japanese, Sharon took great joy in explaining that she was accompanying us on our *shinkon ryoko*, our honeymoon.

Our travels and adventures took us from Japan to Hong Kong, Thailand, and Burma (before it was Myanmar), then to Nepal, back to the beaches of Thailand, and again to Japan. We spent a year teaching English before heading off for more advanced travels, visiting places not even covered by the guidebooks, blank spaces yet to be filled in like the missing continents on a fourteenth-century world map. We spent five months traveling around China, which had just opened to individual travelers as part of its Open Door Policy. We crisscrossed from the southeastern corner of Xishuangbanna near the Burmese border to Shanghai, then back through Inner Mongolia and the western reaches of Xinjiang Province. From there we exited to the west over the Silk Road and the Karakoram Highway into northern Pakistan, which hadn't been open to individual Western travelers since Marco Polo's days. We trekked and traveled in the Hunza region of Pakistan, then headed down to Islamabad and Karachi before swinging back to Nepal and Tibet. At that point, we headed west and made our way home through Western Europe.

That trip solidified our relationship and marriage in a way that, years later, we both agreed was profound, adventurous, and notably egalitarian. We had surreptitiously slept on the Great Wall of China in a crumbling turret; trekked near the base camp of Everest on both the Nepali and Tibetan sides; made an illegal border crossing into Karen-controlled Burma from Thailand; and spent the night at the highest monastery in the world, Rongbuk, experiencing the incongruous specter of Buddhist nuns in maroon robes concealing Pop Tarts left from expeditions, which we eagerly purchased and toasted over yak dung fires. Rebecca and I nursed each other through various bouts of intestinal and bronchial attacks, effortlessly made choices at each fork in the road, and generally had a grand adventure of it. When we returned home and settled into the drama of raising a family, our travel memories served to cheer us periodically like the smell of baking bread.

We conceived a vague plan, when the kids became old enough, to take them traveling, too.

Now, years later, that nebulous plan became a blueprint for my current trip with the kids. And, though I should have expected it, certain places and events randomly conjured up scenes from our honeymoon trip, memories simultaneously stirring and painful.

PK's Jungle Retreat represented such a place because it was so similar in style and clientele to the hundreds of places where Rebecca and I had stayed during our honeymoon.

The kids uncovered deep secrets of their Game Boys as I pulled the van into PK's parking lot and investigated. The polyglot chatter of various Lonely Planeteers—Japanese, British, German, Swedish, French, and Hebrew—filled the front desk area as travelers jockeyed for information about rides back to Cairns, jungle walks, boat rides to go snorkeling, fresh towels, or a dormitory room for the night. We rented a perfectly serviceable cabin for three for about $35 U.S., took a long, hot shower, and availed ourselves of a washing machine, milkshakes, and very marginal cheeseburgers at the cabana restaurant before heading to the pool.

The pool held particular interest for the kids. Earlier that day while they were swimming in the ocean a man with a German accent had come up to me on the beach and said, "If I vas you, I vouldn't let zem svim there. Crocodiles." We had seen signs warning about the crocs, and had even taken pictures of them, but thought the overgrown reptiles were a seasonal occurrence, like the killer jellyfish called stingers. Still, it didn't make sense to take any chances, and I had called the kids in from the water, which pained me because they were finally playing together so well. Still, I could imagine talking to the rangers about my reckless parenting:

Didn't you see the sign?

Well, yes, but I thought it only applied to Australians in the summer.

After dinner and bedtime reading, I concluded that it was okay for me to leave the bickering kids in the cabin and go to the cavernous, thatch-roofed bar to mingle a bit.

Kolya wanted to come.

Zoe didn't want to be left alone.

I wanted to be left alone.

Kolya nailed the reason I wanted to go. "Dad's going to go hang out with a bunch of college students and try to look cool," he opined. That, and needing a way to escape the kids. I needed a moment's peace.

I went.

They stayed.

The bar cabana filled up with early twenty-somethings, gathered in fours and sixes and dozens around beer bottles and plates of French fries. Furious techno pop blared just loud enough to make potential conversation uncomfortable, although I didn't see anybody glaringly interested in making conversation with me, or vice versa. I grabbed a beer, wandered around, and found a corner table from which to regard the scene and fantasize about lithe, tan Danish women with delicate, artistic tattoos and piercings in unimaginable places.

After all, I was not only a single dad, I was a single man. Although traveling with two children hardly made me a babe magnet, I smelled youthful licentiousness wafting around the cabana. Before I'd left on the trip, I'd asked a friend of mine, same age and also divorced, how old the youngest woman he had dated was. He told me that a professor of his once told him a failsafe theorem: Halve your age and add seven. By that calculation, I could still approach a twenty-nine-year-old.

I wasn't sure there was anybody that old in the bar.

I grabbed a second Coopers Ale to take back to the cabin. The kids were snoring in bunk beds across from me, asleep in the time it had taken me to have a brief reverie, down a bottle, observe the Planeteers' social rituals, and realize that I didn't belong there anymore.

STARFISH TROOPERS

I HAD PLANNED two excursions to visit the GBR with the biggest tour operators in the area: one in Cairns and one in Port Douglas. Before leaving the states, I had made contact, through a friend of a friend, with a marine biologist who worked in Cairns. When I called American-born and Boston-bred Robin Aiello, she offered to be our first guide to the reef's science and politics. Robin works for Great Adventures, a Japanese-owned company with a reputation for doing industrial tourism with a conscience. She arranged for us to take a day-long tour, "just going out to the reef with 400 of your closest friends, most of them Japanese," as she put it. Kolya and I could try scuba diving, and, as Zoe was too young to dive, she would snorkel.

I was excited for all of us. My first experience snorkeling, with my brothers in the Indian Ocean, was part of the early courtship that had led to my love affair with the natural world. Only once before, while working on a story, had I gone scuba diving—for a tantalizingly short time. The kids, however, were landlocked Coloradans, and nothing can really prepare a terrestrial animal for the wonder of discovering the undersea world.

We boarded a sleek, hydroplaning craft and enjoyed a cup of tea and biscuits in air-conditioned comfort. The full-day extravaganza began with a stop at Green Island, former home to a fabulous coral reef system that had been transformed into a bleak seascape, victim of a host of coral-destroying influences. The island featured a menagerie of sorts in the form of a crocodile farm and related tourist activities. Besides 10:30 A.M. crocodile feedings of chicken on a stick, the island's concessionaires offered digital camera pictures for sale, souvenirs of the faux–Papua New Guinea Melanesia variety, helicopter rides of the vicinity (one crashed last year), and a hundred gift-purchasing opportunities aimed at Japanese tourists, who are required by unwritten cultural law to bring back *omiyage* from every place they visit for everyone they know. Kolya and Zoe each held a baby crocodile with its jaws clamped shut by a rubber band, and I obligatorily took a picture standing next to the official photographer, whose efforts we could purchase on the way out. Mine was better.

We reboarded after purchasing ice cream, then headed out to the destination reef, where Great Adventures had built a pontoon located less than an hour's boat ride offshore. The Australian government heavily regulates where each tour operator can take guests, and the bigger companies have fixed floating pontoons where they can moor their boats, disgorge the visitors for a furious round of scuba diving and snorkeling, and feed them lunch before taking them back happy and not too sunburned. (At least they are supposed to return with them. One couple on a previous trip had not made it back after a dive, and the boat returned to shore without them. Only shreds of their wetsuits were ever found. Some suspect it was a double suicide. In any case, our boat's crew conducted a vigorous body count before we left the pontoon.)

En route, Kolya and I took a one-hour wonder course in scuba diving, and I could actually sense him being excited by the prospect. He can be so taciturn at times, teen cool and aloof, that it's a great pleasure to watch him display enthusiasm. A cheerful dive master walked us through the basics as we filled out liability forms and signed up for the personalized video of our upcoming dive (supplemental cost). He told us to be ready to scuba as soon as we arrived at the pontoon.

Our destination, Norman Reef, mimics a Discovery Channel dream. Zoe had to wait on the platform as Kolya and I descended down metal steps into the water. The weight of the tanks diminished from our backs and shoulders with each step, and we poised on the edge of this undersea world to receive final instructions: Stay close. If there's a problem, thumbs up to signal that you want to return to the surface. If things are fine, make an "okay" sign with your hands.

I don't know whether longtime divers still experience the complete, counterintuitive thrill of being underwater, but the act of submersed breathing gives way to a truly otherworldly feeling. Kolya's eyes widened as he made the plunge, and after just a few breaths of disbelief, both of us looked at each other through our masks, reflexively making a "thumbs-up" sign before remembering that we meant "okay."

Our eyes widened further as we entered a world of Dr. Seussian dimension and color. We floated through a botanical and zoological paradise of blue-tipped stag coral, vast boulder-like table coral, and coral that looked like an anatomy class—filled with intestines, brains, spleens, livers, all undulating through the lens of a bobbing diver's mask. And the fish, of course, parrot and flute and Maori wrasses, equally flamboyant. One of the wonders of the tropics is how flora and fauna vie for Technicolor bragging rights, not just with hues of the brightest greens and blues, but mixing and matching them with yellows and oranges in improbable combinations. Color, it seems, represents camouflage down here.

Kolya and I exchanged grins, bubbles floating from our mouths like pure, escaped glee. Water seeped into my mask because my smile broke the seal. We were swimming with the fishes.

In a good way.

*

We have driven a long way, from Kampala to Nairobi to Mombasa then up the Kenyan coast to Malindi. We rent snorkeling gear and go out on a boat, then jump in. It is like going through the looking glass, into a parallel world that exists beneath the plane of the ocean's surface. I can see fish that I have only seen before in my stamp collection, especially the flat azure blue one with the golden fin, little neon ones that look like they have an electric filament running through them, pointy-nosed ones, long skinny ones, and brown lumpy ones. They swarm around, don't seem to care that we are there right next to them.

The water is so warm, too warm, we can't even cool off by going swimming. In the early morning, we eat papayas and pineapples and coconut, then just the three brothers take our snorkeling gear out for a morning swim. I have to go to the bathroom, and Bob tells me to just pull down my pants and go right there. The current is strong, it is like a river really, and I watch as my waste floats away from me at a startling speed. My brothers think this is funny, and they decide to go, too.

We take "shit swims" every day we are there. Africa is pretty cool.

After Kolya and I finished, we swam back to the pontoon and exchanged scuba gear for snorkeling gear. Zoe, after being regally disappointed at not getting to put on a tank and breathe underwater, nonetheless experienced an immediate kick when she put her head under the surface to survey the startling scene. Wally, the pontoon's mascot, a five-foot-long aquamarine Maori wrasse, comes by and she pets it. Occasionally she squeals with joy at a new discovery, her glee bubbles floating to the surface. I watch the kids as much as I watch the fish.

What is really cool about where we are right now is that I got to go scuba diving here on the Great Barrier Reef. Doing this was one of the most amazing visual experiences in my life. We got on a big old cruising boat that took us out to a pontoon. The boat ride was horrible, and I felt like puking my guts out for the majority of the ride. I was pretty sure that this was going to be bad, and nothing could make up for the horrible boat ride.

This theory was immediately proven wrong as soon as I stuck my head under the water and took my first breath. I was always scared of drowning, and still am, so taking this breath was a big mental debate for me. I was pretty sure that I was going to try breathing underwater at least, just for the sheer bragging factor. It was just a little hard for me to do.

As soon as I did, it was instant gratification. I loved it, besides the fact that I had an immense fear of drowning. I always loved the water, especially the ocean, so being able to breathe while being underneath, was kind of like a dream come true for me. The next 30 minutes were awesome. We swam around, pretty slow, but we got to see so much awesome stuff, coral, rocks, plants, and the most amazing variety of fish that I have ever seen, pictures included. There is nothing in the world like scuba diving at the Great Barrier Reef (I will let u know if I actually find something better).

We emerged in time to partake of the buffet lunch, catered to Japanese tastes, which was fine with me and okay with Kolya once he realized the chicken curried rice was not the spicy, Indian kind. We were presented with platters of fresh fruit, which Zoe piled high as we sat down to eat with two professional divers, who had been hired, we discovered, to do a most unusual job for Great Adventures: starfish extermination.

The crown-of-thorns starfish, known as COTS, appears to be eating the reef alive. Unusually large, it grows to more than two feet in diameter and can sprout up to two dozen greenish-blue and red arms, which make it look like a spiky undersea punk urchin. The COTS are formidable for other reasons as well. Not only do they consume many times their body weight per day in coral, but when they gather on a fresh patch of healthy coral they emit a pheromone that calls in hoards of other starfish for an undersea feast. Imagine a group of stoned frat boys sitting down to an all-you-can-eat pizza buffet, and by the very act of eating, they emit a call to every fraternity on campus. You couldn't make the pizza fast enough.

Over the past few years, a COTS infestation along Australia's Great Barrier Reef has decimated coral cover over a large area. Coral cannot fend off the swarms of starfish any more than, say, pepperoni pizza can defend itself against an onslaught by Sigma Chi boys. Marine biologists cannot agree about whether *Acanthaster planci* outbreaks represent part of a natural cycle, or human activity inadvertently fuels COTS population growth. If the outbreak's causes are hotly debated, the results aren't: Where COTS proliferate, biologists compare the resulting coral destruction to a forest fire scorching the seabed.

The starfish scourge is probably caused by multiple sources. Land-based nutrient runoff from land clearing for cattle ranching, sugarcane plantations, and resort development all contribute to larger quantities of soil, sediment, effluent, and chemicals spreading into the reef during the prolific rainy season. Plumes of dark goo reach deep into the reef, with increased nutrient loading that favors better survival rates of COT larvae and increased algal blooms, both of which hurt coral. Commercial fishing removes the starfish's natural predators, such as giant triton shells, puffer fish, and shrimp. Subtle changes in sea temperature and chemistry from carbon dioxide and from pesticides and pollution may be slowing coral growth rates. To top it off, 747s full of international tourists, many of them kicking the coral with their rented swim fins and inevitably pouring sunscreen and urine and disposable underwater cameras into the system, probably didn't figure into the original evolutionary plan that brought coral into existence.

Before heading out to the reef, Robin Aiello had introduced me to a scuba diver named Dean Kusenzow. Dean's company, Coral Reef Care, works to eradicate these spiky coral-mongers around the reef-based pontoon sites where Great Adventures operates. He offered a friendly "G'day, mate," introduced me to his partner, Daniel Hill, and suggested we meet after the scuba and snorkeling expedition to discuss his work.

After lunch, Dean showed off the twelve-inch syringes that he and his divers use to probe the reefs for COTS and inject them with starfish-lethal sodium bisulfate, which is essentially swimming pool salt that is harmless to coral. Dean's divers, and others like them, patrol the front lines of an undersea war where the enemy appears to be winning. The divers call themselves "starfish troopers."

I grabbed fins and mask again, and Daniel took me to the edge of the area where they have been starfish pruning. We swam past the scuba-diving spot, and Daniel pointed to the telltale sign of a recent COTS infestation: a bleached white stalk of coral that a starfish had chomped overnight, since Daniel's last trip. The echinoderm actually pulls its stomach out through its mouth, stretches it over the coral polyps, and then coats the coral with digestive juices that kill it and turn it white. At that point, the once-living coral becomes a bleak condo complex for low-income marine life.

We swam a little farther, past the border where the starfish troopers cease their undersea patrol. The scene grew duller, as if we'd passed through a gray filter. We floated through colorless coral skeletons surrounded by gray sediment, and I realized that the throngs of colorful fish now only congregated behind us, at the main diving area. "This is happening all over the place," Daniel said, as I spit out my snorkel and treaded water. We reentered the coral garden around the pontoon, and Wally the wrasse grazed Daniel's thigh.

Great Adventures hires Coral Reef Care to eradicate the COTS in the small coral garden where the company's permits allow it to take tourists. A few other large operators with similar permits for other fixed pontoon sites are doing the same. Daniel and Dean agreed that the problem is far worse than anybody is willing to talk about and may already be completely out of control in certain portions of the reef. "If you go 150 meters in any direction from where we work, it's dead," Dean said when we returned to the pontoon and reboarded the boat. I've already seen what he means.

Once ashore, Dean invited us to his house for dinner. We already considered him an old friend, by travelers' standards. We entered his backyard and gawked at the most Gargantuan barbecue I've ever seen. I turned to Kolya and said, in my best Australian, "Now *that's* a barbie," imitating Paul Hogan in *Crocodile Dundee*, in the scene where he finds himself confronted by a knife-wielding mugger in Manhattan. Hogan, straight from the Australian outback, sneers at the fierce mugger's tiny switchblade and pulls out his monstrous buck knife. "Now, *that's* a knife," he says, and the mugger flees. Kolya concurred about the barbie, mimicking the accent pretty well. The phrase stuck, later morphing into a fill-in-the-blank exclamation: "Now *that's* a _____."

The kids liked Dean. He was the first real Australian we'd hung out with, so they paid attention when we resumed talking about his work. Occupational hazards for the starfish troopers, Dean explained, include chronic cotton mouth from breathing compressed air for two hours each day, tidal currents that slam them against sharp coral, causing infections, and venomous starfish thorns, which get embedded in their fingers. "It's pain, pure pain," he said, making it sound like "pine, payur pine." He was nevertheless pleased with the results of his work: The coral is healthier where they patrol, even though he realizes it's like spraying a gallon of weed killer on a plantation half the size of Texas.

When the living coral spawn, Dean explained, the ocean scene is breathtaking. In summer, when the water temperature is hot enough, all the coral in an area synchronize their mating. Females release up to 60 million eggs in a spawning season, and males respond to the collective female pheromonal onslaught by simultaneously letting the sperm fly. "It's the biggest orgy in the world, mate," Dean said to Kolya, who took note with a sheepish smile.

A few days later, we took a similar reef and diving tour with Quicksilver, based in Port Douglas, about 40 miles to the north. Before heading out, I spoke with Doug Baird, a Quicksilver biologist. He repeated the list of negative influences that could be responsible for the COTS infestation and acknowledged that marine biologists can't seem to firmly conclude that humans are largely responsible. He pointed out one particularly disturbing data point, though: The time period between COTS infestations seem to be closing. It's been relatively easy to track the rate of historic COTS outbreaks worldwide by studying coral fossils, and it is clear that periodic COTS infestations occur from time to time. When the outbreaks occur more frequently, however, as they have in recent years, coral doesn't have enough time to grow back before another horde of spiny and voracious predators descends on them en masse. Whether the cycle is "natural" or not, there is abundant evidence that coral cover in parts of the GBR is diminishing to alarming levels.

The even sadder news is that the GBR is a relative bright spot in oceans full of disappearing reefs. Coral reef ecosystems are gravely endangered around the world. Once-vibrant reefs along the Florida Keys, in the Maldives, and across Indonesia, for example, are virtually destroyed. By some estimates, a quarter of the world's reefs have already disappeared, and marine scientists from around the world collectively report that half or more of the remaining reefs could easily be gone by the time Zoe is my age.

In sum, the COTS epidemic is an ecological parable of our times that is saddeningly, maddeningly similar to so many others. It is perhaps even more so because Australia is such a rich country whose government understands the tremendous economic benefits of ecotourism. "If we can't save the Great Barrier Reef, there's not much hope for other coral reefs, is there?" Doug asked.

Another question hangs out there, almost too overwhelming to speak out loud. Are humans doing something that makes it easier for the COTS to proliferate? What if we believe that humans are contributing to the COTS epidemic, but can't quite prove it?

And what if we can prove it, and it means we have to change how we live in order to stop the starfish from eating a substantial portion of these undersea rainforests? Are humans up to the task?

"MAGICAL, DADDY"

THE DAY AFTER our second reef trip, I spoke by phone with Lyndon DeVantier, a marine scientist based in Townsville and a friend of a biologist I had met in Colorado. Although Lyndon's wife Catherine had just had a baby, they invited us to visit their home on Magnetic Island off the coast of Townsville, which might have the highest per capita ratio of marine biologists in the world.

We drove south to Townsville and boarded the one-hour ferry to Magnetic Island. Lyndon and Catherine greeted us like old friends and set us up in a pair of bungalows they have in their backyard that are frequented at night by possums, which freaked Zoe out.

That evening we visited a neighbor, a single mom with two girls, one of whom was Zoe's age. Zoe glommed on to the girl like a life raft, and I rediscovered one of the most difficult and unanticipated things about this trip. I had wildly underestimated how much my kids needed social interaction with friends and how hard it would be to just be the three of us all the time. Zoe, always a little less self-sufficient than Kolya, seemed to be suffering the most and practically had to be pried away from her new playmate when it was time to leave. I realized that even when Rebecca and I had globe-trotted, we had frequently hooked up with other travelers to bring new blood into our duo—for a meal, for a day's excursion, even for weeks at a time. Here I found very few travelers with kids, and most of the children we met were much younger than Kolya and Zoe.

Lyndon told us that Magnetic Island was renowned for its koala-viewing possibilities, and the next day the kids and I ventured out to spy the marsupial action, or inaction. Koalas, like sloths, are not noted for their activity, especially by day.

The kids dismissed the idea of rising before dawn, so we settled on a late morning start. We hiked up a road leading to a World War II–era fortress called "The Forts" that had been built to stave off an expected Japanese attack. The way was predictably uphill and, for Zoe, immeasurably long and tiring.

"Can I rest? Why can't I rest?" she whined before we had even walked a kilometer.

"C'mon, darlin', let's go to where the koalas are before they go to sleep for the day."

She was still dragging.

"Zoe, I'm very concerned if you can't walk a mile," I said, a little sterner. We planned to leave soon on a five-day backpacking trip on Hinchinbrook Island, where she would have to walk at least five miles a day with a pack on. "Maybe we shouldn't do the Hinchin-brook walk," I said, hoping to prod her on.

"Daaaaaaad," she said, ignoring my implied question.

"What?"

"Can't I rest? You always expect me to be able to do everything that Kolya does."

"Zoe, I know you. You're my daughter. You can walk this far. There's nothing wrong with you. How can I help you? What do you need?"

"I need to rest. Mama let me rest when we went hiking together."

The Mama card. It was always there, lurking. Was she trying to make me feel guilty, trying to tell me how hurt she was? How much she missed her mom? How she was still trying to make sense of everything?

We passed a Dutch television crew filming a kids' show. The producer informed us that koalas were just ahead, which perked Zoe up. We passed a few other tourists before encountering our first koala, which looked very much like the stuffed animal you would like to have next to you for long scary nights of the soul at age six. Soon, we saw other koalas, hanging like furry gray fruit on eucalyptus trees along the path, and other kids, watching the koalas.

Kolya and Zoe seemed as transfixed by two young Aussie kids' banter as they were by the sight of the koalas in the trees.

"Look, it poohed on Sammie," the younger one exclaimed.

Kolya and Zoe looked at each other, barely suppressing laughter.

I knew, and not just from those Quantas Airlines ads, that koalas were big business in Australia. What I didn't realize was that even this "animal ambassador" clings precariously to survival. In Australia, the koala is listed as vulnerable but not yet endangered under the country's Endangered Species Act. The U.S. Fish and Wildlife Service listed the koala as threatened in May 2000, even though the only koalas in the United States are zoo inmates and the regulation mostly affects the importation of koalas.

As I conducted a little research on the koala and talked to Lyndon and Catherine, I learned that the cuddly creatures had almost been hunted to extinction by the 1920s in order to supply Alaskans with exotic koala pelt hats. In 1927, the year koala hunting was outlawed, 600,000 pelts were exported from Queensland alone.

Things went well enough for the koala for a while, enough so that Australia relaxed its export rules by the 1970s and allowed the United States, and eventually Japan, to bring koala refugees to their zoos. The Japanese, in particular, whipped themselves into an anticipatory koala frenzy, with high-level diplomatic talks reaching the respective prime ministers. *Le tout* Japan needed a koala, and the papers blared headlines about marsupial diplomacy regarding quotas of koala immigrants.

Today, nobody seems to know the koala count in Australia, but wildlife biologists do know that koala habitat is being decimated. Although koalas used to be quite pervasive, these days the furry mammals only live in southeast Australia. The nonprofit Australian Koala Foundation reports that 80 percent of the koala's natural habitat has already been destroyed.

As the habitat goes, so goes the animal, and the koala's story is dishearteningly familiar. Honed over evolutionary time to sleep among and eat eucalyptus leaves (both arguably noble professions), the koala crisis provides one more example of the laws of unintended consequences. Not only are the eucalyptus forests being replaced by fast-food outlets, but when koalas are forced out of their trees by urban expansion, farming, logging, and grazing they also face the ignominy of being killed by cars, mangled by pet dogs, and drowned in suburban swimming pools.

Then there's the koala-hugging crisis. In an effort to maximize koala-related profits, several koala sanctuaries allow tourists to hug koalas for an extended photo op in return for a fairly reasonable fee, considering the relative rarity of the experience. For reasons that are not entirely clear, but may have to do with disease transmission, the Australian state of New South Wales outlawed the degenerate habit of koala hugging, allowing only chaste pats of koala heads while koalas are in their perches. The tourism industry protested.

Thankfully, koala petting continues in Queensland.

The kids loved seeing the koalas and ran from tree to tree to take pictures. Ultimately, though, they both tired of watching the koalas do what they do eighteen hours a day. Sleep.

I prodded them to walk to the hilltop where the forts were

perched, commanding a great view of the island, but the kids were tired and dusty and thirsty and hungry and didn't want to. I climbed up anyway, and when I returned they were sitting in the dirt, moping and angry at me for "taking so long."

Suddenly, I was beside myself, furious that here we were, seeing koalas in the wild, and for the kids the thrill of discovery had lasted about long enough to record the experience on a digital camera.

Zoe responded that once again my expectations for them were waaaaay too high. She accused me of wanting them to be different than they are, to be openly enthusiastic about all that they were seeing, what they were learning, at all times. Sometimes, though, they were hot and tired even if they were seeing something amazing.

Fair dinkem, darlin', I told her, which we have learned is Australian for something true or genuine.

I didn't know why I had to keep learning the same lesson. I wondered if I was as diffident as Kolya and Zoe when I was a child, if I mocked my parents when they stopped the car to take in a beautiful sunset or pointed out delicate blue eggs inside a robin's nest? I felt like an old curmudgeon, but I was certain that my kids' generation had a higher hurdle to clear to be engaged in any part of the world not attached to a joystick.

I'd read all about the pitfalls of raising MTV-generation children—of our kids' shorter attention spans and increasingly more demanding requirements for fast-paced entertainment. Teachers bemoan the challenge of keeping students on task when they're accustomed to flashing images that change three times per second. Observing my kids, I had to wonder as well. It's hardly a valid statistical sampling, but when Kolya was Zoe's age, he was a far more engaged reader than his sister. Could it be because he grew up without television in the home until he was nearly ten years old?

I felt like a walking anachronism, complaining about "kids these days" with the same finger-wagging remonstrance once reserved for fans of Elvis Presley or boys (like me) who grew ponytails. But even if it is more difficult to engage my kids' generation in the magic of a slow-motion sunset, I was defiantly dedicated to at least exposing Kolya and Zoe to the finer points of unhurried wonders. It's always been important to me to share my love of the natural world with my kids, even though they'd often rather be playing video games or even soccer.

It's possible, I realized, that they would come to love the natural world on their own. Frankly, I don't remember my parents pointing out particularly beautiful sunsets or robins' nests, although I do have vivid memories of our African wildlife safaris. I discovered the backcountry pretty much by myself around the age of sixteen, when I borrowed a friend's pack, put on Converse tennis shoes, stowed a bunch of chocolate bars and peanut butter sandwiches, and took off into the Sierra Nevada for days at a time. I was hardly John Muir, with his overcoat and crust of bread, lashing himself to the tops of conifers during storms to feel their fury. But my first simple backcountry wanderings were enough to instill in me a serene joy while walking through a kaleidoscopic field of alpine wildflowers or listening to the warning peeps of alarmed marmots on a two-mile-high mountain pass. Over the years I had adventured in various wild places—from the Pyrenees to Mount Kenya, from the Canadian Rockies to the Himalayas and Karakoram. Each place I went, I fell deeper in love—with light, with water, with granite.

I wanted my kids to share my affection for giant redwoods and cholla cactus, to swim in mountain lakes and sleep under streaking stars during meteor showers. When Kolya still wore diapers, Rebecca and I carried him in a backpack to explore the California coast. We car-camped with him from the time he was too heavy to carry until he was nine, when I brought him on his first self-propelled backpacking trip in Rocky Mountain National Park. I will never forget waking up at dawn to the sound of rustling near our tent, and peering out with Kolya to the sight of a grazing six-point elk. My son's look of wonder remains indelible in my mind. On the hike out, he decided that each year, from that point on, we would hike one extra day for each year: next year we would do a two-nighter, the year after that three, etc.

I was thrilled that he had come up with the idea. I wanted to teach my children the language of the natural world, about drainages and ridge winds and north slopes and glacial valleys and treelines and how the temperature dropped 3.5 degrees Fahrenheit for every thousand feet of elevation gain. I wanted them to distinguish a deer poop from an elk poop (deer droppings have a dimple and a nipple), a raccoon print from a weasel print. I wanted them to know what ptarmigan spoor looks like and notice where an elk had made a day bed. What to do if they came across a bear (don't look a grizzly in the eye, but be big and bold with a black bear). What it feels like to be prey.

When Kolya and I hiked, we'd lie in our sleeping bags at night and he learned that you can tell a planet from a star because planets don't twinkle. As we rose in elevation in the Sierra Nevada, we traversed madrone and oak forests into Douglas fir and red cedar stands. We'd conduct impromptu math lessons on estimating, counting annual rings in a section of a fallen tree some 15 feet in diameter, then extrapolating that it must have been 500 years old when it toppled.

I wanted to impress upon them that in our home country, they were part owners of 726 million acres of public land, nearly a third of the country. I hoped they'd learn viscerally the beauty and meaning of words to describe landscapes and natural formations: confluences, passes, gullies, washes, bluffs, draws, swamps, bogs, knolls, mesas, snowfields, meadows, ranges. When does a seep become a rivulet become a stream become a river become a torrent? When is a puddle a tarn, a tarn a pond, a pond a lake, a lake an inland sea? How do you tell a spruce tree from a pine tree, a lodgepole pine from a jack pine? Why don't lynx live in the same habitat as bobcats, and which animals are predators and which eat carrion?

When Zoe turned nine, I began the same ritual, taking her into Rocky Mountain National Park with Tory. We stripped naked to swim in an icy waterfall, I taught her to whittle with her new Swiss

Army Knife, and she snuggled in between us for the warm cozy night. And there was no MTV in sight.

Now, on this trip, I still had to pry the kids away from the Game Boys, but they occasionally feigned interest when we saw something interesting—especially if it moved. One afternoon I pulled the van to a well-marked roadside trail and we walked through the rainforest on a self-guided tour. I was earnestly talking to Kolya and Zoe about all the different life forms and how they interact, from the way leaf cutter ants help make forest soil to the way cassowary poop helps fruit trees reproduce, when Zoe broke into a sarcastically nasal tone meant to imitate a nerdy kid and said, "Oh, Daddy, this is so magical!!!" Even Kolya thought it was hilarious.

Another impromptu phrase entered our lexicon, an encapsulation of how I wanted the kids to appreciate what we were doing, and how unlikely it was for that to happen in real time. From that point on, whenever I prompted the kids to notice something amazing or unusual, they just looked at me with a faux-rapturous look and said, "Magical, Daddy!"

On our way back to Lyndon and Catherine's, we stopped in front of one last koala perched on a limb about fifteen feet away. In the moment we stood there, the koala stuck out its tongue and moved its paw in a gesture that looked uncannily like a good-bye wave. Kolya, Zoe, and I looked at each other and back to the koala. It was still sticking out its tongue and waving.

And Zoe obliged with her now trademark nerdy twang but also with an unmistakable ring of sincerity.

"Magical, Daddy!"

DUGONG MUNCHER

UPON LEAVING the sanctuary of Lyndon and Catherine's hospitality in koala-infested Magnetic Island, we headed north again for Cardwell, where we would pick up permits for our next Australian adventure: a five-day "walkabout" across the world's largest oceanic island national park, Hinchinbrook Island. Several years previously, I had gone backpacking on this rainforest island with a friend for a magazine assignment. As I planned this trip, I had decided that Hinchinbrook would be a great place to revisit with the kids. The 32-kilometer hike and four nights out would be a stretch for Zoe— she had never backpacked for more than an overnighter before. But Kolya was an old backcountry hand by now, and I figured we could take our time and the hike would be a great opportunity to really get a feel for a rainforest.

Before heading off, we paid a visit to Margaret Thorsborne, who at seventy-three hadn't eased up from performing her role as a tenacious guardian of Hinchinbrook Island and its environs. It was a task she had shared for many years with her late husband Arthur— in fact, the trail we were about to walk—Thorsborne Trail—was named after him. The two of them had started visiting Hinchinbrook in the mid-1960s and had eventually become self-appointed protectors of the island and the mainland coast surrounding it, dogging developers and leading protests and campaigns to attempt to stop them.

Margaret, whom I think the kids immediately regarded as a little batty, living as she does in an isolated cabin deep in the rainforest, greeted us in a clearing outside her cottage. Her electricity-free home looked as if it could barely fend off an unrelenting assault of tropical foliage, but Margaret nonetheless appeared the picture of propriety. She invited us in for tea, fresh-baked goods, and little English-style sandwich triangles with a brand of processed cheese that survives in extremely muggy tropical environments.

She talked eagerly about the plight of the Hinchinbrook region and had laid out piles of press clippings, maps, and pamphlets for us to peruse. She expressed particular distaste for a huge development expansion planned for the mainland called Port Hinchinbrook, proposed by a developer named Keith Williams who has a habit, according to many critics like Margaret, of "performing miracles in reverse."

Williams had earned dubious notoriety for building an Australian *Sea World* in a previously untrammeled stretch along Australia's Gold Coast near Brisbane, and for developing the high-rise Hamilton Island Resort in a gorgeous chain of islands called the Whitsundays. That resort, built with much controversy, helped to turn an otherwise beautiful tropical beachfront into something approximating a luxury quadrant of Miami Beach. The British newspaper *The Guardian*, hardly an environmental rag, praised the resort for its luxury—and noted its inappropriate placement: "Despite its obvious pleasures, [it] shames the state government that allowed it to be built."

Williams's plans to develop hundreds of vacation homes directly across the channel from Hinchinbrook Island, complete with private docks and an artificial port, had Margaret fearing for the dugongs, dolphins, and other richly varied marine life that make their living along the channel and around the island.

Not even deigning to use Williams's name, she referred to him as "the developer" and simply could not believe that people would allow construction that would, among other ecological indignities, threaten mangrove forests and bring masses of private boaters out to Hinchinbrook Island.

The dugongs, relatives of the manatees found in Florida, are especially imperiled, she said. These long-lived mammals, which can weigh more than 800 pounds and grow to be as old as Margaret, are also known as sea cows, even though they are more closely related to elephants than to bovines. As in south Florida, where manatees are regularly mowed over by speedboaters on holiday, on Hinchinbrook Island it was likely that joyriding vacationers at Williams's new development would mean fewer dugongs. The species was already endangered by the typical cascade of human influence: over-fishing, land clearing, nutrient runoff, sewage running into seagrass beds, and other habitat-destroying activity. All the essentials of this unique marine ecosystem would be irreversibly damaged if Williams had his way, his slight, gray-haired adversary insisted.

Various species of birds, all of which Margaret could name, flitted by the feeder on her windowsill, and she paused long enough to identify them before returning to her tirade. "It's just monstrous," she continued.

Over several cups of tea and refilled plates of goodies, which the kids dispatched as if I never fed them, her portrait of "the developer" emerged as something right out of a Carl Hiaissen novel—only instead of being set in south Florida this one operated here in Queensland. According to Margaret and other Queensland environmentalists, Williams had strong-armed his way, threatening lawsuits against adversaries and conveniently sidestepping the fact that his former company had gone bankrupt during the development of Hamilton Island, which Margaret clearly disdains as another miracle in reverse.

There was something entertainingly incongruous about the

quiet, mild-mannered Margaret and the vehemence with which she discussed her nemesis. Even Kolya remained attentive as she explained how Williams had promised that the new Hinchinbrook development would bring thousands of jobs to the chronically underemployed area ("an absolute lie") and greased the political skids by co-opting local officials with a piece of the action. Margaret recounted getting arrested at a protest, screaming "dugong muncher" at Williams's henchmen as she and others tried to stop the "swamp dozers" from razing the coastal mangroves.

"Dugong muncher?" Kolya giggled.

She nodded, a slight grin of self-satisfaction crossing her otherwise prim mouth.

The kids remained uncharacteristically polite and listened, even as they were devoured by *mozzies* (mosquitoes) as Margaret and I chatted. But after awhile, they signaled for permission to return to the van and play electronic Monopoly on the laptop. I mimed that they should thank our hostess before they went.

Margaret and I conversed a bit longer as I gathered copies of newspaper stories and scientific reports for my roving library. As I took her leave, I silently thanked the world that people like her still try to fight back the red tide that inevitably follows development-mad people like Williams.

We drove away from Margaret's, heading south for the town of Lucinda about an hour's drive away, where we would meet an outfitter who would ferry us across Hinchinbrook Channel to the island. We drove slowly, following a narrow two-track road through the rainforest that led to the highway. Suddenly, we saw a movement in the bush, and Zoe screamed.

"A cassowary!"

Good eyes. The giant bird skittered into the forest. I turned off the engine and we hopped from the car. Kolya grabbed the camera and trained it on the sounds we heard about thirty yards into the jungle. For the next ten minutes, we caught fleeting glimpses of the enormous cassowary, which strode along calmly despite our presence. After awhile we lost it and ambled back to the car.

The kids were jazzed and animated, as was I. They decided we should hike around, and given how rare it was for them to initiate a nature walk, I let them lead. Their senses trained on any movement anywhere, we moved silently through fairly dense forest with no trails.

Nothing on the trip enlivened the kids so much as seeing wildlife in the wild, even though the excitement can be preposterously short-lived. So far, the lace monitor lizards, crocodiles, cassowaries, koalas, kingfishers, and fish species beyond imagination had all prompted expressions of true wonder, even in my jaded teenage boy. Later in Australia, we'd see kookaburras, kangaroos, wallabies, wombats, and platypuses. By the end of the trip we would see pythons, pit vipers, orangutans, gibbons, proboscis monkeys, macaques, rhinos, eagles, raptors of all stripes, river otters, mongooses, and more.

The glee on the kids' faces when they spotted the cassowary compensated for so much of the day-to-day sibling hassling. I wondered what exactly it is that gives rise to such a sense of wonderment—why we "civilized" humans spend gazillions of dollars on zoos, safaris, animal parks, menageries, and even exotic pets. Deep inside, we must recognize a missing connection that we need to recapture. Something, or a combination of things, about our modern existence has forced us to neglect that connection.

It seems to me that we humans risk losing something indispensable to our most basic nature if we break that bond. For as long as humans have existed on the planet, animals have been inseparable from our myths, our stories, our very existence. Long before we domesticated pigs and cattle, we hunted. We anthropomorphized the animals, giving them human traits in our legends: the wily coyote, the shy possum, the regal lion.

Unfortunately, so much of modern civilization involves distancing ourselves from our animal selves. Maybe we've lost the connection in the multichannel, multimedia world we've created. I wondered, stalking the wild cassowary with my children, if a dim filament of evolutionary biology or psychology was being activated by the sighting.

Harvard biologist E. O. Wilson defined this filament as "the connections that human beings subconsciously seek with the rest of life," labeling it "biophilia," love of life. In Wilson's view, we desperately *need* other living things, because *Homo sapiens* co-evolved with all forms of life. Just because we've invented microprocessors and can buy shrink-wrapped meat doesn't mean that we can disconnect from the natural world.

But why, then, is there such an insufferably huge gap between this theoretical deep-seated engagement with the natural world and the worldwide human behavior that destroys so many of the planet's inhabitants? The question bedevils me.

MONKEY DANCING

THE CASSOWARY sighting was a perfect send-off as we readied ourselves to traverse an uninhabited part of Hinchinbrook Island with nothing but what we carried on our backs. We packed until late that afternoon, and I nixed the Game Boys and the mini-disc player in favor of food, tent, and sleeping bags. As the kids watched me pare down our loads to the essentials, it began to dawn on them how isolated we'd be out there.

The other time I had visited Hinchinbrook, a gruff but kindhearted outfitter named Bill Pearce had ferried my friend and me from the mainland to the island. To my happy surprise, the same floppy-hatted and gray-haired third-generation local greeted us with a curt "G'day" outside his home when we arrived ready to begin our "walkabout." Margaret Thorsborne had told me that Pearce knew Hinchinbrook and its environs as well as anybody—and he certainly looked and acted the part. His meaty, flat feet belonged to a man who had spent a lifetime without shoes, and his no-bullshit demeanor matched what you'd expect from a person who had spent plenty of time chasing crabs—and crocodiles—through mangrove forests.

Pearce took us in his van to the boat ramp a few miles from town, but as we arrived there, I realized with utter dread and mortification that I didn't have my camera bag. My digital camera, a 35-millimeter camera with lenses, *and* the video camera were probably lying by a grassy area near a store where we had hung out that morning. I explained the situation to Pearce, and he wordlessly beckoned me into the van. We drove back to the grassy area where I could see the bag in my mind.

The bag was gone.

I felt crestfallen, utterly defeated. No Zen-like state could countermand the feeling of pure stupidity that swept over me. Pearce strolled into the store and emerged with a piece of paper. An elderly couple staying at the caravan park, it seems, had picked up the bag and left the number of their site with the store owner. They seemed to be expecting me and weren't surprised that I was a Yank. Who else would be rich enough to leave camera gear lying around?

The couple refused any offer of reward but graciously accepted my effusive thanks. I felt like a completely relieved fool. Then I just felt overwhelmed, embarrassed, and, finally, grateful.

I love Australians.

Pearce finally loaded us into his skiff to take us to the southern tip of the island. The low whine of the engine cut through the stillness of the channel, and Pearce eased off on the throttle when I spoke. I asked Pearce a little about the island—what was the drinking water situation, the best places to camp this time of year, what were the top predators? He misunderstood me, thinking I had asked which was the most deadly animal on the island. "Well, the way I see it, if you come up with a death adder, a stinger, or a croc, then you're not likely to get off the island alive," he said in a rural Queensland twang that would make "the crocodile hunter," Steve Irwin, sound like a dandified city slicker.

I figured Pearce was putting on a show for the kids, trying to scare us with threats of venomous snakes, lethal jellyfish, and two-ton prehistoric reptiles. But he seemed pretty matter-of-fact about it, using the same voice as when he suggested we hang our food from fishing line to avoid losing it to the giant rodents called mosaic-tailed rats that inhabited the island. The kids looked at each other with bugging eyes.

The skiff arrived with a soft thud and we tossed our gear onto white sand. "Follow up the beach to a stream, cross it at low tide, then look for a trail sign heading into the rainforest. Just don't go swimming in Zoe Bay, there's a croc who lives by the estuary there." I had told Zoe about her namesake bay and the waterfall that bore her name, two days' hike away, and she proudly decided that it was named after her. Kolya snorted. Still, I hoped that the lure of Zoe Falls, which I had explained to them emptied into a huge pool with one of the world's great rope swings, would keep her going.

We tossed our packs in the sand and watched Pearce hightail it back to the mainland. We had no choice now but to walk 20 miles over the next five days, where we had arranged for a boat to pick us up at high noon at a boardwalk in a mangrove forest. We donned our packs and started up the beach, feeling the excitement and trepidation of explorers.

Hinchinbrook Island lay before us, a mangle of mangroves and granite peaks, unbroken beaches, waterfalls, eucalyptus groves, and writhing rainforest. The channel separated the island from the mainland by a mere mile, but civilization drew a bright line between the two. Except for a small resort at the northern tip, Hinchinbrook remains uninhabited: a bushwalker's paradise. Just past the high tide mark on the beach, a dense rainforest begins, guarded by dozens of yellow and blue butterflies that mark the entry into the forest like sentinels. Once inside, we entered a world full of bloodwoods, lawyer vines, palms, strangler figs, and epiphytes and an encyclopedia-full of bird, insect, and animal species. Above the rainforest, the island transforms into eucalyptus forests that sit below the 3,745-foot granite massif of Mt. Bowen, one of several peaks that play hide and seek in the mountain fog. Over the next four days, we would follow the 32-kilometer Thorsborne trail, which more or less paralleled the eastern shore with detours for waterfalls, rainforest crossings, and a climb around impenetrable cliffs and rock outcroppings.

It didn't take long before we realized why one of Australia's leading conservationists would be so exercised about Hinchinbrook's plight. Following Pearce's advice, we crossed the stream and plunged into the rainforest. Even now, during the dry season, the vegetation appeared to swarm over the landscape. Deeper inland, the whole panorama grew increasingly unfamiliar. The rainforest produces fauna on steroids: butterflies the size of birds; beetles the size of frogs; frogs the size of small dogs; lizards the size of small dinosaurs. Even the flora menaces: tar trees with poisonous bark; strangler fig trees that grow slowly on host trees until they literally take them over as a predator would; "wait-a-whiles," a.k.a. lawyer vine, thin whips with cactus-like spikes that trail like vines, growing smaller until the tips, like barbs, catch you unawares and snare you. The smell, somewhere between an unusual odor and a stench, added to the sense I had of being overwhelmed by the proliferation of life. If I stood still for even an hour, the jungle would simply grow over me.

We camped the first night by Mulligan Falls, a 75-foot vertical torrent deep in the rainforest, and immediately dropped our packs to swim in the giant pool beneath them. We saw a couple other tents and exchanged greetings with hikers who had been going north to south, opposite from us, and would be heading off the island the next day. The kids explored downstream by themselves. I marveled at their spirit of exploration, especially given what I had told them about the first time I had been at that same campsite on my magazine assignment. After an uneventful night, Ted Wood, my friend and the photographer, awoke before first light and stepped outside the tent. "Whoa," he let out, and I scrambled out to see him standing a respectful distance from something moving in the leaves. A python. "How big is it?" I asked, from an even more respectful distance. Like a giant hose being uncoiled, about fifteen feet of nonvenomous snake headed for his day bed after munching on the mosaic rats that I had seen looking for crumbs the night before.

The kids returned, uneaten, and I dried off on a rock and realized that tropical night would arrive with stark swiftness, especially now in the middle-of-July winter. We set up the tent and cooked dinner on my little campstove. Unfortunately, as we sat down to eat, we discovered an embarrassing oversight: I had forgotten to put in any cutlery. Kolya rummaged through his pack and turned up a single spoon, which had probably been hidden there, unwashed, since the previous summer. No matter. It was a find, and as we huddled around our pot of Thai noodles with canned chicken, we quickly abandoned the pretense of passing the spoon around in a circle. With feral abandon, we simply dipped our fingers into the bowl. I told them that in Nepal we would be eating all our meals that way, but that didn't keep them from teasing me mercilessly for my oversight. Mr. Backpacking Guru, forgetting the forks. As far as I was concerned, they were lucky I didn't forget the food and make them scavenge rainforest grubs and grill rats for dinner.

We washed up, climbed into the tent, and read a bit by flashlight. Slowly, Zoe's anxiety level rose as she imagined the long, dark night ahead, and only then did the stories kick in. Now she was petrified of amethystine pythons and giant rodents and noises scurrying in the night.

After a morning swim in the pool under Mulligan Falls, with jungle perch nibbling at our legs, we headed off again. The trail rose inland, past the homes of orange-footed scrub fowl, frog-mouthed owls, fruit bats, rainbow lorikeets, goannas, and wompoo pigeons. En route, we stopped at the top of a gully and picked a swingable vine, then took turns doing our best Tarzan imitations.

We became human pendulums in the rainforest, swinging from vines and jungle yodeling.

We threw our packs back on, kept walking, and inevitably the thrill of vine swinging receded as we entered a state of happy trudging. Zoe walked ahead, singing invented rhymes, and Kolya and I fell into step. He was curious about the world in measured doses and began what would become a regular refrain during the rest of the trip.

"So, Dad," he opened, his warm-up to questions that will range from Uncle Bob's football career to a political evaluation of the Cold War. I loved these discussions as we walked through improbable places together. There on the Thorsborne trail, he wanted to know about the history of civilizations, of European conquests, about how *Homo sapiens* evolved and developed tools and agriculture and formed into permanent settlements and learned to cross oceans and the whole history of the world.

He seemed genuinely interested as I gave him the rap as far as I understood it, but I realized how incomplete my knowledge was of the origins of humanity and human society. Did we evolve from separate groups of *Homo sapiens* in Pangea, or in Gondwanaland? Why are there Caucasians and Negroids and Asiatic peoples? Did they speciate, as it were, or originate more or less simultaneously on different parts of the planet? I had just read Jared Diamond's *Guns, Germs and Steel: The Fates of Human Societies* (1996) and wished I had a better memory. Still, Kolya seemed satisfied with the detail I could recall.

Zoe's period of walking grace ran out about the time we had to climb a hill before dropping down to a cove to spend the night. I had already removed everything heavy out of her pack and now took the whole pack, but she insisted on whining, "Are we almost there, yet?"

I usually try the Zen master response to that question, replying, "But you *are* there. How could you be anywhere else?"

The answer has long since ceased to amuse the kids, although occasionally Kolya will actually say those words to Zoe. But at that moment it wouldn't work, not from me and not from Kolya, and we had much ground to cover before we reached a suitable camping site.

The kids suggested we play a "category game," wherein we pick a category and take turns listing things in the category.

I saw no way out. I suggested "trees."

Too much of an advantage for me. Kolya suggested "bands." This could go on for awhile.

We began, and Kolya unveiled a shrewd strategy by naming *my* bands.

Kolya: The Rolling Stones.

I countered his strategy by naming one of his: Green Day.

K: The Beatles.

D: Blink 182.

K: The Doors.

D: Eminem.

Zoe chimed in. "What about me?" Christina Aguilera.

K: Led Zeppelin.

D: Millencolin. (I know the band because Kolya has a poster in his room.)

Z: Britney Spears. (Kolya has several of her posters in his room, and not because he likes her music.)

K: The Beach Boys.

D: Pennywise.

Z: Aqua.

It didn't take long before Kolya and I switched strategy and reverted to our own bands. Zoe, who listens to more music than I ever did at her age and watches more MTV than I would like, held her own for awhile with the equivalent of modern teeny-bopper bands. The kids have brought me to the verge of contemporary musical relevance, since I will listen to their radio stations during car trips, but I am no match for the quantity of music videos they have seen.

I conducted an unsystematic search in my brain of obscure 1960s bands: Strawberry Alarm Clock.

Kolya dragged out equally obscure punk bands. "No Use for a Name."

"There's no band called "No Use for a Name," I moaned.

"Yes there is."

Who would name a band "No Use for a Name?" I asked. "You're making that up."

"Who would name a band after a bug?" he riposted.

Point taken. Which reminds me. The Dragonflies? The Bees? Bee Gees.

Kolya remembered one of mine. The Monkees.

We started playing associative games.

D: Badfinger.

K: Bad Brains.

D: Bad Company.

K: Bad Religion.

D: Black Sabbath.

Z: Sunday's Child.

K: Poster Children.

D: Kid Rock. (pulling out another contemporary coup.)

Zoe ran out of ideas after trying Christina Aguilera again and Kolya and I snapped competitively, "You already said that." She offered to join forces with Kolya against me, and of course Kolya's first instinct was to balk.

I shot him a glance that said, "We're playing this stupid game in order to distract your sister and make sure we can keep walking through this jungle until we reach a camping spot. Why would you be such a dicknose?"

He gets it, first try, and says, "Okay, Toots, you're with me."

Kolya has taken to calling his sister "Toots," which rhymes with "puts" rather than "roots." For years she was "Toast," or "Toaster," a result of my Cockney-like slang game which started with Zoe, Zo, Zoester, Zoester-toaster, Toaster, and simply, "Toast." Kolya became Kolya-Bolya, Kolster, and Kolya Bear, which simply became "K," which he later informed me he doesn't like. He isn't entirely sure he even likes his name, which is a Russian diminutive for Nicholai, taken partly in honor of my Russian roots but also after a character in Dostoyevsky's *The Brothers Karamazov*, a naughty little waif who gave the saintly Alyosha hell. To name him Nicholas would have been a debacle, since that would certainly have become Nick, and with our last name it just wouldn't have worked.

The way the kids address me has also evolved over time. When they were young, they called me "Papa," perhaps because that's what Rebecca called her Dutch dad. For a short while after Rebecca left for the West Coast, when Zoe started screaming "Maaaaaamm-mmmmm," only to realize that it was only me there to respond, she transformed the word into something like "Maaaaaammmmm-pop." I liked that, MomPop, and for awhile that was what she called me. That shifted invariably to Dad, but on the trip we started something new. When I was feeling particularly goofy, or wanted to make a serious disciplinarian point without seeming too heavy, I shifted into a bad Scottish brogue and an even worse imitation of Mike Meyers, the Scottish character Fat Bastard in *Austin Powers*. "Now, y'ere not goin' to steart screwin' around with yer olde Da, now, eare ya?" So I was Da for awhile.

And even that became whittled down as Kolya began calling me simply "D." Not for my first name, but for Dad or Da. D it is. It felt a little more grown-up to him, I figure, and it felt endearing to me. Zoe stuck with Papa or Dad. Or Daaaaaaaad.

The game continued long enough to easily cover a mile and a much broader swath of intergenerational musical ground. I put Kolya on the ropes with "The Holy Modal Rounders," and he asked if he'd already said "Homegrown," which he had.

We all declared victory and continued walking in relative silence. We crested the hill and I saw our goal, so I could actually and truthfully say, "We're almost there." We descended to a gorgeous cove, which we had to ourselves, settled in comfortably on camp chairs converted from inflatable sleeping mattresses (which I didn't forget), cooked dinner and ate it while fighting over the spoon, then fell asleep early and exhausted.

The next day we climbed over a ridge and dropped steeply, following a pool-laden river, which required many strippings and dippings, until we reached the paradise-within-a-paradise of Zoe Bay. There, we reveled in tropical green pools big enough to swim laps in set at the base of a towering waterfall. As promised, there was the fabled rope swing of Zoe Falls, with a launching point on a rock outcropping 15 feet above the water. With a coordinated leap, grab, and swing, we flew through the air and landed with various splats into the giant jungle swimming pool.

I watched Kolya transforming into a young, competent man before my eyes. That evening he had run ahead with Zoe to set up the tent at dusk as I filtered water, then guided her a half-mile along rainforest track to the rope swing while I tended to camp. He set up the stove, lit it, and boiled water for dinner.

We slept near Zoe Falls that night, then headed onward, spotting sea turtles along the way and capping the day with a dreamy swim in a freshwater lagoon over the dunes from the ocean, fed by a jungle stream. There, our last night on Hinchinbrook concluded with one of the most memorable moments of our entire trip. We camped at the high-tide mark of a mile-long white sand beach, in a clearing under a canopy of palm trees. After four days, we had accustomed ourselves to the rhythms of the island, bedding down early and waking with the dawn jungle chorus.

When I finished with the dishes, the kids dragged me to the deserted beach, a half-moon midway through the winter antipodal sky, which was already black and pockmarked by stars though it couldn't be past seven. The two of them jumped me, and we began a raucous three-way tag-team wrestling match that mostly involved the kids running kamikaze at me and me tossing them to the sand like a benevolent King Kong.

In the tropical night, Kolya and I stripped to the waist, Zoe in her bathing suit. Without a word, we started a kind of simian step, hunching our shoulders up and down and dragging our knuckles on the fine sand. The three of us peered at each other with cocked heads, vocalizing monkey sounds. We started moving slowly, almost in a circle, then faster, and faster, with more abandon and less inhibition. We danced wildly along the beach, rolling around, jumping and screaming. Kolya dubbed it "monkey dancing."

We were monkey dancing around the planet.

THE JERRY SPRINGER SHOW?

I CAN NOW ADMIT the relief I felt when we set foot on the mainland and saw Bill Pearce waiting to shuttle us back to our van in Lucinda. Although the Hinchinbrook hike was popular enough that there would be other hikers along the way in case of emergency, I also knew that we had been on our own out there. We toasted our success with ice cream and returned seamlessly to the land of forks and slightly less feral eating habits.

On the ride back, we observed the first stage of the Port Hinchinbrook development rising where mangroves used to be, listened to the grinding of dredges and the familiar and depressing signs of another natural wonder being carved up at such a high cost. And could only hope that people like Margaret Thorsborne might be able to prevail before Hinchinbrook is added to a long, sad list of places that constitute a miracle in reverse.

Since Hinchinbrook provided one of the only fixed stars in our itinerant constellation, we felt free to proceed as the winds pushed us. We pulled into a shaded caravan park and reengaged our now-familiar routine. The van seemed like a mobile lap of luxury, with sodas in the fridge, cookies in the larder, and portable CD players, which occasioned Kolya to remember a slew of bands he had forgotten under the pressure of our forced march. I walked into town, found an Internet café and downloaded an edit of a story I had submitted to *Outside* magazine before going to Hinchinbrook, picked up groceries, and strolled back to the van. I grilled Australian lamb chops on the caravan park's barbie, tasted the singular delight of the first beer after a hike, and we settled, controversy-free, into our respective berths for the night.

As we drifted off listening to the waves, a coconut slammed into the roof of our van, startling us momentarily. Zoe snuggled close and whispered how peaceful it was to sleep with the sound of the ocean so close by, then fell asleep within minutes of that observation. I smelled and kissed her hair before drifting off myself.

I awoke before dawn and ran on the beach, then called the *Outside* editor to make comments about his comments and put the story—about the starfish troopers—to bed. As I hung up, I pondered the balancing act between considering this a "work" trip and letting it be a noncommercial enterprise. Before leaving, I had lined up three magazine assignments, which combined would pay enough to cover airfare for the three of us. But I didn't want to work too much along the way because I didn't want to defeat one of the main reasons for taking the trip: to focus my attention on Kolya and Zoe instead of on my work.

I took a financial flier on the rest. If the trip drained my savings, I decided, it would be well worth it. With Bob's death driving home the truism "you can't take it with you," and the realization that the prolonged stock-market dive had caused my 401(k) to decline in value by more than I ended up spending on the entire trip, I had taken the plunge.

In truth, my relationship with work remained in flux, as it had been since the divorce. When Rebecca left, I had been forced to reevaluate my professional calling. As a single dad, I could no longer realistically react to breaking news by hopping on the next plane to cover a militia stand-off in Montana or a wolf reintroduction in Idaho. Parachuting into news events at a moment's notice had only been possible with Rebecca available to tend the home fires. I had no choice but to look for another way to make a living—and this adventure presented an opportunity to postpone that search.

Or, possibly, to find what I was looking for.

First we needed to survive the trip.

The next day dawned lazy and we pointed the van south again after I called a family friend near Brisbane and accepted an invitation to spend the weekend at his place three days hence. We lolled around, read, wrote in our journals, and spent the day cruising.

Kolya and Zoe marred the easy mood with occasional flare-ups of sibling sadism, which are so familiar to me. As the middle son, I was both recipient and perpetrator of vile acts during long car rides, even once chipping Steve's tooth by banging his head against a metal bar on our Chrysler New Yorker station wagon (it was an accident). We three boys were more than once threatened with the prospect of being left by the side of the road if we continued fighting, an option that probably seemed a little more viable to my parents on an American highway in the early 1960s than it did to me in Queensland. Ultimately, my parents gave up on road trip vacations.

Our fraternal trio revolved for many years around Bob, the eldest son. Steve and I, less than two years apart, vied for our big brother's attention and only later in life discovered the potential in joining forces against Bob. For much of our childhood, Bob played his younger brothers' rivalry like Iago, pitting Steve and me against each other in repeated tests of love and loyalty.

Only after Bob married and left for medical school did Steve and I begin to bond. When I returned from a trip to Europe, I insinuated myself into Steve's apartment, and for much of our respective undergraduate years at UC Berkeley, we remained roommates. We shared a car and played gasoline chicken with the unwritten rule that whoever actually ran out of gas had to fill the tank. We ran in the Berkeley hills together, discovered that we had more in common than either of us did with Bob, and stumbled into a closer friendship that nonetheless never completely ignored Bob's shadow. Bob drifted further away, lost for years to both Steve and I, as he worked long hours at the hospital and privately engaged in a futile battle with an increasingly untenable marriage.

I frequently wonder how Kolya and Zoe's relationship will evolve. On this trip, balancing the needs of these two radically different kids has proven to be even more challenging than I thought it might be. When I first told Rebecca about my idea to take the kids around the world, she replied, "I can't imagine doing that alone. It's gonna be hard."

I replied that it was hard at home. It wasn't as if the kids didn't fight and things didn't seem overwhelming when we were on our own turf. She agreed, shook her head, wished me luck. And gave me her blessing, slightly wistful that she wasn't coming along. For the first time since the divorce, I felt the slightest tinge of—what?—not regret so much as a sense that she missed our marriage, or at least our family. We even had a brief discussion about whether she might join us during the trip, but we quickly concluded it would be too confusing for the kids, too awkward for us.

A caravan park owner suggested a restaurant to us after we decided to dine out, but the kids balked because I insisted on walking the half a mile to the eatery. Zoe began, in the first 100 yards, by feigning injury to her foot, dragging it Quasimodo-like down the street. I offered her a piggyback ride (though with Zoe at nine and a half years old and about 65 pounds, this was getting less interesting for me), and she accepted as Kolya walked ahead. The cool night filled with munificent stars, and I steered the conversation toward something, anything but how far it was to the stupid restaurant.

We topped a little hill, and Zoe took to her own feet again, sans the Quasimodo strut, and told me after some coaxing why she was so upset. Zoe cataloged the contents of her little black book filled with indignities large and small that I had already heaped upon her since we started the trip. According to Zoe I had:

- called her a pig (I told her not to be "an oinker" at the Red Carpet Club lounge at SFO when she piled her plate with the freebie snacks),
- told her she was a brat (she was *acting* like a brat when she refused to let me talk to an airline attendant about a customs matter),
- said she had a fat ass (I had punched her butt in utter frustration, and in an unfathomably bad choice of words, made the excuse that I had chosen her gluteus maximus for my target because of its abundance of soft tissue),
- said "Shut up" to her, words that I forbade her to use (and forbade myself to use) but just came out after we were unable to choose a book that we all wanted to read, and I almost cried because all I wanted to do was read them a story,
- and had generally not said too many nice things to her since we had taken off.

Zoe's list:

A list of the things my dad said to me bad.
Shut up
Your butt is fat
Pig
Bash your head open
Brat

Of course I wondered if maybe I am abusive, maybe Zoe's right with her black-book listings of fat butts and shut ups and verbal outbursts, which are of course terrifying to her. She retaliates regularly, attempting to right the power imbalance, to take her pound of papaflesh many times over when she wants to, because she has so little power over her world. She would like nothing more than to be home with her friends eagerly awaiting the next Disney film, which they saw the trailer for at the last Disney film, which they saw the trailer for at the Disney film before that, and go out afterward and buy a (non-Disney) Shrek-meal at BK or Mickey-D's and talk about the Shrek cups they collected and maybe trade for all four—they're a perfect set—until the next animated merchandising marauder hits the marketing mainstream.

I apologized to Zoe as we arrived at Scotty's, a typical outdoor/indoor backpacker-type pub/restaurant with something on the menu they could both stomach (but no stomach to order the kangaroo stew). Food always seemed to help, a lesson I relearned about five times a day.

Aussie-rules football blared from a telly in the corner of the room. Kolya and I became transfixed, it being the first time we'd ever seen the sport. Watching football of any stripe on the tube reminds me of Bob, and I hoisted a silent toast to him, actually pointing my beer glass at the TV. Kolya asked what I was doing, losing it completely and toasting televised sport, or what? I replied that I thought Uncle Bob would enjoy watching footie with us. (Did I say "would," or "would have"? It's still unendurable to talk about him in the past tense.) During a break in the Aussie-rules action, Kolya asked for a Bob story, about his football days as a quarterback.

Because I had skipped a grade in elementary school and Bob was held back a year because of Africa, I was in tenth grade when he was a senior despite being three and a half years younger. He was the classic BMOC, star quarterback of the league championship team. I was a young squirt, third string on the B team.

Still, I basked a little in his reflected glory and hung out on the periphery when his buddies would come over after the games and talk about each play, each screw-up, each heroic effort. I would fetch sodas and be the butt of jokes, but I was allowed to stay.

The night of the final game of the season against the cross-town rivals, Coach let me play for the first time all season. Despite being about 5'5" and a whopping 140 pounds, I was a linebacker. I played during the fourth quarter, made two tackles, and saved a touchdown.

After the game, the B team crossed paths with the varsity coming out of the locker room game-time intense. I was out of my mind with excitement and mobbed Bob. "Bob,Igottoplayand Imadetwotacklesand Isaveda-touchdown!" I rambled in one long syllable. Bob, immersed in his pregame tenseness, just having no doubt vomited as he did before every game, broke into a smile. "Hey, my brother Danny made two tackles," he announced to the team.

Man, what a moment.

A little later, Kolya returned from the bathroom disappointed once again. Ever since we had arrived, he had been searching for a dunny that spun counterclockwise. He somewhere had learned about the corealis force and, with much anticipation, had checked with slightly obsessive enthusiasm the direction of the flushes in toilets that, to date, had operated with a straight down suction rather than a spin in any direction.

The footie game wound down late and we walked home, Zoe's hand slipping into mine. Back in the van, the kids cozy and cuddled up around Papa, I read *The River* (1991), by Gary Paulsen, to them. It's about a boy lost in the wilderness with a traveling companion who's been struck by lightning and falls into a coma. At a chapter break, I placed the book on my chest, just lying there with one arm around each of them. A random association spurred them to ask about the divorce, about Mama's departure, about her announcing that she was lesbian. Zoe recalled the time I walked in to the kitchen and screamed "shit" to Rebecca after she had told me about her first woman lover. Zoe was in the next room and it had made a big impression.

Of course it did.

I always try, though sometimes it's hard work, to be magnani-mous toward Rebecca in front of the kids. But at times I want to tell the kids everything, that their mom was very, very hurtful, no mat-ter what her reasons were, reasons that I can pretend to begin to understand but mostly still can't. Tonight I duck and dodge.

"Why were you so angry?" Zoe prodded. Kolya, as almost always when the subject comes up, wanted nothing more than to talk about something else.

"Mama hurt my feelings."

"But she wouldn't hurt anybody on purpose."

"No, darling, I don't think so. But she did something that hurt my feelings a lot, and I was angry."

"What?"

"It was all about her beginning to realize that she didn't want to be married to me anymore. That was very hard for me."

Kolya interjected, "Can we read now?"

But Zoe persisted and said, "But you can understand why she couldn't be with you, that she was with another woman?" She was referring to the girlfriend Rebecca moved in with when she left for the coast. Somehow, Zoe had decided that since her mom had jumped the gender preference fence, it should all make sense to me, that it was nothing personal. It isn't that simple, but how in the world could I begin to explain the process of disillusionment to her when I couldn't even explain it to myself?

"Mama's girlfriend wasn't even in the picture yet, darlin'. That was later."

"Yes. Sort of. Let's read."

Zoe started crying on one side of me, and Kolya whispered to me that he had a question to ask me later, when Zoe wasn't around. He had an insight to share with me about Mama becoming a les-bian and all that. But now, could we read more?

When Zoe went to the bathroom, I asked Kolya what he wanted to share.

"Oh, yeah," he said. What he wanted to know was, when his mother was having her first affair with a woman, was she lying to me about it?

I was taken aback. I didn't recall directly talking to him about it and I didn't really think he knew. I told him no, she was for the most part contemporaneously truthful, but that didn't make it any easier. He was satisfied, at least, with the issue of truthfulness. It is one of my parental axioms that if either of the kids screw up, the consequences for the infraction get multiplied by a factor of three if they lie about it afterward.

I kissed him good night; he kissed me back and hugged me.

We licked our wounds at irregular intervals. We licked each other's wounds as well, as best we could.

The kids fell asleep. I didn't. I pondered how they were dealing with all these momentous concepts of sexual preference and identity.

I remembered when Rebecca and I decided that Kolya must be told something to help him make sense of our divorce. She wanted to come out to her son, as if that would explain things.

We sat our eleven-year-old boy down uneasily in our comfortable living room, which was festooned with small and meaningful mementos of our extended honeymoon: a Tibetan religious painting called a *thangka* we picked up in Bhaktapur, Nepal; a red wedding-style carpet we bargained for hours to obtain in a bazaar in Karachi, Pakistan; a woven picnic basket with carved wooden figures we purchased in Shanghai; a wood-block print we found in a thrift shop where we worked as English teachers in Hamamatsu, Japan. We still owned a few items from when my family lived in Africa: a snakeskin drum we bought in a village market; a carved ebony walking stick from the merchants at outdoor stalls in the middle of a Kampala roundabout.

In this living room crowded with travel treasures and their stories, the three of us sat down, more formally than we ever had, on our hand-me-down couches, whose pillows we and the kids had pulled off and rearranged over the years with blankets and sheets to

make impenetrable fortresses and hideouts and story-time sanctuaries. I was curious to hear what she would say, how she would say it.

"Kolya, your papa and I are getting divorced because your mama
needs to be in relationship with women. I'm a lesbian."

Kolya, tears streaming to his eyes despite every effort to contain
them, looked to the ceiling with anger and mortification.

"Fuck," he exclaimed, looking at her, then at me.

I tried but couldn't imagine what he was feeling and thinking.

"Great, what's next?" he asked plaintively. "Are we going to be on
the *Jerry Springer Show*?"

SEX, DRUGS, AND THE PLURAL OF PLATYPUS

WE NEVER made the *Jerry Springer Show*. But I came to learn that we'd have been in the midst of a crowd if we had. After Rebecca left, I was taken aback to hear how many women friends had self-identified as being lesbian at some point in their lives; how many men told me stories about an ex-wife or ex-girlfriend leaving the relationship to be with a woman; and how many people knew cousins or friends who had gone through similar trials.

The concept of a person "coming out" in middle age didn't shock me. The world is full of men and women who discovered their homosexuality or bisexuality long after they became heterosexually active. It's no secret how hard it is to be gay in our society, and it's no surprise that it takes many people a long time—and much courage—to come out. Among our network of friends and neighbors, the kids and I knew three formerly married women who were now living with other women. Two of them were also mothers, and one of the children was a good friend of Kolya's. Clearly, something is floating in the air, or the water, or the times. Or are we just talking about it more?

People have asked whether it was easier for me that Rebecca left for another woman rather than for another man. The simple answer is that it was easier *and* it was much more difficult. Easier because I believe that human sexuality is such an integral part of our nature that it is hard to argue with something so basic as sexual orientation. Easier because I believe that homosexuality has clearly been a part of human experience since recorded time and that many people have no choice but to be with mates of their own gender. More difficult because Rebecca had been my lover for so long, because I didn't see it coming. More difficult because I couldn't compete; I couldn't become a woman to save my marriage. More difficult because the disintegration of our marriage couldn't be explained away that simply.

My kids quickly developed a more sophisticated view of human sexuality than most of their peers. They surely wrestled with the obvious and complicated questions about how their mother could live with their father for seventeen years, then decide she wanted to be with women. But they understood more than most kids their age how human sexuality comes in many different flavors. As hard as it is at times, I know that's a good thing. Humans are messy creatures, almost any way you look at it.

One of the many reasons that I contrived this trip was to simply *be* with the kids as they struggled with these grand and novel questions, in addition to the run-of-the-mill horrors of preadolescence and adolescence. One truism of parenting that I subscribed to was that kids spell "love" T-I-M-E. I didn't want to simply make them snacks when they came home from school and take them to soccer practices and nag them to do their homework or clean their rooms. Kolya, in particular, was in a very dicey spot, I felt, reeling from the divorce and Uncle Bob dying, hanging out with older kids who pushed him to accelerate his already MTV-accelerated maturation. Like most teenagers, he wanted nothing more than to be grown-up completely. But like most thirteen-year olds, he still wasn't ready to fend for himself. Sex, drugs, and (punk) rock 'n' roll were fast becoming the currency of his consciousness. The simultaneous end of my marriage and the beginning of his adolescence provided spectacularly potent catalysts for him to expedite his experimentation. And I desperately wanted to slow him down.

The year before our trip, Kolya had returned home from school one day after a seventh-grade drug-education class either misinformed or confused. Somehow in conversation he mentioned that pot was a hallucinogen, and I took it as a signal that it was time to "talk to your kids about drugs," as the ubiquitous full-page newspaper ads suggest.

We sat on his bed, his room festooned with posters representing a four-subject catalog of current interests: teen sex goddesses in low-cut suggestive poses, snowboarders in sick mid-air poses, skateboarders in sick mid-air poses, and punk bands in simply sick poses. I matter-of-factly walked him through the mind-bending array of drugs—where they came from, what they did to one's brain, how addictive they were, everything I could think of: marijuana, hash, hash oil, acid, mushrooms, mescaline, peyote, speed, ecstasy, airplane glue, angel dust, downers, cocaine, cough syrup, heroin. As a Baby Boomer who came of age in Berkeley of the early 1970s, I am an authority on drugs, either from personal experience, my friends' experiences, or the many years I worked as an in-house security guard for Bill Graham Presents, the largest concert promoter in the San Francisco Bay Area. Before the concert began, we could predict the crowd's predominant drug of choice by the band's demographic appeal. I have worked at San Francisco's now-defunct Winterland for Grateful Dead concerts, where at least half of the 10,000 people in the hall were on acid, and was actually bitten by a rabid Johnny Winter fan who had ingested a particularly violent combination of PCP and Southern Comfort at a day-long outdoor concert in Oakland.

Like many in my demographic bulge now finding themselves raising teenage kids, I knew I would eventually face a day of reckoning when I would confront how much to reveal about my own past experiences and experimentation.

I had definitely inhaled.

Kolya decided the day was upon us. He listened fairly attentively as I walked him through my purposefully clinical listing of the pharmacological and physiological properties of various mind-expanding contraband.

Glad we had this talk, son.

"Dad?"

"Yes."

"Have you ever taken acid?"

Pause.

How do I answer that question?

"Yes, but only a couple of times. I didn't like it." The simple, unadorned truth. My experiences with LSD *were* limited, but notably included going to Disneyland with Bob (who nobody ever thought would have dropped acid) and standing outside of the haunted house for a long time, trying to figure out if a spider on a wrought iron fence was real or imagineered. Bob worried that a security guard would see me and think, appropriately enough, that anybody peering at the spider for so long was probably tripping, and so big brother dragged me off to the Matterhorn.

Next Kolya question: "Have you ever smoked pot?"

"Yes."

And that was that. He hadn't yet learned the journalist's prerogative of the follow-up question.

Two days later, I checked in on the way to soccer practice. "Kolya, how was it for you to hear that I've taken acid and smoked pot?" I asked.

His answer confirmed that I had done, if not the right thing, at least something vaguely correct. Kolya shot me a sideways glance and deadpanned: "I'm just glad you didn't lie to me, 'cuz I wouldn't have believed that an old hippie like you never smoked dope." I found some solace from a pamphlet I came across from the organization Partnership for a Drug-Free America:

For many parents, a child's "Did you ever use drugs?" question is a tough one to answer. Unless the answer is no, most parents stutter and stammer through an answer and leave their kids feeling like they haven't learned anything—or even worse, that their parents are hypocrites. Yes, it's difficult to know what to say. You want your kids to follow your rules and you don't want them to hold your history up as an example to follow—or as a tool to use against you. But the conversation doesn't have to be awkward, and you can use it to your advantage by turning it into a teachable moment.

I asked him if he had ever tried smoking dope, and he said nah, he hadn't. How about his friends? There was a rumor that a kid in eighth grade had done it, but basically, none of his friends had, either.

The summer before he entered seventh grade, I had taken Kolya on a backpacking trip with my twenty-year-old nephew and an old friend of mine. Evidently, as we scrambled over granite passes in Yosemite, my nephew told Kolya that everyone, including grown-ups that Kolya knew, smoked dope. Probably even Uncle Danny.

Thank you, nephew.

Weeks after the backpacking trip, Kolya had posed a new and inevitable question: "Do you *still* smoke pot?"

This one was tougher to answer. I had read about kids who were told by school officials to turn in their parents for drug use, and although I didn't think Kolya would do that, I wondered what he would do with the information.

I swallowed and opted for the truth again. "Sometimes."

I also sensed that Kolya had gone further in the six months since our last conversation, and it turned out that he had. He said he still hadn't tried smoking anything, and I believed him. But more of his friends had tried marijuana and he was getting really interested. He was barely thirteen. I really didn't want him starting now.

We talked more about drugs. I told him that I suspected that he was going to be under pressure, or at least he'd soon have the opportunity, to try it himself. I also told him that I thought he was much too young, and that it was a bad idea. I knew that the "Just Say No" message would seem particularly hollow now that he knew about my early experiences, combined with what I knew about his temperament.

So I tried a different tack: "Just Say Not Yet."

I told him that the pot these days was extraordinarily strong, that it messed with your memory, that his brain was still developing, and that, although I didn't expect that he'd wait until he graduated from college to experiment, I wanted him to hold off for a few more years.

With that as background, the next stop of our tour was a wild chapter in the education of Kolya Glick, as well as that of his father.

Call it "sex, drugs, and the plural of platypus."

After our Hinchinbrook hike, we headed southward, where we had arranged to meet a family friend for the weekend—whose name, for reasons that will become obvious, has been altered. Darren Pearlman was a wild man, a wealthy fifty-something professional who evidently lived his life on his own terms. He owned fast cars, had expensive tastes, and greeted us like long-lost relatives in his elegant home on Australia's Gold Coast not far from Brisbane. I had, in fact, only met him once before, on my previous visit to Australia, and had no idea what was in store for us.

As soon as we walked into his home, furnished in contemporary bachelor with indigenous art from places around the globe he had obviously been to, the kids were smitten. The barrel-chested, gregarious Darren was a divine manifestation for Kolya and Zoe, after living so low to the ground with their tightwad dad. For lunch, Darren barbecued the best steak any of us had ever eaten and uncorked a bottle of French burgundy that I would have reserved for my fiftieth wedding anniversary had I stayed married long enough to have one. He poured the kids glassfuls without asking if I minded, and we feasted on his veranda while he talked nonstop of his plans for us.

He told us about his neighbor, a single mom with three kids, and said we would all jet-ski that afternoon. Later we'd dine out, tomorrow we'd picnic on the beach, and if we were available to return the following weekend, he would take us out on his house-boat.

The single mom, we'll call her Samantha, arrived with her three kids, a fourteen-year-old girl, a twelve-year-old boy, and a ten-year-old girl. The eldest, "Francesca," appeared at a glance to be far more sophisticated than Kolya. With a European dad and an Aussie mom, she'd traveled back and forth between the two continents enough to be thoroughly world-weary before she could drive. She offered opinions about what Darren wore, the music we played on the stereo, and the thoroughly distasteful parochial school her mom forced her to attend, all the while checking Kolya out through the corner of her eye.

And vice versa.

The kids headed to the swimming pool, and the three of us grown-ups sat around and talked. I suddenly felt enormous relief that I didn't have to entertain the kids nonstop.

So we jet-skied, Darren's daredevil driving eliciting shrieks of laughter and even a small grin from this vehement tree-hugging opponent of the machine's two-stroke polluting engine. We ate out, the eight of us cavorting around the streets peering at menus and debating the relative merits of Indian tandoori versus oriental grill. The adults retired to Darren's living room, and the kids scattered throughout the house to play.

On the trip, when talking to new friends, other travelers, or a host, I often eventually found myself telling a story about my life with Rebecca. At such times, I awkwardly attempted to find an appropriate term for her relationship to me. I hate "ex-wife," although it's accurate enough. "The kids' mother" begs too many questions, such as, "Who's their father?" "Ex" is expedient but still unsatisfying. So I had to muddle through. I felt the kids listening more intently whenever I mentioned their mom, and I wondered what they were wondering. I also was beginning to feel that the story was getting easier to tell, even easier for them to hear. It was beginning to feel like a fact of life, like my height or deteriorating vision, that I am a divorced single dad.

That night the kids were otherwise occupied, and Darren disappeared into his bedroom before returning with a pipe and a leafy substance that was obviously not tobacco. I was, to be honest, aghast. I worried that the kids would burst into the living room at any moment. I didn't want to have the drug talk with Zoe yet, nor to explain the upcoming compromising situation to Kolya. I told Darren that I felt uncomfortable getting high in front of the kids, and he responded that I didn't have to smoke if I didn't want to.

I tried again, telling him that I'd been trying to give Kolya the message, "Just Say Not Yet," and that I didn't want to mix him up by flagrantly adding, "but I'm going to right now." He blithely said that he thought Kolya seemed mature enough to handle it. He lit up, passed it to Samantha, who offered it to me. I abstained, and nonetheless enjoyed listening to the Stones "Let It Bleed" on his exquisite stereo at an appropriately robust volume.

The kids did not come in, and when I could talk about this to Kolya later, I learned that he had no clue what the grown-ups were doing.

He was occupied with other business.

The next day we attended the promised picnic on a bluff overlooking the shoreline. The children went down to the beach, but after awhile, Zoe and her new friend came back with an announcement: Kolya and Francesca were "sucking face."

Samantha and I looked at each other, wondering if the other was scandalized. Being the father of the boy, I felt a tinge of responsibility. Then I realized that Francesca was an eminently willing participant.

Then, to my astonishment, Kolya and Francesca appeared, holding hands, and stopped within eyeshot to suck more face. Kolya looked very pleased with himself, and Francesca clung to his hand as if she had found a handful of gold coins in the sand.

He had told me of a stray kiss during a "Truth or Dare" game, and I think a spin-the-bottle smooch or two, but I was pretty sure this was the first bona fide girlfriend kind of affair. He was growing up quick, without the benefit of an older brother like mine to guide him through a transition or two. I had little doubt that his current experiences would stick with him forever.

The year we lived in Africa, 1968, our mom traveled around doing research for a book about languages in Uganda. Dad worked at the medical school, and in between family vacation safaris, we had tons of free time. At ages sixteen and twelve, Bob and I constituted the oldest and the youngest of an undersupervised group of ex-pat kids, mostly American and British, who roamed Kampala. That was one of the coolest things about living there; all the parents were so happy to have cooks and gardeners and night watchmen that they thought that they had babysitters, too. So a lot of the kids had parties when their parents were at cocktail parties or whatever.

Bob didn't so much enjoy my company as put up with it, partly I think because I was a little more adventurous and maybe also because one of my friends, who was fourteen, had lived there for more than a year and spoke way more Swahili than we did. I'd tell Bob about how John and I would ride the local buses, the only mzungu, *or white people, scampering over huge piles of green bananas in the aisle of the bus to get to seats, the collective astonished murmur of all the people on the bus saying* mzungu *sounding like a beehive or something.*

One weekend there was going to be a party out by John's house and Bob came with us on the bus to spend the night at John's. His house was out of the city about seven miles, and John and I routinely stopped at an African market on the way there. It meant we had to get off a stop early and walk the last mile, but we'd buy cigarettes and smoke them on the way, talking about the girls in the market, suspecting that they didn't wear any underwear. The time Bob was with us, we each bought five Ambassador cigarettes from a lady with a bad leg, and she carefully pulled one match from a box she was selling, just barely hit the corner of the flint so nobody would notice that it was a used matchbox, and lit our cigarettes.

The market was much more interesting than the pretend American stores where I had shopped with our African cook William, which were stocked with cans of yucky English food but nothing really good like root beer or taco shells. It smelled like so many things, like papaya trees and breadfruit leaves and big red anthills and Indian pastries called samosas. In the market you could buy all these strange animals, and if you wanted they'd kill them for you after you felt them all over to see if they were plump enough. That day a woman bought a huge snake and the man chopped its big head off and skinned the whole thing in one motion, as if he were taking off his socks or something. He looked at us and laughed, but I don't think he really knew how weird that would seem to the guys back home.

We stopped off in bat valley before we went home to John's. Every night at dusk, thousands of fruit bats would take off and fly across the red equatorial sky, filling it with small black dots like dirt on one of those observatory telescopes. It was so loud in the valley when the bats took off, we could barely stand the high-pitched shrieks, which sounded ten times worse than the woman we heard once who was being beaten by her husband in their hut. John said that if we threw a tiny pebble in the air, the bats would think it was an insect and dive to eat it. The pebble would be too heavy for the bat, and it would fall to the ground helpless. We tried this for a long time, but it never worked. I don't even know what we would have done with the bat anyway. They're really pretty creepy looking, like rats with dirty cellophane wings and tiny bones that look like veins.

The party started and soon we were sitting around in a circle spinning an empty bottle of orange Fanta. When it turned to me, I had to kiss Chris, the English girl. It was my first kiss, sloppy and awkward. Later, I saw Bob making out with Chris, making her one of two girls that I know Bob and I both kissed with amorous intent. (The other was a girl *in high school, when I was in tenth grade and he was in twelfth. It was an ill-fated romance for both of us in turn.)*

Somebody had a bottle of waragi, *the local gin made out of green bananas. (They made everything out of green bananas. I could never figure out how they could make* matoke, *which actually tasted a little like mashed potatoes, and also liquor, out of bananas.) I got so drunk I was sick. I tried to make it to the toilet but threw up on the bathroom floor. I covered it with a bath mat. Bob must have known that I was in trouble, because he came in, took me by the shoulders from behind (I think he didn't want me to rolf on him), and led me outside. I don't remember going back to John's, but I think Bob took me there. He never told Mom and Dad.*

I wonder if he cleaned up the mess I made. I doubt it.

I never asked him. And if he didn't, I'd really like to apologize.

The next day, we bid Darren, Samantha, Francesca, and everybody goodbye and promised Darren we'd be back in a week for the houseboat overnight. Kolya and Francesca sheepishly held hands. Then we piled into our van, which suddenly appeared cramped and dirty, and headed south to the surfing paradise of Byron Bay. Kolya had extracted a promise of surfing, and surfing it would be. I surfed when I was a teenage Southern California boy before my family moved to Berkeley, but I hadn't been on a board in thirty years.

We are in a town near Brisbane, sort of half way between Cairns and Sydney. There is a friend of the family's here named Darren (my Dad says we can't use his real name). He has been extremely hospitable to us while we have been out here. I think he is a really cool guy. Just by listening to him and Dad talk, I've learned more than a few things.

This isn't even close to the best part about Brisbane though. Darren has some neighbors a few levels down in the apartment building. The mom's name is Samantha, and she has three kids: a girl named Francesca who is 15 or something, another girl who is somewhere around Zoe's age, and a guy about my age. My interest was of course in Francesca. She was really good looking, and was someone who was finally up to date in some current affairs besides politics. The first night we were with them, we went out to a noodle place, then me and Francesca sat on Darren's porch all night and just talked about shit. That was so nice, even though she wasn't really into the same music as me, we had a few bands in common, and had plenty of other things to talk about.

It was really fun, but the second night in Brisbane was the absolute fucking greatest. There was a picnic of some sort that Samantha and her family was invited to at a place called the cliffs. Zoe and Francesca's little sister were constantly following me and Francesca around, obviously expecting something to happen. They kept following us there, and wouldn't stop.

They were looking for something to see, so me and Francesca sat down on a park bench and gave them something to look at. At first they just sort of put their hands over their eyes and peeked, but then they just looked on with awe. Zoe then made the smart-ass comment "you guys are faking it, you aren't using tongue."

We proved her wrong there. After about 5 minutes, they got tired of watching us, and went back up to the picnic. We kept going for what must have been a half hour down on that park bench in front of the Brisbane River. That was absolutely great. After we got tired of that, we went up and got a little of what was left of the picnic dinner food. Then went into their '68 jaguar, and made out some more, right in front of my dad, her mom, and our little siblings.

I was in euphoria.

We pulled into a fabulous caravan park right near the beach, signed up at a surf school, and proceeded to enjoy an utterly glorious and lazy vacation-within-a-vacation. Each morning we'd call to see where the surf would be best, drive to the designated beach, and join a small group led by a tanned Aussie surf bum, who taught the three of us to successfully stand up. In between surf sessions, we'd lounge, read, swim, eat, and stroll into town for ice cream, with Zoe and I teasing Kolya mercilessly for his *liaison dangereuse* with Francesca.

> I went serfing yesterday, and I really surprised myself. It is so much easyer then I thought it would be and its really fun.
>
> I have a lose tooth that is killing me. I went to a friends house he had a jet ski and I rode it and went soooo fast and I saw my brother French kiss a girl about 1,000,000 times. I felt really weird.

At the end of the week we met Darren at the marina where he moored his boat. We provisioned up and pulled out in his cabin cruiser on a beautiful, warm afternoon with light winds, heading for the South Stradbroke Islands.

Just before dusk, we dropped anchor in a little channel between two small islands. Darren cracked a bottle of wine and we soaked in the sunset. After a bit, he went below and let out a "Damn." He had counted on there being beer on board as well. He whipped out his cell phone, placed a call to what I presumed to be a roving boat-delivery service for essentials like this, but received no response. He decided instead to hop on his jet ski and go to a little store on a nearby island. Zoe called after him, "Get Parmesan cheese, too."

I said, "Zoe, take a look around. Do you see where you are? How do you think he's going to get Parmesan cheese?"

Darren returned, triumphant, less than half an hour later, with wine, beer—and freshly grated Parmesan cheese. We settled into our meal, watched the stars come out, and the kids recounted our cassowary stories to Darren with appreciable excitement, which he shared.

Darren went below and rummaged around for another bottle of wine and his pipe. "Bedtime," I pronounced hastily to Zoe, when I figured out what he had retrieved. After a short fight, she acquiesced. As I passed Darren in the galley, I made a fateful decision.

"Go on, if he wants to, let Kolya try it."

I read to Zoe, and half smiled, half cringed as I heard Kolya coughing from the deck. Zoe was so tired she drifted off as I read.

I headed up, unsure what would happen next. I looked at Kolya, saw the pipe, and whispered as Darren peed off the back of the boat. "Did you???"

Kolya looked me in the eye and shook his head in an emphatic "no." Then he shook his head the other direction, grinning wildly, with an even more emphatic "yes." I know he was caught between not wanting to lie about it and not wanting me to be angry because he violated my "Just Say Not Yet" policy. Darren hadn't told Kolya that I had given the green light.

"It's okay, Kolya. I told him it was okay this time."

He grinned again.

"Do you feel anything?" Whispering.

Emphatic "no" again.

"Wait a little."

Then Darren returned, loaded the pipe, handed it to me.

I looked at Kolya. Another moment of truth. Then I lit up. Somehow, it seemed right, with the waves lapping and the offshore breeze and the adult supervision, however flawed *that* line of thinking was.

And I worry that I've unleashed a genie.

And I'm sure that I will receive hate mail.

And I don't regret it at all.

So much has happened since I last wrote in this, oh my god. Now, almost all of the stuff that I was wishing for came true. I have three things my dad promised me that are done now: I've gone scuba diving, surfing and I got to drive the van. I think I am all set for the Australia part of the checklist.

I have also checked off one more thing on my personal "to do" list that I had set at the beginning of the trip. After the whole Francesca thing, I was pretty damn happy about getting with a hot girl. The "checklist" has a lot of things on it, some fairly reasonable, and some way the hell out in left field, this is one of the things that I was not really planning on doing, but I did it, at a time and place completely unexpected.

The real fun started when the sun went down. My dad was being pretty chill about things during dinner, and gave me a glass and a half of wine, and a few sips of his beer. I might have had a little buzz going at the time. We went outside after dinner to the other table and just sat and talked for a little. I would've been very happy with the night at that point.

It started getting better when Darren busted out a small Nepalese piece, and a film container. Zoe was really entertained by it, and was squirming around Darren to see what it was. When she asked what it was, he said tobacco, and a pipe. After this, dad quickly escorted Zoe to bed. While he was gone, I asked if it was really tobacco. He answered "of course not, it's dope."

I wasn't very surprised at all when he started smoking, or when he offered me some to smoke. I took the risk that he hadn't talked to my dad about it, because I was fairly sure that he did. When my dad came out, Darren loaded another bowl, and we smoked one with my dad. It was one of the best nights of the trip so far. And I got to smoke weed on the trip, which is something that I wasn't planning to do at all, and if at all, only in Amsterdam.

The next morning, after a bacon-and-eggs breakfast, we motored back to harbor, bid farewell to Darren, and headed out more purposefully in our rolling home. I had booked our onward passage to Bali for ten days hence, and we needed to accelerate our southerly pace toward Sydney.

We had discovered an array of *divertissements* to pass our driving time, such as quoting popular culture characters out of context. One disgusting favorite of theirs was Mike Meyers in the Austin Powers films. Luckily, I had seen both I and II and could begin to relate when they took up after Fat Bastard, screaming, "Frisky, are we?" which Kolya would say to Zoe when she started up with him or challenged him. Zoe never simply said, "I have to go number two, dad, could we please find a toilet?" Instead she would put on her best brogue and say, "Ah got a crrrrap on boarrrd that'd chohke a donkeh." So we'd look for a rest area.

One stop, Eungalla National Park, promised to be more than a restroom break. Here, the literature promised, we might sight a platypus. Kolya wryly noted that it might be better not to wonder about the plural of platypus. The joke flew past Zoe.

She wanted nothing to do with platypus hunting, so Kolya and I walked upriver to the platypus viewing area. Standing on a wooden platform above the water, I seized the first private moment I'd had to discuss *l'affair Francesca*.

He bashfully listened to my awkward "let's talk about sex, son" opening, then quickly informed me, to my moderate surprise, that he'd already been exposed to more than simple spin-the-bottle games. At home I'd placed parental control filters on his Internet access, but he laughed at my naïveté if I thought that meant he hadn't seen any porn. I knew he had found *Penthouse* magazines while doing the recycling, but I didn't realize that he and his buddies had access to scenes I hadn't *ever* seen.

I would have killed to have access to digital downloads and CD burners at his age.

He didn't want to talk about Francesca much, but he let me know that one of his pet peeves about traveling with me and Zoe had been that he hadn't had much opportunity to talk to or meet girls. He had had fun with Francesca.

No details, Da.

Fair dinkem.

A Puppy Pile in Sydney

Two DAYS later we arrived in Sydney at the home of friends of a friend who live in Narrabeen, just north of Sydney proper. We had never met Dave and Leonie, but I had e-mailed and spoken with Leonie several times already, most recently from a pay phone 100 miles from Sydney. She had enlisted a friend of hers, Alice, to help play tour guide and hostess. Our main orders of business were to return the rented van, pick up a Vietnamese visa for later in the trip, and mail our excess camping gear home. We made an obligatory pilgrimage to the Sydney Opera House after returning the van and dropping off our passports at the Vietnamese consulate.

With a couple days to kill while our visa was being processed, we organized a visit to Leonie's family vacation home in the Blue Mountains west of Sydney. Kolya, Zoe, and I took the train to meet Leonie, who was already in the area on business.

En route to the mountains, I noticed Kolya and Zoe peering out of the commuter train window with uncharacteristic fascination, commenting on what they were seeing. I put down my book, leaned over, and tried to figure out what they were talking about.

"They have some pretty good taggers here," Kolya remarked.

Graffiti. They were looking at Australian graffiti art. As I started seeing through their eyes, what had appeared to me as standard-issue urban/exurban blight opened up into a world of stylized signatures and graceful caricatures. Kolya and I discussed the fine points of vandalism vs. individual expression. He informed me which friends of his were taggers. In incremental, incidental ways, I learned new things about Kolya's world all the time.

We spent a quiet day and a night up at Blackheath in the Blue Mountains, making several stops to a renowned "lolly" (Australian for sweets) shop and hiking to view the natural rock formation called the "Three Sisters." We telephoned Rebecca, though we'd been updating her periodically via e-mail about our whereabouts, and Zoe couldn't *wait* to tell Mom about Kolya's amorous escapades. Kolya seemed bashful and a little proud, and both of them related our adventures with more enthusiasm than they generally showed me. That night, as I put the kids to bed, Leonie came upon the three of us doing what we call our "puppy pile," a wrestling-snuggling routine that we do when the stars align and the kids feel affectionate.

Later that night, she told me she was quite taken with the three of us, our adventure, the way we behaved together—how beautifully affectionate I was with the kids and how much they seemed to love their dad. Stuck as I am in their day-to-day bickering, her words reassured me. Leonie and Alice, over a bottle of Australian cabernet, all but gushed, "I wish I had had a dad like you." I fed on this, although it felt so—*transparent*—the ego of it all. Still, I took it in as another moment of grace, sitting before a crackling fire in the Blue Mountains, the kids snoring peacefully in the next room, the warmth of our puppy pile fresh in my mind.

Back in Sydney, the kids and I began, at my insistence, to pare down before we embarked for Asia. Without the van, the idea of lugging our stuff around humid cities to unknown destinations filled me with dread. I tried to jettison nonessential items, and the kids parted with a few favorites. They still insisted on DVD cases and MP3 players and Game Boys, but in the end we managed to reduce our loads to a backpack and a daypack apiece. Plus my traveling guitar and Kolya's skateboard. The next day, we sent our camping gear back by slow boat and picked up our passports with newly stamped Vietnamese visas, which we wouldn't need for another month.

Leonie cheerfully drove us to the Sydney airport at an unreasonably early hour, and I surveyed the Sydney skyline with a profound sense that the trip had started on a very soulful note. Our six weeks Down Under in the land of Oz drew to a close. Now it was time to meet Tory, produce new, Asian adventures, and, I hoped, continue our monkey dance around the planet.

PART 2

"SHE'S NOT OUR MOM"

*Tory, Kolya, Zoe, and the author in the Monkey Forest
outside Ubud, Bali, in Indonesia.*

Return of the Sardine Eater

The cloud cover below obscured our view of the great Australian outback en route to Denpasar. Having never visited Bali or anyplace in Indonesia, I felt flush with the pure thrill of exploring new territory—that same untempered excitement I had experienced stopping over in Cairo and Khartoum before arriving in Entebbe more than three decades ago.

I recalled my first visit to Asia, when Rebecca and I had roamed the streets of Niigata, a Japanese port city, a week after our wedding. Everything had seemed so foreign. We couldn't read the street signs, the storefront names, or the menus because everything was written in *kanji*. As uninitiated westerners, we felt like we couldn't even go to the bathroom without implicating ourselves in some horrible cross-cultural taboo.

Now, as the kids and I were about to arrive in Indonesia, I couldn't even imagine what Asia would seem like for them. The cultural, political, and ethnic differences they would soon encounter made our Australian sojourn seem like a trip to California. Even simple things would be a challenge because of the language barrier. Although

Indonesian is written in letters we recognize, Vietnamese, Cambodian, Thai, and Nepali each have an entirely different alphabet.

Our itinerary for the next few months consisted of a few fixed destinations and a fair amount of room for improvisation. Moving northward from Australia, we envisioned two expeditions in Indonesia. The first would be to Bali, a tiny island just east of the island of Java. After that, we'd head to Borneo, the largest of Indonesia's islands. Then we'd make our way to Jakarta, Indonesia's capital (on the island of Java), and fly to Singapore, the small city-state perched on the tip of the Malay peninsula that separates mainland southeast Asia from Indonesia. We'd fly from there to Vietnam and then head overland to Cambodia, where an old high-school friend of mine lived with his Khmer wife. From there, we'd almost certainly visit Thailand and Nepal. China and India remained tantalizing possibilities.

I felt a nervous energy creeping in as well; during our Australian stay, I had monitored news accounts and the U.S. State Department Web site concerning the political situation in Indonesia, which was sketchy. About the time we were backpacking on Hinchinbrook Island, the People's Consultative Assembly, Indonesia's parliament, impeached President Abdurrahman Wahid. The blind sixty-one-year-old Muslim cleric had been accused of massive graft (he was later cleared of those charges), ineffectual leadership (the vote was 592–5 to impeach), and widespread corruption (he was emphatically not cleared of these charges). Wahid defiantly stated he would not step down, and Indonesia-watchers expected a military crackdown.

When we emerged from the Hinchinbrook wilderness, Australian newspapers were filled with talk of Indonesia's looming constitutional crisis, the potential for violence, and the possibility of renewed martial law. Indonesian news is big in Australia, way bigger than Canadian news is in the United States, and I began wondering if we would have to bypass our Bali and Borneo legs. Kolya saw the headlines, too, and asked if I was worried. I reassured him that probably none of this would affect our plans, but privately I knew I wasn't ready for a month of living dangerously with my kids.

Just weeks before our intended arrival in Indonesia, while we were still in Queensland, Wahid declared he would step down. His rival, Vice President Megawati Sukarnoputri, came to power in what the Aussie newspapers called an "unorthodox but legal and constitutional presidential transition."

Bali was a go.

On the plane, we fell into our trio again, heading off to unknown adventure after hanging out for more than a week with Leonie, Dave, and Alice in Sydney comfort. In the airport waiting area, people smiled at us, a dad and his two kids, how . . . cute? *(Where's mom?)* Could people see what an amazing trio we were, different, not the typical boorish American family on vacation? But travelers! Adventurers!

Still, I remained nervous about traveling with the kids in Asia, the world's most populous continent. Even more than the threat of coups, insurgencies, and rebel groups, though, it was negotiating the crowded streets of Asian capitals and staying together in swarming marketplaces that worried me.

We rehearsed, with renewed urgency, the "what if" contingencies we had developed in Australia. "What if" one of them were lost? "What if" something happened to me? I carried all our passports, plane tickets, and traveler's checks in my under-the-shorts money belt. Now they would both begin wearing their own hidden money belts containing a photocopy of all our passports, an array of emergency phone numbers, travel medical insurance information, and cash. Our action plans, should we become separated, included elaborate contingencies:

- Plans A, B, and C, respectively: Don't get lost; don't wander off; keep me in sight at all times.
- Plan D: If separated, return to the last point where we had all been together, if it was obvious—a shop, a street corner, a

restaurant, our hotel. I would quiz them on the names of our hotels, tell them to look around at all times for landmarks, remind them to be thinking about where they were. I'd stop them when we were in a crowded shopping area and say, "If you were lost now, what would you do?" I tried to make it a game rather than a morbid, rabid obsession.

- Plan E (in capital cities only): Find someone who speaks English and call the American embassy or consulate.
- Plan F: Look for a policeman or a soldier in uniform (always a crapshoot in the developing world) and tell them your story. I would search for, and find them, somehow, at a police station. Hopefully.
- Plan G: Call Mom.

I harbored frightful, unsettling fantasies. White slavery. Organ transplants. The heart-wrenching image of Zoe standing alone on a street corner, completely disoriented and frightened beyond measure. Like most parents, I'd already experienced adrenal surges in America whenever I turned around at a playground or mall and couldn't immediately spot one of the kids; I would probably keel over from acute adrenaline poisoning if I had a similar experience in, say, Jakarta.

I warned them to increase their vigilance about our stuff and watch our packs at all times. I didn't want to make them paranoid, but after Australia, where Good Samaritans returned our cameras to us after I carelessly left them lying about, we needed to be more cautious. In Asia, we were more susceptible to theft from stealth than from violence.

Next up were health issues. No drinking tap water. No brushing teeth in tap water. No drinking shower water. No drinks with ice unless we could ascertain the water's origin. (The good news: They could drink more bottled sodas than I usually allow.) We would eat only fruits or vegetables that were peeled or cooked. Bananas, pineapple, and papaya worked fine. Tomatoes and lettuce didn't. No great hardships there, especially for Kolya.

After filling Kolya and Zoe's heads with cautionary words about dysentery-inducing microbes, military coups, preying pickpockets, and teeming masses of opportunists and beggars, I briefed them about important Asian cultural mores: Don't point your feet at people if you prop them up on anything, don't touch anybody's head, don't eat with your left hand. I explained that they might have to go to the bathroom while squatting over porcelain (or even dirt) holes and finish their business with water rather than toilet paper (that's where the left-hand issue comes in). I told them how in most Asian countries, a basin filled with water is set next to the toilet alongside a small bucket. The people dip the bucket into the basin and pour the water into their cupped left hand to wash themselves "down there." People then use soap and water to clean their hand in another basin or sink nearby. This possibility alone seemed to be keeping them both awake at night, and Kolya began stockpiling toilet paper in every pocket of his clothes and day pack in case he ran into what the two of them had dubbed "big dippers." Each time, from then on, one of them entered a toilet, they reported to each other. "It's a big dipper, big brother. Better bring some toilet paper."

We moved on to other cross-cultural matters. I told them that in many Asian cultures, it's not unusual to see men holding men's hands and women holding women's hands—it didn't reflect on their sexuality. I figured, correctly, that Kolya and Zoe would have questions about that, given their heightened sensitivity to the subject.

What else? I racked my brain. Bali was a Hindu island in a sea of Muslim Indonesia, which meant they'd probably see mystifying temples and offerings and ceremonies. The Balinese version of Hinduism would be different from what we'd see in Nepal later in the trip, mixed as it was with a worship of spirits and animist traditions, monkey gods, and volcano spirits as well as Brahma, Shiva and Vishnu, Ganesh, Kali, Rama, Krishna, Hanuman, and the whole polytheistic crowd.

This flight definitely represented a transition time. As we neared our destination, I realized that when we met Tory, people would see us and think we were just another family taking two weeks off from our well-salaried American life, spending stacks of traveler's checks on a Balinese vacation. (And that when we returned, we would present a themed slide show to our friends. We would wear batik sarongs we bought at the hotel gift shop, play CDs of indigenous music we purchased from a native crafts store, serve Balinese dishes we made from a cookbook we bought at the cooking school, and talk excitedly about the taxi driver who drove too fast on our way to the airport.)

It would look so . . . normal.

I wondered if I originally had not wanted Tory to come because it would mess up my self-image. I mean, how could I be a brave single dad wandering around the world with my kids if she joined the team? The schema would change, become less special. People would think, momdadandthekids, and we weren't.

Still, I knew that to move on after my divorce, if there was hope for this new relationship to grow and thrive, the four of us needed to amass the stuff of legend together: epic bus rides, festive holiday meals, unexpected gifts, the shared experiences that bind people together in collective memory. I wanted to invite Tory into our gang of three, but I was nervous and worried about being caught in the middle, between the kids' needs and Tory's expectations. I couldn't wait to send Kolya and Zoe into their own hotel room and to share one with Tory (for lots of reasons), but I fretted that the kids would feel abandoned when I unveiled the new bedtime regime.

Tory had hung in there as I vacillated before the trip, and as our rendezvous approached I felt increasing clarity that we had made the right decision to stick with it. Zoe loved Tory, Kolya liked having her around, and they had enthusiastically supported my decision to invite her to join us in Bali.

Tory and her ex-husband, both former National Park Service rangers, had opted for other adventures and had never had children. They had spent four years as winter rangers in Yosemite's Tuolumne Meadows, seven isolated months a year fending off bear attacks, ice dancing together on frozen alpine lakes, and braving blizzards to rescue wayward backcountry skiers. They had traveled to Nepal for mountaineering expeditions, and Tory's work as a wildlife biologist and naturalist had brought them to beautiful places around the western United States.

After divorcing, Tory had departed her native California for Colorado to attend Naropa University in Boulder. We started our relationship dance while she earned a master's degree in Buddhist studies and reinvented herself as a Buddhist minister, teacher, and facilitator. As she passed forty and I definitely cut off the possibility of conceiving more children, she still chose to remain with me. Tory stepped into the netherworld of step-girlfriend with as much grace and compassion as I could ever have hoped for.

She would need reservoirs of both in the next couple of weeks.

Kolya, Zoe, and I landed at the Denpasar airport about an hour before Tory's scheduled arrival and picked the line with the world's slowest customs official (that is, until we arrived in Kathmandu). We sprawled out on the linoleum floor to play cards and then heard the announcement that Tory's plane from Hong Kong was delayed by an hour.

The kids balked. Why couldn't Tory meet us at the hotel? Would we *always* be waiting for her? How long would she travel with us, anyway?

I had moved slowly with Tory, as the self-help postdivorce books suggested, and hadn't even introduced her to the kids until after we'd dated for six months. They took to her easily, enjoying her openness. Kolya was impressed that she had once been a climbing ranger who jumped from helicopters to rescue injured rock climbers in the Grand Tetons. Zoe loved having another female around, having announced on numerous occasions that being in the house with two males watching hockey playoff games very closely approximated her idea of hell.

Which didn't mean that this was gonna be easy. Because of my earlier ambivalence about traveling together, Tory and I had remained open-ended about how long she would travel with us. At a minimum, she'd accompany us through Bali and Borneo, our next stop. She and I schemed that, if all went well, she might continue on with us through Vietnam and Cambodia and possibly beyond. Because of this uncertainty, I had been vague with the kids about Tory's itinerary.

As Kolya trounced Zoe and me in a game of cards, I reiterated our plans for the next couple of weeks. We'd probably stay in Bali a week before the four of us moved on to Borneo together to visit the orangutans.

"That's bullshit," offered Kolya, diplomatically.

"What's bullshit?" I wondered, genuinely perplexed.

"What do you mean Tory's going to Borneo with us?" Kolya demanded.

"I thought this was supposed to be a *family* trip," contested Zoe. "If you married Tory she'd be family, but she's just your girlfriend and that's not the same."

"Hey guys, what's up?" I answered. "I thought you *liked* Tory and wanted her to be with us. We talked about this."

"Yeah, but you said she'd meet us in *Bali*," whined Kolya. "You didn't say anything about *after* Bali.

"Guys, I did too. Tory was *always* going to go to Borneo with us, and might stay longer, too."

"That's bullshit," repeated Kolya.

"She's *not* our mom," Zoe added, definitively.

Tory bribed the customs official with twenty dollars because she didn't have a return airplane ticket with her, since our plans were so noncommittal that she had decided to pick up tickets as we went along.

It was great to see her, a visceral relief to have pulled off this rendezvous mostly arranged from Internet cafés in Queensland.

Despite the kids' earlier tirade, Zoe flew into Tory's arms and Kolya allowed a genuine hug.

Tory had reserved two rooms at a modest hotel in the tourist center of Kuta, an overrun beach town a few miles from the airport on the southern coast. The hotel had promised to send a driver who would meet us outside in the muggy heat amid the throngs of touts, drivers, tourist guides, and hustlers—with Tory's name prominently displayed on a handwritten sign. Tory and Zoe peeked outside while Kolya and I guarded the bags. I immediately felt a sense of relief that the child-to-grownup ratio had changed. Until now, I had played a zone defense; now we matched up well with a man-to-man, or at least 1:1.

Tory returned with Zoe. No sign approximating her name, she reported. We called the hotel.

Driver coming.

We waited.

No driver.

We called again.

Driver coming soon.

No driver.

After an hour, which we considered to be a reasonable "soon," at least by Western standards, we hired a taxi, even though we'd already paid for the phantom hotel driver. We stuffed the four of us and all our backpacks into two diminutive Asian cabs as one driver told us, in broken English, that a festival had necessitated the closure of the road near our hotel. The drivers could drop us off "about 200 meters" from the hotel, which seemed a reasonable trek. So we hopped in.

Well, the "festival" turned out to be a countrywide celebration of Indonesia's independence from the Dutch on August 17, 1945. Our ride from the airport to Kuta passed nonstop parades and music and thronging crowds. The drivers dropped us off at the village square. Toting our backpacks, day packs, a camera bag, Kolya's increasingly incongruous-looking skateboard, and my traveling guitar, we proceeded in the direction of the 200-meter-away hotel.

About half a mile later, we asked, then asked again, and heard differing versions of how many more 200-meter stretches we had to go. We finally dropped our packs after covering a mile and Tory scouted for the hotel. I hung out with the kids at the edge of the infamous Kuta beach, observing three decades of world travelers' influence on this once-sleepy Balinese beach town.

When we were there, Kuta was a poster child to demonstrate the downside of the "ecotourism" revolution; later, in October 2002, we were shocked and saddened to hear that it was the site of the terrorist bombing in Bali. Such an event was unthinkable as recently as 1969, when Kuta was a fishing village of about 30,000 residents. That was before the construction of the Ngurah Rai International Airport, which opened mass tourism to Bali like a broken irrigation ditch gushing too much water into a painstakingly terraced rice paddy. With the tourists came hotels, restaurants, curio shops, land clearing, coral-killing sewage runoff, and an industry of aggressive beach masseuses, boogie board rentals, Fanta vendors, hashish dealers, hookers, hair plaiters, and hawkers of trinkets, hats, and sunscreen. Sometime in the early 1990s, the number of visitors to Bali surpassed the number of Balinese residents at around 3 million. Nowhere else have I seen such aggressive, concentrated commerce on a beachfront stretch. I had heard about this, heard that Kuta had devolved into a caricature of itself, summed up by the T-shirt that vendors gleefully sold in a self-parody:

NO
Transport
Hashish
Mushrooms
Pot
Massage
Tours
Hotel
Boogie Board
Drinks
Girls

While waiting for Tory, Zoe whispered to Kolya that topless European women were sunbathing on the beach, and he disappeared to check it out. "I'm going to look at the waves," he said, before Zoe revealed to me the real object of her brother's reconnaissance mission. Meanwhile, a Balinese woman peddling massages on the beach adopted Zoe. The smiling woman invited Zoe to sit in her lap, and Zoe looked to me to see if this was a problem. It seemed okay to me if it was okay with Zoe. She settled in to the woman's lap and let her hair be stroked.

As a veteran Asia traveler, I found this entire bumpy arrival scene more amusing than distressing. Money tends to insulate American and European tourists from the places we visit, and it actually felt good to me that we hadn't been whisked away in an air-conditioned van and reached our destination without being exposed to the rhythm of this pulsating scene. The parades and the music and the dances were not staged for the tourists, although tourists watched.

Most amazing to me was that the kids seemed to feel the same way about our arrival adventure. Here we were, on a stifling eight-degrees-below-the-equator afternoon, slogging upstream through a crowded parade, with Balinese marching bands and costumed schoolchildren and hawkers asking us where we were going and did we want a massage or to rent a boogie board, and the kids were enthralled. Kolya began to worry (as did I, a little) when dusk approached with no sign of Tory. I could think of no better course of action than to sit tight, however, at least until darkness fell. Then we could think about a Plan B.

What a joy for me to rediscover my confidence in serendipity that I had honed during many Jack London– and Jack Kerouac–inspired on-the-road years. I first set out at fourteen, pedaling a ten-speed bicycle down the coast of my native California from San Francisco to Los Angeles with a friend, sleeping on beaches and in artichoke fields. I graduated from high school early and started university at sixteen, but by the time I was seventeen the road beckoned again and I dropped out of college for the first of what would be four times. That spring and summer I hitchhiked and rode freight trains across Canada and back. Along the way, I canoed in Nova Scotia, hiked with friends in Montana's Glacier National Park, and backpacked solo in the Canadian Rockies. The call of the wild lured me deeper into nature's mysteries. Picking wild raspberries, watching bear cubs wrestle on a distant glacial cirque, and paddling through rising morning fog became as intoxicating as the smile of the beautiful woman from suburban Chicago who once picked me up hitchhiking and took me home with her.

I remembered that serendipitous summer's end, which featured a kamikaze hitchhiking trip from Canada to California to catch Bob before he moved across the country to medical school:

After I hike out from a ten-day solo backpacking trip near Mt. Assinaboine south of Banff, I note the late-August date on a newspaper and realize that Bob would be leaving for medical school in Philadelphia in a day and a half. I look at a Rand McNally atlas in the same gift shop and calculate that if I'm really lucky, I can be home in time to surprise him.

Following road etiquette, I stand at the end of a long line of hitchhikers heading west from Banff on the Trans-Canada Highway. Within minutes, a metallic blue Porsche 911S slows, and I flash my cardboard sign, which says, enigmatically, "Home." He looks me over in his rearview mirror, I follow him with my eyes like a sunflower tracing the arc of the day. He nods, pulls over. Another hitchhiker starts toward the Porsche, and I holler, "He's mine!"

"Where's home?" he asks, rolling down a window to check me out.

"California."

"Where?"

"Berkeley."

"I'm going to Sacramento. Hop in."

We pass the U.S. border into Idaho. He asks if I would drive so he can nap; he's in a hurry to patch things up with his girlfriend. I cruise until we need gas at the junction of Interstate 80 at Elko, Nevada. He wakes up, refreshed, takes the wheel, and the next thing I know we're passing Truckee in the Sierras. It's been less than 24 hours since I've left Banff.

He leaves me at a truck stop and I, riding this stroke of luck, quickly snag a ride that will take me to within an hour of home. Unfortunately, the driver lets me off at the intersection of two interstate highways, and it's approaching midnight. I'm so close, and Bob will be leaving in the morning, and I figure it's increasingly unlikely anybody's going to slow down from 65 mph to pick up a scruffy teenager standing under a street lamp with a sign that says, "Home."

I hoof it to a gas station a mile back and call my younger brother Steve. It's a secret, I tell him, but I want to say goodbye to Bob. Would he come and pick me up in Vacaville?

He would.

I arrive home at just past three, fall right into bed after extracting a promise that Steve will not tell anybody I'm home and will wake me in time to say goodbye.

In the morning, Bob is preoccupied, he is about to move 3,000 miles away to medical boot camp, but he's surprised and pleased to see me. We are alter egos, he and I. Somewhere around high school we flipped roles—he becoming studious and intent on medical school, marrying, following in Dad's footsteps, and I dropping out of college and vagabonding around the continent.

I tell him about the Porsche, the ethereal green northern lights above the Saskatchewan plains, the hard-looking toothless hobos in the rail yard in Klamath Falls, my standing on Highway 505 in the middle of the night trying to get here to say goodbye.

"Have a great time in Filthadelphia," I say.

"It's gonna be a bitch."

"I'm going back to bed."

"See ya."

At nineteen, I dropped out of college again and flew to Europe, where I worked as a migrant worker picking grapes, peaches, cherries, asparagus, beans, and peas on various farms alongside French,

German, Spanish, Portuguese, Sri Lankan, Dutch, and Moroccan coworkers. I was invited to have a cup of tea at the home of a Swiss woman, Martine, who had just returned from a vacation in California, and stayed with her for four months. I followed the ghost of Hemingway into Pamplona and hitchhiked to Finisterre, the end of the earth as I knew it, in Galicia, the northwestern corner of Spain. The road was magic for me. I loved not knowing or caring where I would sleep that night, trusting in whatever came my way. I learned to be alone in ways that have not always served me well when I've been in relationships; I'm sure my self-styled independence has seemed like a formidable barrier at times—even with Rebecca.

I recalled my nineteen-year-old self standing in the Jura mountains in Switzerland, heading for France, holding up a cardboard sign in three languages: *Irgund wohin* in German, *N'importe ou* in French, and *Somewhere else* in English. A farmer dropped me off in the middle of nowhere, not a structure or town in miles, late in the afternoon. My pack contained a tin of sardines, half a baguette, and a liter of water, in addition to my sleeping bag and a flute. I was set. I knew that, in due time, a car would appear and move me along. It always did.

But in recent years, my confidence in benevolent fate had been sorely tested. After the divorce and Bob's death, a therapist I was working with had referred to that hitchhiking youth in the Jura mountains as my "sardine eater." I had definitely lost touch with my sardine eater, and he suggested that I find a way to reacquaint myself with this lost element of my youth.

Our round-the-world trip promised to be the matchmaker I needed, something to remind me of that essential belief I once held without thinking about it, the central tenet of my faith: A car will always appear and take me where I need to go. Even if I don't know exactly where that is.

Here on Kuta beach, with Tory in search of our hotel, with Kolya ogling bare-breasted European women and Zoe being snuggled by a Balinese masseuse, I felt a reassuring wave wash over me. I leaned back on my pack, surveyed the scene, and grinned like an absolute idiot. My sardine eater sat in my lengthening shadow, grinning back at me.

Tory turned up with our driver, who *had* tried to meet us at the airport but had been waylaid by Independence Day traffic. Just before dark, we arrived at our comfortable bungalow in time for my first Balinese beer, a *Bintang*, and Kolya's first Balinese satay, grilled meat on a stick with peanut sauce—which he lived on for the next two weeks. Tory and Zoe sipped tropical fruit drinks like princesses on vacation. Tory and I held hands with the anticipation of newlyweds.

The day provided a perfect introduction to Asia, a reintroduction to the travelers' way. Bali proved to be a gateway in more ways than one.

PEEING MONKEYS

TORY AND I couldn't leave the overwrought tourist scene in Kuta fast enough, although the kids would have been happy to stay at the beach, body surf, and ogle. We negotiated a taxi ride up to Ubud, Bali's cultural capital, driving on narrow, crowded roads where pedestrians, bicycles, motorcycles, and cars improbably followed unposted rules for various right-of-way hierarchies. Unlike other parts of Asia I'd visited, the rules did not dictate that the most aggressive driver with the loudest air horn won the game of road chicken. The road was busy, but it still seemed civil.

In Ubud, we settled in to a comfortable pair of bungalows hidden off the main Monkey Forest Road and surrounded by tropical wonders: frangipani, hibiscus, wild orchids, bamboo, and banana trees. During the week, we watched the banana leaves unfold daily and listened to falling coconuts, drank tea served on our veranda, and sought refuge in the compact but refreshing swimming pool.

It took about fifteen minutes in Ubud to begin realizing that what we had heard about Bali was eminently true: that despite the onslaught of tourists, the rhythms of Balinese life continued.

Amidst the tourist hoards, the Balinese continue their affirmation of the sacred amidst the undeniably, ubiquitously profane.

As we carried our packs down a narrow path to our rooms, a procession of mourners passed by on their way to a cremation. First came the men wearing sarongs and rubber sandals, their heads wrapped in *udeng*, the traditional cloth headdress folded into a triangle shape. The women followed, costumed with more elaborate, flowered headdresses and carrying offerings, fruit and banana leaves tied into small boxes filled with flowers and incense. We sat to the side of the narrow pathway, catching the eyes of the marchers, feeling neither intrusive nor particularly wanted or unwanted. Zoe stood transfixed, observing what each woman wore, down to the ankle bracelets.

We later strolled to the famous Monkey Forest at Padangregal on the edge of town. Since monkeys are believed to be the descendants of General Hanuman, the monkey warrior who helped the Indian prince Rama save his wife Sita from certain death, they hold a divine status. In the Monkey Forest, long-tailed macaques find a refuge. They love to terrorize tourists with impunity.

If monkeys are descendants of gods, as the Balinese believe, they are gods with a sense of humor. We pay the 6,000 rupiah (75 cents) family entrance fee (there are certain advantages to being momdadandthekids) and enter. One monkey in a tree above the entrance took aim and peed on Tory, for no reason other than to be mischievous. The kids howled at the unofficial initiation ceremony that brought Tory closer into our circle.

We arrived at dusk and had the park almost to ourselves. We wandered to a temple by the river, and there, on every stone statue, fountain path, vine, tree, hillside, and step, we saw monkeys: long-tailed, mustachioed, long-armed, flat-nosed, black-faced macaques. The big males swaggered and expected all the others to give wide berth. Monkey kids hung off each other's tails, and monkey infants clung like opossums and suckled at their mothers bloated teats.

Tory, whose naturalist training makes her a much more knowledgeable guide than I am, explained the monkey relationships. When they scattered as if on cue, she noted that the monkey tribe followed the dominant male to an unknown destination.

Our imaginations ran wild as the monkeys scampered up the stone- and moss-covered steps. We felt certain the macaques were heading to a giant monkey dance and tried to follow them to their meeting spot. We envisioned a monkey bacchanalia, total simian abandonment, congo-playing monkey musicians, bewitching monkey courtship, cigarette-smoking monkey teenagers, burly monkey bouncers, frenzied monkey hip-hop. We wanted to monkey dance with them, but couldn't penetrate the secret monkey-dancing venue.

After dinner, Tory headed to an Internet café and the kids blindsided me. They demanded to know why I hadn't corrected the various hotel clerks and taxi drivers and fellow travelers who had referred to Tory as my wife or to them as Tory's children.

The kids didn't want people to think Tory was their mom, not because they didn't like her but because it wasn't true. I had noticed Zoe rolling her eyes when one shopkeeper, in broken English, remarked that she looked so much like Tory.

I told them that I had no problem explaining our situation, in abbreviated form, to other travelers. But for the casual conversation with a restaurant owner or a hotel worker, the momdadandthekids assumption didn't bother me.

I suggested we should brainstorm an action plan. How did they want to tell our story to people? To whom should we tell it? How in the world *could* we tell it? I modeled for them a conversation with an imaginary hotel clerk:

Actually, no, the woman with the brown hair isn't my wife, and she isn't the mother of those two children, either. She's my girlfriend, who used to be married to a guy named Brent. The teenage boy and the girl in the purple sarong are my children, but their mother is a lesbian who lives with her girlfriend a thousand miles from where we live in America.

*The kids and I are traveling for five months together, but we've invited
my girlfriend along for a few weeks to see how well we get along.*

The kids giggled, understood the obstacles, but still wanted me
to tell the truth as much as possible.

Kolya then took the opportunity to protest that since Tory
arrived, I had "sided" with her while ignoring him and Zoe. His
case in point was our quick departure from Kuta, and no amount of
protestation could convince him that it wasn't just Tory's idea, that
I'd wanted to leave, too. Zoe chimed in that I hadn't shown proper
deference to her since Tory arrived, and especially that I didn't
understand how much she wanted to sleep in the same room as
Tory and me.

We heard Tory arriving in the next room, and I quickly kissed
the kids good night, knowing full well that we hadn't resolved
much. I joined Tory, and the subject of Kolya and Zoe dominated
our conversation well into the night. Tory sensed that this transition
posed big challenges for me and for Kolya and Zoe, the intrepid
traveling trio, and of course it did for her as well.

I tried to shield Tory from the kids' recent outburst. For starters,
I figured their concerns would pass like a cloudburst once the four
of us hit a groove. I also knew that Tory would be crushed to hear
Kolya and Zoe's plaints. Like a rookie trying to crack the starting
lineup by displacing a beloved but aging veteran, Tory faced a challenging task. And not just vis-à-vis the kids.

Throughout my budding relationship with Tory I had fought
with memory pangs from my marriage. I'm certain that when she
arrived in Bali, Tory sensed she had waded into a chilly sea of
ambivalence. I tried reassuring her, reminded her that transitions
are always difficult, for adults as well as kids. I asked her to be
patient.

The difficulty I faced telling our story to strangers symbolized
my efforts to move beyond a fifteen-year marriage and start again. I
hadn't made the commitment to Tory that she wanted, to remake a
new family of four (whatever that might look like), and the kids

knew it and Tory knew it and I knew it. I tried moving closer to her, in word and in deed, but I felt myself pulled to show the kids that they remained my first priority. Tory, I believed, would be willing to take on more responsibility for the kids, but I didn't want her to and couldn't trust anybody nearly enough yet.

Lying in bed after Tory and I said goodnight, I submerged myself into another despairing moment. Was I capable of feeling the same intensity of *belonging* with Tory as I had with Rebecca? Did the kids pick up on my tentativeness and use it as a self-fulfilling wedge? (Kolya had told me, "She's not family, legally or mentally.") Even if I announced that Tory and I planned to marry, would the kids accept it? Not that I was ready to remarry.

I wasn't even prepared to fully engage in a relationship yet. Whenever I felt a torn allegiance between Tory and the kids, I felt myself standing squarely with the kids.

Which put all four of us in an awkward situation. It's understandable. Tory understood, we all understood, we were a basketful of understanding. But the configuration of my emotional landscape left all of us in uncomfortable terrain.

How do people do this?

At least once a day during our Ubud stay, the four of us returned to the Monkey Forest. Kolya dubbed one macaque a "loco monkey" because he observed it eating a cigarette butt and spinning wildly in circles. The loco monkey mounted Kolya's shoulders as he sat on a bench, then sat on Kolya's head, turning his butt toward Kolya's forehead and parading like a Davy Crockett hat. We all cracked up at Kolya's look of surprise mixed with fear and waited to see if the monkey would pee on Kolya. (He didn't.) Precious, unforgettable moments, the kind that wipe out a hundred screaming fits.

We flew to Bali and it is soooooooooooooooooo beautiful there are tempols everywhere and women with their tops off! We went to a

monkey forest and Tory got peed on and I saw about 1000 monkeys and two pulled on my sarong and held my hand then one of
them stoll my chips!

Despite the omnipresence of tourist shops, Ubud was a revelation.
Along with incessant offers for "transport"—taxi drivers and tour
guides trolling for business every ten feet or so on the main
street—we encountered signs of Bali's unique religious cultures
everywhere. We passed small shrines and intricately carved wooden
and stone temples as well as citizens who spend hours of their day
preparing offerings to the gods, spirits, and demons whom the Balinese believe are engaged in an interactive dance with humans.

I tend to refer to myself as "spiritually challenged" and have no
formal religious training or current practice. Yet I also believe that
the divine resides in all living things, in nature and in people. I am
unabashedly a tree-hugger, having wrapped my arms around giant
redwoods in California and loblollies in Georgia and banyans in
Hawaii with equal wonder. I am enchanted with the variety in my
own species. I cast my lot with the American naturalist Aldo
Leopold, who said that, when it came down to it, there were really
two things that interested him: the relationship of people to the
land, and the relationship of people to each other.

Had Leopold been to Bali, he might have added, "and the relationship of people to the spirit world." I am enthralled by the Balinese version of Hinduism, with its combination of rituals that
define relationships among people and honor the relationship of
humans to the spirits of all animals and objects. Here, animism
meets Hinduism, which is already a religion replete with a phantas-
magoric array of gods and spirits. In the Balinese worldview, spirits
and demons abound in rice paddies and in mongrel dogs, to be
assuaged and cajoled and bribed and worshiped. Every morning we
awoke to the sight and smell of young men placing *pebantens,* or
offerings, in front of our rooms. These are fastidiously prepared

square trays created from banana leaves and artfully arranged with flowers, rice, and incense. We found these not just in front of our room as a cute "authentic" tourist trick but on the doorstep of every shop in town, and they were replaced several times a day. We each experienced accidentally kicking one of them while walking and wondering if we had committed a cultural gaffe of unforgivable proportions. Nobody seemed to care. The value of the pebantens, it seemed, resided primarily in the act of offering rather than in the offering itself.

Not everything in Bali is spiritual, to be sure. In Ubud, the kids went crazy buying tourist kitsch with the allowance I had given them for souvenirs and impulse buys. Kolya and Zoe were astounding, easing into Asia even more quickly than I could have dreamed. Within a day we had settled so comfortably into Ubud that Zoe and Kolya forayed out shopping by themselves as Tory and I took long walks through the rice paddies in the countryside.

When we all met in the hotel room, the kids regaled us with tales of their bargaining prowess. They showed off their booty of surfboard key rings, fake Rolexes, sandalwood incense, cheap wooden carvings, scarves, and sarongs. They explained their good cop, bad cop technique for bargaining: Zoe would get excited about an item and call Kolya over. He would whisper, loud enough to be heard, that the same item could be had much cheaper at the store next door. The shopkeeper immediately lowered the price, the kids conferred and sealed the deal. Kolya was so proud of himself, sporting a new batik shirt and several Rolexes (Dad, they're *certified Rolexes,* he said with a grin, knowing full well they were cheap knockoffs not worth the eight dollars he'd just spent on them). For the first time in what seemed like years, he jettisoned his backwards baseball hat.

Within two days, Zoe amassed the same ensemble she had seen the local women wearing in the cremation procession. She couldn't figure out exactly how to tie her sarong, so I asked a woman who kept an outdoor stall near our guest house where we bought bottled water and snacks if she would help Zoe. The shopkeeper beamed pleasure and taught Zoe the secret Balinese sarong knot.

That night, we walked arm in arm, father and daughter, down the street, Zoe wrapped in a blue silken sarong and maroon ceremonial-style crepe-type top, with a yellow sash tied around her waist. She looked like a Balinese maiden heading for a ceremony. She turned Balinese heads, elicited *beyouteeful* from the passers-by, and beamed with pleasure, and I fell in love again with her amazing style and enthusiasm. "American fashion is so boring," she stated, emphatically. "I love this place." And she sighed. "Life cannot get much better than this," she pronounced, her arm hooked through my elbow as we walked to a Balinese dance performance. I glanced back, saw Tory and Kolya engaged in conversation, squeezed Zoe's hand, and felt the same way.

The next evening we attended a dance performance at a temple, sort of a *Readers Digest* sampler version of the lengthy Balinese performances that celebrate the many stories of the Ramayana, the epic Hindu story. Zoe was transfixed by the costumes and the dancers, Kolya by the musicians.

In the middle of the show, Kolya offered to give Zoe his much nicer seat if she'd find out where the bathroom was. She did, even though it was a dark hole of the variety that he seemed to fear more than just about anything in Asia. But she came through and received half an hour in his chair as a reward. I smiled, watching the scene from a vantage point ten feet away. Bob used to send me on his errands all the time.

It is rare, these moments of grace between the two of them. I predict they will get much closer in the coming years, perhaps when Kolya is in late high school and he solicits Zoe's advice about girls. I wonder if their shared stories of the divorce and this trip will bind them—or send them off in different directions to escape the repetitive memory of pain.

*

Three nights later (the kids would only take small doses of cultural force-feeding), we walked to a shadow-puppet show, a condensed Ramayama skit for the westerners that is funny and intricate but bores the kids silly. The rift between an American MTV generation kid used to racing millisecond images and a Balinese child who might sit through an eight-hour shadow-puppet performance is bigger than the ocean that separates them.

After the show, Kolya and I fell in step together and he began probing for more details about my youthful drug experiences. Perhaps because he has seen men holding hands everywhere, he and I walked with our fingers interlaced without a hint of self-consciousness on his part. I noticed that his paw was already as big as mine, he rose above my shoulder already, and our strides matched.

He asked if Grandma and Grandpa knew that I got high when I was younger.

Since the ice had emphatically been broken with our Australian experience, I told him about the first time I smoked dope with my parents. He was incredulous and amused to picture his grandparents getting high. It happened when my dad's parents were about to visit. I was a little older than Kolya, and my mother was apprehensive because she didn't get along with my grandmother. At that point, Mom and I had tacitly admitted to each other that we had tried marijuana, but we had never said anything about smoking together. I walked up to her and told her, "This is my last joint, Mom. But you need it more than I do," then struck a match. She stood there, feeling no doubt the same kind of inner conflict I had felt with Kolya, and took me up on my offer.

Kolya and I walked hand in hand, taking in the smells of rotting fruit, incense, and the exhaust of motorcycles. Then the spell broke and he silently pulled his hand away. I savored his momentary display of affection like a waft of frangipani in the warm Balinese night.

THE HIIST MOUNTIN IN BALI

WE DIDN'T expect to spend more than seven or eight days in Bali before moving on to Borneo. But Ubud sucked us in, and before we knew it a week had passed and the rest of Bali still beckoned. We rented a Kijang, a Chinese-made mini-SUV that's perfect for the narrow roads of Asia, though it will never catch on in the United States. The quirky car had been mishandled by many tourists before me, and the cheap rental price (about $8 a day) reflected the car's condition. The treadless tires practically gleamed, but I checked for a spare and a jack and accepted the deal anyway, knowing that we wouldn't be driving great distances in compact Bali. The key was slightly bent, and I later discovered that the ignition switch occasionally responded to it with dull silence.

Nevertheless, over the next week we nearly circumnavigated Bali in our idiosyncratic Kijang. Negotiating Bali's roads required constant vigilance after the ease of driving in Australia; it was like going from riding a tricycle in a driveway to negotiating Boston rush hour traffic in a jalopy. Despite the fact that I was now more accustomed to driving on the right side of the car and the left side of the road, our departure from Ubud was pure, confounding Asia. We threaded through unexpected detours, followed a circuitous route without signposts, stopped and turned around, and crept slowly down noisy narrow streets crowded with bicycles, mopeds, and Balinese "minivans" of mom, dad, and three children packed onto a 125cc motorcycle.

Our first destination, Amed, was a sleepy fishing village with great snorkeling and beach massages—and which sat within view of the volcano Gunung Agung, the highest mountain in Bali. At 10,308 feet, Agung is one of the most sacred sites on Bali and is reputed to be the home of *Mahadewa,* the supreme manifestation of Shiva. Shiva, along with Lord Brahma and Lord Vishnu, represent the holy trinity of deities in the Hindu pantheon. The volcano, which hadn't erupted since a months-long outburst in 1963, towered over the beaches and terraced rice fields. For me, it was an immutable reminder of the awesome geothermal power held within the earth.

We learned that it was possible to climb Agung, if the kids were up for an early start and a long, hard uphill hike. To my surprise, Kolya and Zoe *liked* the idea of rising just after midnight to gain the summit by sunrise, and we hired a local man to guide us.

We awoke at 1:45 and by 2:15 started driving. Illuminated by motorcycle headlights and dim bulbs in small villages, a hidden Bali flitted by as we passed markets in full bustle at 3 A.M. We asked our guide, Nyoman Corea, why the markets started in the middle of the night. The answer must have made more sense to him than it did to us. "That's when the markets start in these villages." Good enough for me.

At 4:00 we hoofed up 300 steps to the temple that marked the beginning of the pilgrimage. From there we would climb more than 3,000 vertical feet to the top of the volcano rim. Zoe and Kolya trooped on, scampering with flashlights up steep and often slippery terrain, clamoring over roots and through fine volcanic dust that crawled into our socks and soon piled up like little dunes inside our shoes.

As dawn hinted of its arrival, the summit remained a steep half a mile away, and Zoe, like a donkey that would prefer to be shot rather than to move, suddenly refused to go on. She hid behind a rock windbreak and curled up. I told Tory, Kolya, and Corea to continue and reconciled myself to staying behind. In a few minutes Kolya returned, offering to stay: "You would like to see the sunrise from the top more than I would, Pop."

I wondered if I was crazy to leave them alone on the mountain, but I could see no imminent danger. I hustled to catch up with Tory and Corea, sucking wind as I approached 3,000 meters and the oxygen quotient in the air diminished. We reached the summit half an hour after dawn, arriving at the barren, rocky volcano's rim lit by the slanting rays. The entire island of Bali hid below the morning cloud blanket, but the horizon opened up clear to the nearby island of Lombok, with 12,224-foot Mt. Rinjani jutting above the cloud cover.

Tory and I embraced, stood gaping into the volcano's cavity, and watched Nyoman Corea pay homage to the mountain spirit. He tucked himself out of the wind behind a rock and faced the crater, lit incense, and meditated, his eyes closed, the dawn light on his serene face.

After a snack, we scooted back down and found the kids happily napping out of the wind behind a wall of rocks. We descended to the temple and car, tired and satisfied.

I climed the hiist mountin in BALI! Which is a valcano it erupted in 1963 it is sooo beautifull. We had to get up at 2:00 in the morning if we wanted to get there before sun rise and we did and we could see the hole island.

On the way back, Corea showed us his village and his home. His extended family lived in a series of small but neatly maintained houses abutting a section of rice field that the family owned and worked. We met his parents, his brother, his brother's wife, and assorted cousins and nephews, as well as a few chickens. In Bali, the family unit is still remarkably intact, especially in contrast to the social dysfunction and mayhem that passes for extended family in many parts of America. Seeing their simple compound, I felt embarrassed by my earlier efforts to bargain about his guiding price. In the end, I paid him more than we had agreed on—about $50.

We thanked Nyoman Corea, then drove back to Amed, crawled into our bungalows, and napped until almost sunset. As the sun caressed the western sky, I had a breathtakingly welcome massage on the porch. I let my mind wander and realized that my face had suddenly become wet, as if the masseuse's strong hands were kneading out my tears. In my periodic grieving for Bob, random events, thoughts, or tangents had triggered an unseen "play" button in my memory; I relived another of Bob's dying scenes. This particular play button, I realized, was a delayed reaction to Nyoman Corea pointing out his brother's house next door to his.

Bob called to give me the news that he had found a lump. He had been showing his wife Renda how to do a self-breast exam when he felt something hard near his nipple.

When they cut him and tested the tissue, the stains on the pathologist's slides were unmistakable, the therapeutic choices pretty clear-cut and reasonably optimistic. The oncologist recommended that Bob schedule surgery right away. They would remove the nipple on his right breast and all the fatty tissue.

Bob said they could do the surgery in three weeks.

Three weeks?

"C'mon, Bob, what are you waiting for? You're a doctor, for Chrissakes. Get this done."

"It's not going to make a difference. And that's when our best guy is available. I know him. He's good."

I flew to California to be there for the mastectomy, my first time in a hospital for such a painful and horrific event. Hospitals meant nice things to me, all in all. I had loved visiting my dad at Kaiser after my eye

doctor appointments, seeing the picture of his three boys on his desk, surrounded by diplomas and OB-GYN magazines, and him in his white
coat. *The nurses were always so nice to me.*

But I had no experience with post-op waiting rooms, even if the surgeon, the anesthesiologist, and the internist were all Bob's colleagues. We
waited interminably, time audible on faintly clicking institutional clocks.
Because this was Bob's hospital, we knew he wouldn't get better care here
if he were a king.

The anesthesiologist entered the waiting room in scrubs toward the
end of the operation to reassure us. It was taking a little longer than
usual, he said, but only because they were being extra careful. They
thought they had removed it all, but we would have to wait for the
pathology reports to be sure. The surgeon was doing a bang-up job with
the scar, he told us.

And when the path report came back, we cheered as if the war were
over, the home team had creamed the arch-rivals, we'd all been accepted
into the colleges and medical schools of our choices, and our child had hit
a triple with the bases loaded during the Little League All-Star game.
They'd removed it all. The nodes were clean. No microscopic cancerous
cell-devils to be found, except for the contained lump, which was removed
and treated with extreme prejudice, jettisoned into the hospital's furnace
maw of diseased tissue and malevolent biochemical mutations. Bob
would be okay, but there would still be chemotherapy.

Just to be sure.

After dinner, the four of us stood together on the beach and stared
at the backlit silhouette of Agung, rising an improbably high distance from where we stood. As if in recognition of our efforts, the
mountain shed its cloud cloak and revealed itself completely. Tory
and I stood with our arms around each other, Zoe snugged up next
to Tory, and I pulled Kolya in. There, on the beach in Amed, in the
shadow of Shiva's home, we held each other in a promising four-
way hug.

*

Driving around the east and north coast the next day reminded me of our sound-track-to-a-movie moments in Queensland. A hand-painted sign beckoned us to detour from the main coast road in order to visit the "higgest [sic] waterfall in Bali." The road led up from the coast to a small village, where we parked and walked fifteen minutes to the falls.

Passing through banana forests and bamboo thickets, we emerged into a startling clearing. Hundreds of feet of cascading clear water tumbled with a deafening crash from the rainforest above. We massaged our shoulders under the cool torrent and met a young man who had taught himself English but had never been able to afford to go to school. He apparently approached tourists like us for a chance to practice his English, and perhaps to pick up a few rupees from being an unofficial tour guide. He walked with us back to the village, and we gave him one of Zoe's books and some money, which he didn't ask for.

As we drove back to the highway, we segued into a deep conversation about the relativity of wealth, monetary vs. spiritual, first world vs. third world. I seized the opportunity to talk about our American privilege and also about the relativity of all things. About guilt over being wealthy, about the importance of finding meaningful work, about how having more money doesn't necessarily mean having a better life.

Kolya and Zoe had never considered that there might be kids who couldn't go to school because their families couldn't afford a few dollars a month in school fees. Zoe felt proud of donating her book to our new friend, but she wished I'd given him even more money. Even at home in Boulder, she often begged me to hand money to panhandlers at stoplights. And so I explained to her again that I donate money each year to organizations that help people in need. There is so much need.

The masseuse hadn't squeezed all of the tears out, evidently. I broke into tears again during the money-isn't-everything section of the morality lesson. I had said something about how much I'd give to be able to live in a dirt-floor compound with my family like Nyoman Corea does, with Bob alive again next door and Steve on the other side, my parents nearby. Kolya and Zoe became subdued, but whether it was out of introspection or embarrassment I could not say. Tory reached over to hold my hand.

Our hair still damp from our waterfall pummeling, we stopped at a small *warung*, or eatery, and had our *nasi goreng* (fried rice, Zoe) *nasi campur* (rice and vegetables, Dad), *Gado Gado* (a mixed vegetable dish with peanut sauce, Tory), and *satay ayam* (grilled chicken with peanut sauce, Kolya). These were the foods that had become the staples of our Indonesian fare. We had all learned rudimentary Indonesian phrases: hello, thank you, how are you, goodbye, beer, and grilled chicken on a stick, please. The kids are blessed with remarkable linguistic memories, and every word they uttered brought a smile to a Balinese face.

We were following the northern coast, lulled by the softening afternoon light and falling into our own reveries, when suddenly a clamorous "pop" brought us to attention and scared the kids. A blowout. Great. I pulled quickly to the side of the road and felt very savvy for having checked on the spare and the jack and tire-changing tools when we rented the car.

I had forgotten, however, to see if the jack worked and if the spare was worth a damn. No on both counts. Two men on a motorcycle pulled over to try to help, but they couldn't make it work, either. A third man went to retrieve his jack when it became apparent that ours was kaput.

One glance at the spare, however, and I wondered if it was even worth the effort. Most of the tread had already been deposited in various potholes over what may have been several decades of use. Upon closer examination, the tire appeared as if it might have been pulled out of a dump somewhere to give a false sense of reassurance to people like me. Since the nearest major town was Singaraja, eight kilometers away, we had little choice but to put on the spare and wobble there as best we could.

We arrived at about 5:30 P.M., found a gas station, and the attendants told us that the only tire shop in town had already closed. Or maybe not. They pointed us 200 meters away to where a Dunlop sign appeared like a savior.

Zoe had fretted out loud ever since the blowout with a series of "what if" questions. "What if the tire shop is closed?" "What if they don't have tires that fit?" "What if we get stranded here?"

Tory appreciated the chain of events as an adventure in the making. In turn, I found one more thing to appreciate about Tory. We tried to impress the kids with the idea that whatever happened would be fine. Although the thought of spending the night in that unspectacular town wasn't high on my list of things to do in Bali, I was in sardine-eater mode and had confidence that things would sort out.

Which they did. I purchased two new tires, replacing one of the remaining threadbare rear tires with a new one and designating the old one as a new, improved spare. Amidst much laughter, one of the tire-changing boys flirted shamelessly with Zoe. She later declared that she was in love with the raven-haired teen with a perfect complexion, swooning all the way to dinner.

While we waited at the tire shop making small talk in pidgin English with the owner, I ventured an Indonesian saying I had learned: *Tidak apa-apa*—roughly translated as "what are you gonna do?" Every Asian language I know has a similar phrase expressing an obligation to relinquish the illusion of control over events. In Thai, it's *mai pen lai* ("it doesn't matter"). In Japanese, *shoganai* ("there's nothing to do"). In Nepali, *ke garne* ("what to do?"). The tire-seller taught me that in his language, Balinese, it's *sing ken ken* ("everything's going to be okay"), which embodies the Asian concept of karma, of submitting gracefully to the unseen forces of the universe.

The Balinese expression evokes the sense of fate, of the pure fact that humans don't control the universe (though we seem to be trying to exert ourselves mightily to alter the face of the planet) or even our day-to-day travails. It's sort of a Murphy's Law for Buddhists, Shintos, Muslims, and Hindus, without the ironic twist. When something bad happens, like our flat tire or a plane being late or, as I've come to think about it, even Bob dying, there is really nothing to be done *about* it. Except to grieve, to let the waves lap and crash upon us whenever they arrive, to breathe in between onslaughts. Sing ken ken.

Selamat Malam, Papa

Dawn greeted us as we sputtered out to sea in a small, bamboo-pontooned, festively painted boat captained by a young Balinese man who might not have been older than seventeen. We had set out from the fishing village of Lovina in search of dolphins, watching the sun rising round and red over the mainland like a giant red-dotted Hindu tika blessing the sky and the day. We gazed landward to see volcanoes, palm trees, and the smoke of morning cooking fires rising from the villages dotting the narrow coastal plain. Though we saw no dolphins, we weren't disappointed. Kolya tried out our new phrase, Sing ken ken. You can't tell the dolphins what to do.

We spent the rest of the day snorkeling off Menjangan Island, where the underwater views easily rivaled the ones we'd seen at the Great Barrier Reef. On a bus ride back to the hotel, Zoe once again proclaimed this "the best day of my life." Before falling asleep on Tory's lap, she mumbled, "What else could you ask for?" Kolya sat up front talking with the driver, and I allowed myself a moment of conscious contentment.

The events of the past few days—climbing Mt. Agung, getting a flat tire, looking for dolphins, and snorkeling—had affected our quartet like cornstarch in a cake mix, adhering our disparate ingredients into a whole. With each shared adventure, Kolya and Zoe clearly grew more comfortable with Tory's presence. As a bonus, the kids soon discovered that she could be their ally, a good cop countering their dad's bad one when my temper flared or my patience grew short. When we returned from our snorkeling expedition, the kids had begged for ice cream and I erupted in frustration that they were never satisfied. Tory calmly backed the kids' utterly reasonable request, offering to take them for ice cream while I sat on the veranda and chilled with a Bintang.

I sipped my beer and tried to recall my satori at Wonga Beach, reminding myself to just freaking lighten up, grateful for Tory's presence.

We returned the Kijang in Ubud without incident and settled in for a couple more nights at the now-familiar hotel. We had made airplane reservations to travel to Java on my birthday, September 2, so Tory and the kids surprised me with a lavish feast our last night in Ubud, September 1.

We walked to a family-run guest house that specialized in elaborate traditional dinners and sat around a large table for the feast, served family style. The host's daughters brought out an opulent array of dishes—smoked duck, satay made with minced, spiced meat and skewered on a bamboo stick, jackfruit, and particularly memorable versions of the other Balinese staples we'd eaten at cheap *warung* around the island.

Kolya liked the rice wine best.

I surveyed the scene at this lavish table, slowly panning to take in my two children dressed in their Balinese best, and Tory, sunned and glowing in the warm night. I was enjoying my own glow from the rice wine. I had never spent much time imagining what my life would be like at forty-five, midway (I hoped) through life's journey.

But I don't think I could have dreamed my present circumstances: a dead brother, an ex-wife living a thousand miles away with another woman, two children I was raising more or less by myself, and an evening at a guest house in Bali filled with the sound of geckos and assorted birds whose calls I could recognize but whose names I did not know.

After dinner, I telephoned Borneo to make arrangements to visit an orangutan research station, then walked the back streets to Nick's Pension. During our stay, we had made passing acquaintance with most of the vendors, shopkeepers, and young men who roosted along the alley adjacent to Nick's. It was past 10:00, and most of the shops were closed. The woman who had helped Zoe with her sarong, with whom we had exchanged greetings ever since we began learning the difference between good morning (*selamat pagi*) and good evening (*selamat malam*), paused while closing her metal tambour shop door, then turned to me and smiled.

Selamat malam, Papa, she said.

On my actual birthday, we bid Ubud and Bali goodbye, taxied down to Denpasar, and caught a flight on the Indonesian airline Merpati. Our plane from Denpasar was delayed and we landed in Surabaya, on the southern coast of Java, just five minutes before our next plane was scheduled to depart for our destination, Semarang. We frantically followed the only other Caucasian deplaning with us, a thirty-something American named Sean with the world-weary look of an ex-pat. Sean planned to catch the same plane to Semarang but didn't seem at all concerned. He queried the man at the ticket counter in impressive Indonesian, then informed us the second plane was delayed as well. We finally boarded and only then realized we wouldn't be arriving in Semarang until well after dark and had no hotel reservations. But we didn't care. We were all becoming sardine eaters.

Zoe sidled up to Sean on the Semarang flight and chatted him up. She told him today was her dad's birthday and we just came from Bali and Australia and we're on an around-the-world trip and that's my dad's girlfriend Tory and god knows what else. I went back when Zoe headed to the bathroom and informed Sean that if Zoe bugged him, please say the word and I'd pull her back to her seat. He replied that he was thoroughly enjoying the conversation, no worries.

Sean exported Indonesian-made furniture from a factory near his house, an hour's drive from Semarang. When we arrived at the airport, he had a car and driver waiting for him and asked if he could he give us a lift. We said sure, but that we didn't exactly know where to get a lift *to*. He invited us to pile in, then offered to take us to dinner at a fancy hotel nearby—it was my birthday, after all. After dinner, he would take us to a hotel in our price range. We gratefully accepted all his offers.

At dinner, the kids pulled out the birthday presents they had carried surreptitiously from Bali, saving something special for my actual birthday. I had been suspicious when Tory had given Kolya something she had hidden in her pack before we entered the restaurant, but I couldn't have guessed at their planning. They recounted with pride how they had shopped and bargained and bought the presents by themselves, using their own money. This was extraordinary, since the kids, to the best of my recollection, had never given me a birthday gift or Father's Day gift that was not orchestrated by their mom or a schoolteacher.

Zoe presented me with a one-inch-high wooden carving of an owl.

"Because you are so wise," she said, without a *soupçon* of irony.

Kolya unwrapped and presented me with a beautiful walking cane with an intricately carved dragon head and a long, tapered, scaly body.

"Because you are so old," he said, and he, Zoe, and Tory giggled.

Sean encouraged the kids to have dessert, called on his cell phone to make hotel reservations for us, dropped us off, and disappeared like a vivid dream about flying. We took two rooms, and I went to the kids' room to tuck them in. The three of us exchanged happy amazement at the serendipitous encounter with Sean, and I reminded them that the next day we'd really be heading off for some adventures when we flew to Borneo. I thanked them for their gifts, and we nuzzled in the three-way, nose-to-nose-to-nose embrace and snort that had become our trademark-monkey kisses.

I stood in front of the mirror, brushing my teeth with bottled water and examining my lengthening crow's feet, which seemed to depict my age like human annual rings.

Selamat malam, Papa, I repeated to myself with a chuckle. Good night. And happy birthday.

ORANGUTAN BREAST MILK

BORNEO HIT US like a blast furnace. The air conditioning in the Blue Kecubung Hotel waged battle at full power against a sustained assault of equatorial air, but the A/C was clearly outmatched. After the electricity had been out for an hour, however, we began to appreciate its heroic efforts. With the unexplained power outage, our rooms in Pangkalan Bun began to feel as if somebody had cranked up the thermostat in a spectacularly potent steam room. The smell of mold infiltrated my brain like a disease. The kids, who had discovered with glee that even in Borneo there is satellite television reception with MTV Asia, stared at the blank tube in horror, sweating miserably.

The young women who worked at the hotel strolled down the corridor planting candles on the linoleum floor and handing them out to patrons in a practiced ritual. The increasingly sweltering room only grew hotter with the candles, and Tory and I convinced the kids that we couldn't just stay and swelter; we needed to venture forth into the Bornean night. After a brief, cranky rebellion, we waded into the downtown market scene of south central Kalimantan.

A brief geography lesson here: Borneo is the largest of the Indonesian archipelago's 13,000 to 17,000 or so islands (depending on who's counting) but is geopolitically divided among three countries: Indonesia, Malaysia, and Brunei. Most of the northern third of Borneo is part of Malaysia. Brunei is sandwiched in, and the southern part, known as Kalimantan, is part of Indonesia. (To the many, many people who asked, "What about their *schooling?*" I replied smugly that while Kolya's eighth-grade class remained at home studying world geography, he would be learning about it firsthand. Dozens of indigenous peoples call Borneo home, including the famed Dayak "headhunter" tribes, who probably don't really care if they're considered Indonesian, Malaysian, or Bruneisian.

Escaping the oppressive heat of the Blue Kecubung, we walked down the dark streets of Pangkalan Bun. No Dayak headhunters appeared, but Borneo still felt, as Kolya put it, "out there." Not only were we in a land-of-no-McDonald's, but when we reached the main street in town it was apparent that tourists were a relative rarity. We saw no beckoning signs advertising jungle tours in syntax-garbled English, nor were we badgered by offers of transport or tickets to witness authentic cultural experiences. The guidebook warned that Pangkalan Bun was nothing but a dusty market town, devoid of fruit smoothies and Internet cafés.

The streets would have normally been dusty, but after a deluge of not-quite-monsoonish rain that had fallen that afternoon (swamping the town's electrical system), they became impressively muddy. Unfamiliar sights and sounds bombarded our senses, and the smell of peculiar-looking vegetables and overused cooking oil emanated from street stalls tucked into alleys. Most people dressed in Western clothes—the men in cheap polyester shirts and pants, the women in long skirts—and we no longer saw the impressive costumes and sarongs of Bali.

The darkness and the olfactory overload began to take a psychic toll in the sultry night, and the kids wanted to go *home* (to the Blue Kecubung). Instead, Tory and I led them into a warung to drink a bottled soda. We plunked ourselves at a table surrounded by mostly men eating plates of *mie goreng* and *nasi goreng*, fried noodles and fried rice, respectively. We watched the head cook busily stirring the contents of a giant wok situated in an alcove at the storefront overlooking the street. He and an assistant frenetically fried up batches of noodles and rice, a propane fire raging under the well-worn wok. They casually tossed in ladlefuls of spices from plastic containers on the counter: garlic, chilies, lard, and unfamiliar others, then onions, cabbage, other vegetables, and the noodles. The hot oil sizzled and the pungent smells of spices were released into the room.

We ordered Fantas and I asked if the kids were hungry. Kolya shot me an "Oh-no-Dad-we're-not-eating-*here*-don't-even-think-about-it" look. I told him that this was a perfectly fine place to eat, his momma and I had eaten at hundreds of places like this during our travels. Sucking on his straw as if it were a life-giving oxygen bottle, Kolya remained obstinate, afraid of the provenance of this food and wanting the relative safety of the overpriced hotel restaurant. I didn't press the issue as we drank our sodas. The kids were transfixed by the sweaty cooks, who by this time had noticed the kids noticing them and chatted together, smiling.

Seven o'clock rolled around and Zoe, bless her heart, decided that yes, she'd eat here. I ordered two plates of mie goreng, which I could now do in pidgin Indonesian, and Kolya waited for Zoe to taste it before he grabbed a fork and dug in, too. Tory and I exchanged a greasy, smiling glance in between bites, gratified that the kids had just crossed another traveling threshold.

We have come here to investigate part two of our quartet of global environmental case studies: the orangutan—literally the "person of the forest" in Indonesian—and one of the world's most endangered primates.

While researching the orangutans' plight before leaving the states, I had contacted Dr. Gary Shapiro at Orangutan Foundation

International (OFI), a small nonprofit based in Los Angeles that has taken on the daunting challenge of trying to save orangutans in the wild. Shapiro briefed me on his group's efforts in Kalimantan, and especially about a research station founded almost thirty years previously by Dr. Birute Galdikas with several goals, including repatriating orphan "ex-captive" orangutans into the lowland forests they call home.

The Canadian-born Galdikas, now approaching sixty, began her career as one of three female primatologists trained by Dr. Louis Leakey in Kenya in the 1960s who ultimately made significant contributions to our understanding of primates—and to ourselves. One, Dian Fossey, became extraordinarily famous by the seductive combination of being violently murdered in 1985 at the age of fifty-three and being the subject of a Hollywood film. Her character had been played by Sigourney Weaver in *Gorillas in the Mist* (1988). Rounding out the trio known as the "three angels" was Jane Goodall, who has written and lectured extensively about her groundbreaking work with chimpanzees. Fossey had her Karisoke Research Station in Rwanda; Goodall had headed up Gombe Research Station in Tanzania. For Galdikas, the base of operations became Camp Leakey in Indonesian Borneo, an area with the highest densities of orangutans in the world.

At least since curious baboons interrupted my tennis game with Bob back in 1968, primates had captivated me. How could we humans not be drawn to animals so similar to us that looking at them is like peering into the mirror through an evolutionary lens? Geneticists say that orangutan DNA is 97 percent similar to ours, and the behavior, expressions, and intelligence of *Pongo pygmaeus* reflect that similarity. I'm not even sure I share 97 percent of my DNA with certain neighbors.

We may be drawn to watch television specials about primates, but we're brutally unkind to them in the wild. Nearly everywhere orangutans make their home, humans make life almost impossible for them. We decimate the lowland forests, hunt them as pests, and capture them to sell as exotic pets. *Homo sapiens* are, figuratively at least, committing cousin-cide. If the current pessimistic predictions are correct, by the time Kolya and Zoe are my age, the only orangutans left in the world may be living in enclosed, simulated orangutan environments recreated by humans and located inside zoos and artificial safarilands.

I had called Shapiro in Los Angeles before we left Australia, hoping for a trustworthy update on the political situation in Borneo. He had just returned from Camp Leakey and reported that although the impeachment crisis had passed, vicious fighting had broken out between the indigenous Dayaks in Kalimantan and the immigrant Madurans from Java. The Indonesian government, attempting to alleviate population pressures on Java, had embarked on a massive and controversial government relocation program to move Madurans to the more sparsely populated Kalimantan.

Around Pangkalan Bun, where we now sweated, the program had resulted in bad blood, burned houses, and prevailing tenseness. Local Dayaks, who are mostly animist and converted Christians, rebelled against losing their traditional lands to the immigrant Muslims. News reports suggested that Dayaks had also reclaimed their nearly lost tradition of headhunting, and Maduran heads literally rolled.

Shapiro didn't think the conflict would affect tourists, though.

We had originally made arrangements for Zaqie Al-Ichlas, or "Mister Jackie," OFI's point man in Borneo, to meet us at the Pangkalan Bun airport. He was inexplicably delayed, but Mrs. Ibu Waliyati, who works for Dr. Galdikas, had helped us check in at the Blue Kecubung. (*Ibu* means "mother," we found out later. Many Indonesians go by one name.) The next day, she offered us a trip to the Orangutan Care Center outside of town, where orphaned orangutans live for up to eight years before they are old enough to be released into the wild. At the center, local humans pair up with orphaned orangutans for daily walks into the surrounding jungle, ostensibly to help the orangutans access an instinctual core and, over time, learn how to forage for food on their own.

I'd read that OFI's "ex-captive" rehabilitation program, and Galdikas herself, had been targets for criticism from wildlife biologists and conservationists—not to mention the Indonesian government. Galdikas began her career in Borneo with groundbreaking studies that described the solitary orangutan's social behavior and habits. Over the years, her shift toward promoting the ex-captive program drew fire. Certain primatologists objected to the low success rate of reintroducing orangutans to the wild, while others worried that ex-captive orangutans could introduce diseases such as tuberculosis into wild populations. Others criticized OFI because it is so expensive to care for orphans, and conservation dollars might be better used for habitat preservation. The Indonesian government routinely hassled her for her high-profile campaigns to expose feckless environmental policies.

Galdikas has articulately defended her work against the charges. I had spoken to her from a *wartel*, or public phone station, in Bali, when she was still in Pangkalan Bun. Unfortunately, she would be leaving town before we arrived, but we chatted about her approach to conservation in a country as complicated as Indonesia. In Borneo, a lethal mix of land clearing for palm plantations, massive logging operations, destructive gold mining, and government corruption posed a clear and present threat to the orangutan's survival.

Although OFI uses pictures of cute orangutans for fundraising, there's nothing doe-eyed about Galdikas's conservation strategies. After thirty years in the country, she understands that if she lectured locals about the importance of biodiversity or the spiritual necessity of saving humans' closest relatives, she'd be laughed out of a Dayak long house. When she works the locals these days, she said, "I don't even talk about orangutans anymore."

Instead, she talks about how the forests and the rivers provide more jobs and better livelihoods when they are vibrant. Workers wielding chain saws in the forests and manning the sluice pumps on the rivers make little more than subsistence wages—at tremendous long-term cost. Galdikas and Mr. Jackie brought a new message: If rivers are poisoned in the name of a few ounces of gold dust, or forests decimated for a short-lived timber harvest, was that worth lifting a few people temporarily out of poverty and making a few others, mostly foreigners, very rich?

In critical areas of Tanjung Puting National Park (which Galdikas was instrumental in creating in 1984 from an area that had previously been, nominally, a reserve), illegal logging had already declined significantly. By offering "bonus pay" to the local police, plus perks such as cigarettes and food, OFI had convinced the police to maintain roadblocks on the rivers in the park—the only way into this remote and roadless region to transport logs. The roadblocks, Galdikas said, had been an almost complete success, and illegal logging in one part of the park had come to a virtual standstill.

Unfortunately, an equally destructive gold rush had brought thousands of miners to those same river basins. All around the park (and throughout Indonesia), illegal miners dig tons of riverbank, then process the slurry using mercury to find relatively small amounts of gold dust. The mining poisons the waterways and kills the fish and other animals that depend on them. I would soon witness the devastation.

"The only people who can make a difference are the police, and they can only do it if they have the support of the community," Galdikas said over the crackly phone. She expressed frustration that multinational groups have been so slow to address the number one problem in Indonesian conservation: "An endemic culture of corruption." I knew from a cover story on international conservation work that I co-wrote for *Newsweek* in 1993 that Indonesia was a black hole for corruption, especially when it came to black rhino programs. Conservation organizations working to save the rhino finally quit when they realized how frequently corrupt officials siphoned off program money.

As far as the criticism about the ex-captive program went, Galdikas told me that in a species as endangered as the orangutan, it's important to save individuals. While reintroducing ex-captives into the wild is time-intensive and sometimes fails, she acknowledged, orangutans have fared reasonably well.

As in so many international conservation efforts these days, OFI's central approach is to show local people that intact forests mean long-term economic activity—from tourism, environmental protection programs, and sustainable harvests from vibrant rivers and intact forests. "Right now [in August 2001] we employ 180 people," Galdikas said—from those who clean the camp to people who attend the orangutan orphans. "I hope to employ 1,000. That would create a powerful political constituency."

Galdikas said goodnight and left me with a sobering thought. "The war for conservation is never-ending," she said. "Eternal vigilance is the price you pay."

Despite Galdikas's efforts, orangutan adults are being killed and baby orangutans are being orphaned in alarming, almost epidemic numbers. The Orangutan Care Center has become a repository for primate refugees from the rainforest wars.

We entered one room where a baby orang, perhaps six months old, sat in a human child's bassinet. Even without any knowledge of what to expect from a baby orang, I saw something was wrong. The baby was lethargic, dull-eyed, and seemed to have trouble moving its arms to hold the bassinet's handle. Somebody had killed the mother then struck the baby on the head, causing permanent brain damage. "That's sooooo sad," Zoe moaned.

We walked down a corridor lined with mostly empty cages, since most of the 170 orangutan inhabitants were in the forest with their human handlers, acclimating to the eventual day when they might be released into the wild—if enough wild remained for them to be released *into*. A few orangutans stayed behind in their cages, and we approached to observe the remarkable similarities between orangutans and humans: their expressions, their morphology, their *being*.

I don't like anthropomorphizing animals, but these orangutans didn't need much anthropomorphizing to make them seem so close to human. As we stood in front of one large female, she casually sucked her own teat, then proceeded to spit the milk at Kolya, who was stunned by the mischievous squirt. Zoe shook hands with one, giggling and obviously noticing how amazingly human they seemed, with their long fingers, expressive faces, and roguish actions.

Unfortunately, orangutan biology conspires against their survival in these disturbing times. Mother orangs only give birth once every four years, since their babies often remain with them for that long. Orangutans don't reach sexual maturity until about age twelve. For the most part, they are solitary animals, although they can share overlapping territory and are known to "talk" to each other by vocalizing sounds that can be heard from a great distance. Like humans, immature orangutans aren't able to fend for themselves, and orphaned orangutans often need to stay at the Orangutan Care Center or Camp Leakey for years before they can be considered for release into the wild.

Many of the orangutans at the center had arrived after their mothers died at the hands of palm oil farmers, who regard orangutans the way American ranchers regard wolves: as varmints. Others had been maimed or wounded by machetes. We met a Spanish veterinarian volunteering at the clinic, Rosa M. Garriga, who wore the sallow look of a doctor in a war zone. Here, as in a battlefield hospital, the facilities are spartan, the casualties come in endless waves, and the futility of being there is only outweighed by the necessity of being there.

"There are more coming in all the time," Garriga sighed. Even if orphaned orangutans show promise for reintroduction into the wild, she said, unlogged and intact rainforest diminishes in supply each day. Orangutans are solitary animals, requiring a good supply of fruit and a rainforest to roam. "It's getting worse all the time," Garriga said, shaking her head slowly in disbelief. "They are so close to us," she added, dragging on a cigarette and looking at the brain-damaged baby orangutan. She exhaled, shook her head again in what seemed like an acquired involuntary motion. "It's just so unfair, what is happening to the rainforest."

Walking back to the car, I pulled Kolya aside and asked if he felt sad to think that orangutans might be extinct in his lifetime. I have tried to keep what Kolya calls my "hippie tree-hugger" stuff to myself, but I wanted to know how seeing the orangutans affected him. He answered enigmatically: "I'll get back to you on that."

THE CRACK HOTEL OF KUMAI

BY THE TIME we returned from a repeat visit to the fried noodle restaurant after touring the Orangutan Care Center, the power was humming again in the Blue Kecubung and our rooms were merely uncomfortable rather than unbearable. We had been in Borneo less than thirty-six hours, but it seemed like a week. We had already seen burned-out Dayak houses, Kolya had been spit on by a roguish orangutan, we had endured several power outages, and we had expanded our culinary horizons. We returned to our hotel for a second night with a fresh array of new images waiting to be processed in our sleep.

I worried about the accelerated pace of our travels from now on. After our leisurely five weeks in Australia and nearly two weeks in Bali, we would be moving relatively quickly for the rest of the trip. I wondered whether we would be able to fully "arrive" in each place before logistics and mental momentum would pull us to the next.

I planned to rent a houseboat *(klotok)* and spend four or five days in Tanjung Puting National Park, and I suspected that our river trip into the jungle would stress us all even further. Kolya was already a little uncomfortable in the relative comfort of the Blue

Kecubung, and I didn't expect the boat's onboard lodgings to be an improvement. After our visit to the Orangutan Care Center, he told me, "Okay, we've seen the orangutans, let's go to Vietnam." But seeing orphaned orangutans in their cages was a little like seeing orangutans in a zoo, and I wanted to press further into the jungle to see them in the wild if we could.

Which, it turned out, was easier hoped for than done. The next few days were wait-and-see, a lesson in Indonesian letting go, tidak apa-apa. Mr. Jackie still hadn't shown up, although we had spoken by phone several times and he assured me that he would help us rent a klotok that would take us upriver to visit Camp Leakey and environs "soon."

The kids remained cloistered in the depressing but well-meaning hotel watching MTV Asia and Hindi movies in French with English subtitles while Tory and I ventured into the heat to explore the town. We wandered down narrow wooden walkways to the Kumai River waterfront, a busy thoroughfare with brown, silted waters specked with klotoks and water taxis, speedboats, and ocean-going cargo ships. Along the waterfront, which was lined with a rickety boardwalk, we passed wooden shacks and fish drying and children swimming and people washing and pooping and doing laundry in the same water.

Like Rebecca and me, Tory and her ex-husband had traveled extensively in Asia. Our occasional walks without the kids offered the opportunity to exchange stories: of our marriages, our adventures, our lost dreams, and, cautiously, our new dreams. We talked about the kids, and I was anxious to hear her perceptions of how they were doing. She sensed heightened anxiety in both of them since we'd left the comforts of Bali, as did I. We shared how challenging this trip was for all of us, and we bucked each other up in the draining tropical heat. It was easier to talk about the kids than to talk about where the two of us might be heading—a place unknown to both of us.

*

We spent two long days in Pangkalan Bun watching the power go on and off, and then Mr. Jackie showed up. Zaqie, from Jakarta, appeared to be in his mid-forties and sported longish hair, a mustache, and glasses. He had come to Borneo originally to research proboscis monkeys. Then he met Dr. Galdikas, whom he and everybody else calls "the Professor." Galdikas roped him into orangutan conservation.

We drove about half an hour to the neighboring town of Kumai to negotiate with Mr. Imul Mulyati, the klotok captain, about our home for the next five days. Zaqie told me that it was a little more difficult getting klotoks these days than it used to be, since the police and OFI rented many of them to conduct river blockades in order to staunch the flow of illegal logging. We were in luck, Zaqie said, that Mulyati's klotok was available. After good-natured but hard-nosed bargaining, we settled on about $35 per day, including a cook and a first mate, shook on it, and agreed to leave early the next day.

Zaqie had to return to Pangkalan Bun for the night. He dropped us off at the Hotel Garuda in Kumai, which made the Blue Kecubung seem like the Ritz Carlton. Our $6 rooms theoretically had A/C, but the power went out almost as soon as we turned it on. A shy young man entered, apologetically bearing candles, which warmed up the already stuffy rooms.

This was the first hotel we had stayed in with Asian-style bathrooms. The tile floor slanted to a floor drain, and the toilet, a porcelain fixture set flat into a slightly raised tile platform, had no seat. Kolya and Zoe stood over the porcelain hole in the floor, aghast. Next to the hole sat a tiled basin filled with clean water that served a dual purpose: We would use a plastic bucket to scoop water over us to bathe, and also use the water to wash after going to the bathroom. The kids quickly dubbed it "shit water" for its latter purpose.

After a few fairly good nights of sleep at the Blue Kechabung, I had some pretty high expectations for the next hotel, and the town that surrounded it. This made it even more surprising when I stepped out of the car, and first caught a glance of the hotel. It was a small white building with the paint coming off; it had a little paved area where there were more cracks than actual pavement. Up above the door, it looked like it might have had some lettering, but there was only one letter still hanging so it was hard to tell what the name of the place was.

I wasn't too disappointed until I stepped into the room itself. It was about the size of an office cubicle. It had a little bench, 2 tiny beds that were barely still standing. The bathroom was the worst that we had seen in a hotel yet. It had no shower at all, no TP, all there was was a squatter, and a big dipper (which I still haven't used, and still intend not to).

The only moment of delight in the whole night's stay in Kumai was when they said that they could get us a TV. Zoe and I were quite thrilled. They then carted in an 8-inch TV with a VCR built in. It was about six-o-clock when we got back from dinner, and Zoe and I got comfortable, turned on the TV and for about 5 minutes, we were engulfed in scrambled "MTV Asia", then the power went out.

We all took it in stride except for Zoe, who gave us a little fit. I was happy about the size of the fit, it could've been a lot worse. Tory seems to still be a little surprised at the frequency of the meltdowns, but dad and I are fully used to it by now. We had candles delivered to our room promptly. These were great, and almost gave off more light than the little bulb in the ceiling.

After our dipper showers, we got a little bit of another problem. The mozzies were just about as bad as outside. We put 3 mosquito coils around the room, and they still were buzzing around us. We put up with this pretty well, though we all woke up with bites all over us. It was about eight-o-clock when dad said "Okay kids, we've got a big travel day ahead of us, and I want you to get some sleep. I'll wake you when it's time for breakfast."

Then Zoe and I retired to our room, and dad and Tory did the same. I lay in my bed long enough to realize that I wasn't gonna get a good night's sleep, then my bed broke. The part of it that was holding up my feet collapsed under me. This of course woke Zoe up, and she did a little bit of pestering me while I moved the inch-thick mattress to the floor where I tried to get to sleep again. This time, I tried for a lot longer to get to sleep because "We have a big travel day ahead of us."

The biggest of my problems while sleeping on the floor was that the mozzie coils had gone out, so I was bitten to hell while hearing Zoe's droning slumber noises coming from the bed above me. I finally gave up on sleeping at midnight, when I pulled a cheap plastic chair, a candle, and a mozzie coil from my Australia stash, and *The Three Musketeers* (by Alexander Dumas). This was the highlight of my night.

250 pages later, I couldn't keep my eyes open, and at 4 in the morning, I fell asleep on my "mattress" on the floor only to be woken up 4 hours later for a much welcomed breakfast.

Later that day on the boat, I was listening to The Atari's song *Teenage Riot*. In it, it says "another night, we'll be staying in some crack hotel." Right then, that is what I dubbed the Kumai hotel, and it stuck: The Crack Hotel of Kumai.

The four of us collectively might have put together one good night's sleep, and rising in the morning was actually a relief despite our fatigue. We ate an unexpectedly tasty breakfast of saffron rice and hard-boiled eggs dipped in a red chili sauce, which for reasons that are mysterious to me stands out as "the best breakfast in the world" to Zoe.

We humped our packs down to the pier and loaded them onto the 55-foot-long klotok. The boat immediately impressed the kids (a relief), especially because the crapper was Western-style, even though I had to contort myself into a ball in order to crawl into the tiny toilet space.

Mr. Aji, the klotok's cook, then took us on a shopping spree, first stopping at a dry goods store for staples: canned wieners, cookies, and bottled water. Then we accompanied Mr. Aji to the outdoor market, ducking through rain-puddled plastic canopies to shop for fruit, vegetables, chicken, rice, and more. Properly provisioned, we carried overstuffed plastic bags back to the boat.

We took our places on the deck, Mr. Aji cast off the lines, the muggy air moved, and we were off. Captain Mulyati turned the boat up the main Kumai River, then headed for what looked like an overgrown riverbank. As we approached, we passed the confluence where the Sekonyer River emptied into the Kumai. Captain Mulyati pointed the klotok upstream and deeper into the jungle, and we all felt a deep sense of anticipation, and, truth be told, a little trepidation.

As we skimmed upriver, successive wildlife sightings drove home the full import of where we were. After we turned up the much narrower ribbon of the Sekonyer, we felt civilization receding with every chug of our diesel motor. Signs of human settlement dwindled, green jungle crept down to the riverbanks on each side, and macaque monkeys jeered at us from the jungle canopy. Sitting on the deck of the *Harapan Mina III,* feeling as if we had entered a scene from *Apocalypse Now,* we watched a huge reticulated python duck under water as we gaped.

"Now, *that's* a snake," Kolya offered in his best Australian twang. I concurred.

Guerrilla Conservation Tactics

Before I left Colorado, and from Internet cafés in Bali, I had researched Indonesian environmental politics—and especially orangutan politics. Although Indonesia is surpassed in population only by India, China, and the United States, I knew precious little about it, and even less about Borneo. In my research, I discovered that Indonesia, like so many countries formed by conquest rather than by tribal or topographic boundaries, consists of an unnatural hodgepodge of distinct ethnic groups of people who collectively speak more than 650 languages and dialects. The lingua franca, Indonesian, is widely taught in schools, but it's a second language for many in a country that stretches over a distance about equal to the span between San Francisco and New York.

Indonesia is a grindingly poor country, wracked by political changes in recent years that have accelerated environmental destruction of the country's incredibly rich forests and coral reefs. After Indonesia declared independence from the Dutch in 1945, one repressive authoritarian regime after another ruled the country, centralizing power in its capital, Jakarta, on the island of Java. In

1998, the perpetual president since the mid-1960s, Suharto, lost power. The aforementioned and ultimately impeached Abdurrahman Wahid took over as the first (arguably) democratically elected president.

Unfortunately, democracy treated Indonesia's natural splendors more harshly than dictatorship had. Previous regimes certainly entertained and profited from massive logging and mining operations, which already threatened the orangutan and everything else that depends on the forest to make a living. But as the central government's dictatorial control fractured under Wahid, the door opened for provincial officials to profit from resource extraction. Indonesia's environmental crisis intensified.

What happened in Indonesia mimicked events in the breakaway Soviet republics after the dissolution of the Soviet Union in 1989: The loss of central control unleashed natural resource extraction mayhem. In Indonesia, as in Russia, it became every crook for himself.

Indonesia was overripe for the picking. Its coral reef resources rival the Amazon rainforest in terms of biodiversity. But Indonesia's reefs—nearly 15 percent of the planet's irreplaceable supply—are being quickly decimated by over-fishing and pollution. If the Great Barrier Reef has problems, they are magnified a hundredfold in the coastal waters of Suluwesi and Sumatra. Similarly, the rainforests of Indonesia hold untapped troves of flora and fauna whose names we may never know because they are being destroyed so rapidly.

This environmental destruction spells huge trouble for many species across Indonesia, which hosts nearly a fifth of all the world's known animal species (including more than 500 mammals) with a little more than 1 percent of the planet's landmass. Indonesia also ignominiously hosts the longest endangered species list as well, including the clouded leopard, the Sumatran tiger, the Javan rhino, the sea turtle, the proboscis monkey, the sun bear, and many other less charismatic megafauna. "We have megadiversity here in Indonesia," Zaqie had told me. "But people don't care."

The endangered list includes the orangutan, whose prospects

for long-term survival appear grim. The lowland forests, freshwater swamps, and peat swamp forests that orangutans call home also happen to be home to many highly valued hardwood trees. Orangutan habitat also makes a great place to plant palm oil plantations, which means orangutan habitat is being stripped bare so people can cook french fries and make soap. And as with many "indicator species," if the orangutan disappears, you can bet that the rest of the system will crash, too.

If there's one thing I've learned by talking to conservation biologists, it's that everything in nature is connected to everything else, even if we humans haven't figured out the details. In the case of rainforests, however, certain things are known. When loggers or farmers pierce the forest canopy, plants and animals in the forest are exposed to increased sunlight. One result is increased likelihood of fire, as happened during the El Niño of 1997–1998. In that drought year, the great forest fires of Kalimantan aired on the U.S. evening news as 12 million acres burned—clouding the skies over much of Asia. After the fact, scientists discovered that logged areas burned more completely than untouched areas. Much of the extensively burned area was orangutan habitat.

The orangutan didn't need that kind of unnatural disaster, since it was already in deep jungle muck. Once upon a time, the orangutan, the only one of the four great apes found in Asia, roamed a vast tract of Southeast Asia. As human population increased, orangutan habitat decreased—and eventually most of the orangutans were driven out except for small populations on Borneo and the island of Sumatra.

Since the 1980s, orangutan habitat has declined by 80 percent, and since the early 1990s, orangutan populations worldwide have halved. Orangutans have other problems, too: They are routinely sold as pets in Jakarta markets for $2,500, an unfathomable sum for any of the villagers living in settlements along the river. Some researchers have suggested that as few as 15,000 wild orangutans remain. The trend charts a decline that could mean their extinction in the wild before Kolya turns twenty-five.

Does anybody else think this is an insane trade-off—making movie-theater popcorn butter from Indonesian palm oil, or pool cues and cheap futon frames from exotic Indonesian hardwoods?

Zaqie arrived in Kumai the morning of the "best breakfast in the world" with news that he wouldn't be coming with us on the houseboat. Instead, he would meet us "soon" at Camp Leakey. He gave me a letter of introduction to the camp manager, handwritten in Indonesian, a note for the police, and strict instructions to me not to introduce myself as a journalist. Zaqie helped load the boat, then we motored off with Captain Mulyati, Mr. Aji the cook, and the third mate, Ahmed Nazir. Between the three of them and the four of us, using English and Indonesian, we could pretty much communicate about how hot the weather was and what to have for dinner.

After the python sighting, the rest of the river trip proved relatively uneventful; we only saw a pit viper, one crocodile, and a bunch more monkeys. Captain Mulyati took a right turn on a yet narrower branch of the Sekonyer, motored past a police post set up to halt illegal logging in the park, and followed the smaller tributary about five miles up to Camp Leakey. Immediately after the turn, the water changed color from a cloudy green-gray to an almost jet black. With limited common language, we couldn't get a clear answer why. Until later.

We arrived at a wide spot in the narrow river, where a worn wooden floating dock led to an equally worn wooden pier. We tied off and walked a quarter mile up the pier into Camp Leakey, a ragtag assortment of outbuildings, bunkhouses, and a small information center. A sign greeted visiting tourists:

Please do NOT:
feed the orangutans
eat in front of the orangutans
or touch the orangutans

The camp manager, Togu Simorangkir, glanced at my letter of introduction and announced that we were just in time for the afternoon feeding. The four of us followed Togu and another camp worker on a trek along a well-worn forest path for a mile or so to a wooden feeding platform in the middle of the jungle surrounded by trees. The feeding program provided one piece in the long program of acculturating these ex-captive orangutans, several of which had come from the Orangutan Care Center we had visited. Togu shouted out orangutan calls, and one by one the orangs arrived, swinging on trees and sliding down branches to the platform, where Togu had placed bananas, pineapples, potatoes, and milk. He knew each animal, and in many cases knew from field research reports where the orang had spent the night and whether it had come to the previous day's feeding. A few orangutans, Togu explained, spent many days in the forest between human feedings. Soon, perhaps, these orangs could be transplanted to the wild.

Togu warned us to sit quietly, since the orangutans were outrageously strong and could be aggressive toward humans if they felt threatened. He told us not to approach the orangs no matter how friendly they appeared, and never to act menacing in any way, even if they came up and tried to take things from us. Kolya and Zoe sat next to each other on a makeshift bench, and Tory and I sat on another. The kids at first watched the orangutans arrive with interest if not necessarily awe, observing the human-like movements and familiar interactions. Mothers with their offspring. Juveniles fighting over food like siblings. (Zoe elbowed Kolya knowingly when a larger orangutan stole a milk container from a smaller one.) The orangutans climbed up and down, swinging from trees and vines, vocalizing to each other.

It didn't take long, however, until the kids whined that the mosquitoes were bugging them and that they were hot and tired. They wanted to go back home to the boat.

I fought my familiar disappointment at Kolya and Zoe's lack of enthusiasm. We had traveled halfway around the world, were sitting about fifteen feet away from a bunch of orangutans hanging from branches and stuffing their faces with bananas and pineapples, and they wanted to return to the boat and play some Game Boy inanity called Frogger.

I wrestled with my unspoken expectation that they would actually be *exhilarated* by what they were witnessing. Even if they didn't show it, I told myself that some of this *was* sinking in. I had to believe that *some* of this was making an impact.

We awoke the next morning to the reassuring sounds and smells of breakfast cooking. We peered out of the boat toward the dock that served as the national park entrance and saw that several orangutans had come down to watch us eat breakfast, including a shaggy, red-haired mother with her suckling baby that Zoe dubbed the Munchkinmonkey.

Soon the volunteers from the orangutan research station began arriving to take their morning baths in the river. The wide spot in the river serves as Camp Leakey's swimming hole, washing area, social gathering zone, washing machine, recreation area, and orangutan observation post. The British volunteers and Indonesian camp workers arrived, towels draped over their shoulders, soap in hand, and proceeded to wash, splash, and swim.

Zoe and Kolya, who had been freaked out at the thought of pythons and pit vipers, suddenly perceived the water not as a haven for monstrous beasts but as a jungle swimming pool. Tom, a Brit who was the chief volunteer, matter of factly told me that the human activity of daily washing and bathing and occasional tourist boats ensured that this stretch of river was snake-free. A crocodile had mauled a policeman earlier in the year, but that was several miles downriver. Tom and I squatted on the splintering wood dock while the kids screamed, "C'mon, Dad, the water's great!"—as if they were wading into the Pacific Ocean on a hot summer California day. The previous day's fear evaporated in their glee. They discovered how to conduct tandem swampings of the leaky wooden dugout canoes and began doing cannonballs off the boat's top deck. Soon, the three of us were leaping in unison into the brown water.

I climbed back up to the deck and surveyed the scene. Earlier, I had spied a river otter on the opposite bank, sliding around the rocks. I pointed it out to the kids and we sat together, enthralled, watching until it moved out of sight. The dawn chorus of birds, insects, and tropical life echoed all around in the not-yet-unbearable morning heat, the enveloping green like a living thing. I allowed a grin to temporarily transform my worried face as the kids scrambled up on either side of me.

We held hands, counted to three in Indonesian.

And jumped in again.

Suddenly, I felt as if I had nailed the most difficult, crux move of a difficult rock climb. I realized that it didn't matter if the kids were occasionally bored and snotty and indifferent. That they fought and whined and resisted. Whether or not Kolya and Zoe would eventually come to agree, for me this trip was unforgettable, worth every tantrum.

I let my doubts wash away in the milk-chocolate brown waters of the Sekonyer River, to be eaten, for all I cared, by crocodiles downstream.

The next day we joined Togu and a biologist—whom we had dubbed "the bird man," because he knew every sound of every bird in the forest—for a longer walk to try to see wild orangutans. Zoe balked at the jungle trek and decided to stay put with the boat crew and British camp workers. Kolya didn't really want to go, either, especially when I told him he couldn't bring his mini-disc player and listen to punk music as we walked. But given the alternative of staying with Zoe, he acquiesced.

We walked three or four miles on increasingly smaller footpaths until Togu stopped, gestured for us to be quiet, and made an orangutan-like call. From a distance, the call was answered. We continued and met up with an Indonesian researcher who tracked wild orangutans to observe their behavior. Togu pointed to a tree, and we could see a mother orangutan with a baby less than a year old clinging to her. This pair, Togu informed us, was wild—they'd never come to the feeding station.

Tory and I looked at the wild orangutans, then at each other, then grinned. I glanced over at Kolya to see if he was impressed and noticed him viciously swiping at mosquitoes without even looking at the orangutans. He wore the batik shirt we had purchased in Bali, which was soaked in sweat, and appeared far more miserable than enchanted.

He cheered up when Togu announced it was time to return. Kolya and I trailed behind, and I decided not to ask if he thought the wild orangutan baby was cool. Then, of his own accord, Kolya answered the question I had asked at the Orangutan Care Center, about whether seeing these orangutans had changed his otherwise nonchalant reaction to extinction. He said that before seeing the orangutans, the idea of them being endangered was "too abstract." Now that he'd seen them firsthand, he allowed, "I'd be sad if they were all gone."

Yesterday started like any other day that we had had on the boat, or the rest of the trip for that matter. It was our third day on the boat, and we had a full day planned out for us. Zoe threw a minor fit at the beginning of the day to get out of going on a hippie nature walk with Dad and Tory. Frankly, I didn't want to go, but I had finished *The Three Musketeers* yesterday, and I wasn't about to spend a day on the boat alone with Zoe with nothing to read. So I decided to go on the nature walk.

It turned out to be about as hippyish as Zoe had expected. I somewhat regretted going, but then thought about "playing" on the boat with The Toots, and just grit my teeth, and kept going, listening to Tory consistently list off the names of every living organism that we saw, smelled or heard. This would've been OK, if I could have remembered a single word from this conversation, but I didn't, so it was just a boring hippie hike. The only good part was that we saw an orangutan that had never been in captivity, or anything of that sort. This was okay for five of the thirty minutes that we sat staring at it sleep high in a tree with its baby.

Even as I am writing this, my dad is telling me to "Write my thoughts on seeing an endangered animal in the wild". He really doesn't realize that I don't really think too much of it, or most of the stuff that he tells me to write about. I thought it was okay, and I am glad that I saw it, but the only thing I gained from seeing it was bragging rights and enough mozzie bites to make me look like I have a second case of the chicken pox. This is true for many of things that we have done so far on this trip.

The day got better as we crawled out of the forest into the sunlight of Borneo. Just laying on the boat and listening to music contented my needs. Except the buzzing of Zoe, who can not sit still for over ten minutes. The deal that I eventually made with her involved me jumping into the python infested waters with her for an hour, then I got 30 minutes peace until I had to swim again. I am not going to pretend that I didn't like jumping off the boat, but I would much rather sit there and listen to music. But the combination contented everyone on the boat, so I was happy, and happy to give dad and Tory some reading time, though they never sacrifised themselves with Zoe so that I got reading time.

In Bornio we went on a house boat the water was soooooo dirty. When we were quietly mindng my own businis I heard my dad say Holy shit. There was a huge pathon his head was 20 feet. After that my dad saw a pit vaiper that I did not see. We parked the boat on a little river side bank and after that we hung out and then the cook on the boat said there is crocodileses near here. That scared me. We went to a place where you can see arangatans. They are big freaking animals. The boat was very nice the bathroom is the littlest thing and one day Kolya went to the bathroom after he was done I said Oh gross.

He said what?

I said, is that your turd?

Oh, he said.

It is floating down the river and boy let me tell you it is not a pretty site. Then Kolya said oh it is moving and little minnos are pecking at it.

And then we went swimming.

Zaqie arrived two days later with a story about a run-in with the local constabulary. He brushed it off, remarking that he lives with the fact that his natural enemies—illegal loggers and miners—also occasionally include local officials. Especially when said officials receive kickbacks from the natural resource poachers. Zaqie had been negotiating with government officials to increase patrols in the park, with moderate success. It didn't hurt anything that Julia Roberts had recently dropped by to film a television special on the orangutan's plight. Even provincial governors in Kalimantan know *Pretty Woman.*

Mr. Aji, who performed culinary wonders with the food we'd purchased in Kumai in his tiny shipboard galley, announced that dinner was served. The last of the volunteers retreated from the dock, leaving us with the sound of Mr. Aji's propane cookstove and the nighttime forest noises. We sat on the boat deck listening to Zaqie talk about saving orangutans, the reflections of the candle-light dancing in his glasses.

Zaqie recounted the travails of the past years in more detail than I had heard from his OFI colleagues Galdikas and Shapiro. Effective conservation work here, it became apparent, consisted of pursuing the art of the possible in the face of overwhelming opposition. Zaqie is a guerrilla conservationist, working in the field every day, maneuvering through obstacles with a combination of his wits, his unassuming charm, and a magnificent resolve. But Zaqie is nothing if not a realist. "This is Indonesia," he said, when I asked him about prospects for more government support. "It's like another planet."

Wrapped by the warm blanket of tropical night, Zoe placed her head on Tory's lap as we listened to Zaqie's stories and the occasional rustle from the shore. Kolya and I munched on weird Indonesian wafer cookies the kids had picked out at the Kumai market, and Zaqie's passion saturated the already humid air.

In fluent but heavily accented English, he recounted that the area near Camp Leakey had been included in a 100,000-hectare expansion of Tanjung Puting in 1997, an expansion that The Professor had lobbied for. Unfortunately, local people had cleared this parkland for agriculture—especially palm plantations—and claimed it as their own. The next year, Zaqie continued, a group of about a hundred mostly illegal loggers stormed an American researcher's camp and threatened westerners who were accused of stealing the locals' land. Zaqie suspected that the bigwig timber barons had organized the protests. The angry mob lay siege to park equipment, sinking boats, breaking windows, and sacking computers and files.

After the siege, Zaqie, along with Galdikas, brainstormed the idea to fund "bonus pay" for police patrols and river blockades. The patrols effectively stopped the illegal loggers from getting their booty to market, even as it strained OFI's resources. "Police are expensive," he said, matter of factly.

Since that time, Zaqie said, the Camp Leakey stretch of the fork of the Sekonyer had remained relatively intact while the bulk of the illegal mining and logging continued along the other fork. OFI made a strategic decision to safeguard what Zaqie called "the heart" of the park, saving the fight to protect the surrounding area for later. If later isn't too late.

The next day, Zaqie offered to take me back to the main fork of the Sekonyer River then up the main stem to a place called Aspai, where miners had created a floating camp. Our large klotok couldn't make it upstream because the water levels were so low in this month before the monsoons began. So Zaqie procured a small speedboat, which, unfortunately, couldn't hold the kids and Tory as well. Tory agreed to hang with the kids so I could learn the source of the river's discoloration—and see firsthand the growing threat from mining.

When we hit the main fork of the Sekonyer, the water again transformed, this time from black to muddy green-gray. Zaqie solved the enigma. Upstream, mining activity churns up tons of riverbank, which stirs up so much sediment that the water is a different color all the way to the Kumai River. That, combined with mercury that the miners use to extract minute particles of gold from vast quantities of sand, fouls the water for miles. He said that a survey from 1995, well before the current gold rush, already showed that mercury levels in the river were seventy times normal. Zaqie was fearful that the towns downriver would soon show birth defects and other mercury-related problems. I couldn't help but think of the infamous case of Minamata Bay in Japan—which became the horrific poster child for mercury poisoning in the 1950s and 1960s. After industrial waste from a manufacturing plant spread through the marine food chain, nearly 1,000 people died from eating contaminated seafood and tens of thousands became plagued by debilitating ailments and birth defects.

As we turned up the murky main stem of the Sekonyer, the driver throttled the 40 horsepower Enduro to full, dodging logs that looked like crocodiles and crocodiles that looked like logs. We saw several kingfishers and a hornbill as well as more proboscis monkeys. When Zaqie first came to Borneo from Java to study the monkeys, he discovered, among many things, how smart they were. He'd watch bands of them waiting on the shore, and when a motorboat passed by, they'd scurry into the water and cross en masse.

"Do you know why?" he asked.

I didn't.

"Because they'd learned that the crocodiles don't like speed-boats."

On either side of the river we passed signs of abandoned logging operations, with crude wooden ramps laid out like sloppy railroad ties disappearing into the dense underbrush. The loggers built sleds that they would pull by hand for miles over the ramps to bring wood to the river. It struck me how hard people are willing to work to do this. The prospect of hauling a two-ton sluicing machine through this landscape is mind-boggling. Poverty and greed are both powerful motivators.

We passed a bend in the river and came upon a strange sight: two women's frightened, bobbing heads appeared in the river next to a capsized dugout wooden canoe. We slowed and realized they must have been swamped by a passing klotok. We helped them to their canoe and gathered half a dozen ten-gallon cans filled with water. The women had been sent by the men at the mining camp to fetch water from a small tributary that wasn't hopelessly polluted from mercury and silt.

Zaqie turned to me to see if I understood the import of what I had just witnessed; even the miners realized that they were polluting the water where they worked and wouldn't drink it.

We approached Aspai, the center of the most intense mining activity. Before we saw any miners, we saw signs of their presence, or former presence. The riverbanks turned from verdant green to bleached desert white; the sandbanks looked like lifeless dunes for hundreds of yards on either side of us, and a few abandoned wood structures remained in this apocalyptic scene. It looked like a napalm bomb had been dropped.

Then we arrived at the real mess, one of the most depressing sights I've ever witnessed. Even before we reached the spot, we heard chugging from diesel engines rising over the noise of our own motor. Then we turned a bend and beheld an eerie and surreal scene.

There's a children's book by Dr. Seuss called *The Lorax* that depicts otherworldly destruction by a factory emitting "gluppity glupp" and befouling the air, the land, and the water. Here I witnessed Lorax-like destruction. Groups of men manned their "units"—floating barges with huge engines powering conveyor belts and pumps, sucking the riverbank up, and running it through a series of crude filters. Oil and gasoline smells permeated the jungle air. The stretch of river might as well have been the middle of the Sahara for all the life that remained on the once-lush riverbank.

Zaqie introduced me to a miner, who, if I understood correctly, receives a little stipend from OFI in return for intelligence about the other miners' doings. He offered us tea, and I hoped that I didn't insult him by declining. Itas Tasrip was thirty-eight but looked closer to sixty, his sun-dark skin and facial furrows as developed as a river system. He told me he owned land near Kumai, where he used to farm. When the riots between the Dayaks and the Madurans began, he fled up the river with his family to mine.

Itas explained that he paid rent to his boss, a man who owned the engine bolted to a floating wooden platform, which formed a "unit." He lived with his wife and three of his five children on a small, floating shack. "Every day I work to earn enough to pay for food," he told me, as Zaqie translated. He earned between $7 and $8 per gram of gold dust. Itas displayed the paper receipts he had received over the course of several days from middlemen who had bought his dust: 2.4 grams, 3.5, 3.7, 2.35, and one bonanza day when he found 9.35 grams.

Like all miners, he said he dreams of the magnum find and recounted how a buddy had found enough gold in one day—13 million rupiah worth ($1,600)—to buy two new motorcycles. But Itas didn't have many illusions about what he was doing for a living. "The workers don't get rich," he said. With a bemused but resigned laugh, he added, "Only the bosses get rich."

Itas poled us across the river in a canoe to a spot where two of his sons worked with a dozen other shirtless men in their teens and early twenties. The deafening noise of the diesel engines made it impossible to talk. I watched the boys and men stir up sediment and maneuver a hose that sucked up sand to the top of a conveyor belt about 15 feet off the ground. The belt ran the silt down and across a carpet-like strainer. At the end of the day, Itas takes the carpet, hopefully sprinkled with gold dust, and runs it through a process where he adds mercury. The gold, if there is any, binds with the quicksilver.

Itas guessed that there were about 300 "units" moored along this three-kilometer stretch of river, worked by about 1,800 men. Seeing the mucky output of Itas's three rigs, I realized it was no wonder that the river changed color back to the confluence of the Kumai River a dozen miles away.

A Kumai local, Itas acknowledged that his work fouls the water and kills the fish. "In my heart this is a big problem," he said. "But it is the only way I can make money for my family."

We motored back to the camp, veered up the tributary, passed the police checkpost, and glided at dusk along the jet black water to Camp Leakey. I felt absolutely baked from my day in the sun and despondent over what I had witnessed. I asked Zaqie how he kept going in the face of depressing specters like Aspai.

"We still have optimism," he said. "But right now we are running in place."

We headed back to Kumai at first light and caught a ride to the airport, where the police actually encouraged Kolya to do skateboard tricks on the sidewalk. This impressed him more than the orangutans because the police at home always seemed to hate skateboarders.

We flew back to Semarang, indulged at the airport's Dunkin' Donuts, and put up at the same hotel where our friend Sean had taken us on my birthday. Without a doubt, we were all relieved to be back in the relative splendor of Javan civilization. We boarded a plane for Jakarta and on to Singapore the next day.

Which was, incidentally, September 11.

PART 3

THE WORLD TRADE CENTER CLAPST

Kolya and Zoe in front of the former U.S. embassy
(now consulate) in Saigon, September 15, 2001.

September 11, 2001

On September 11 Tuesday someone highjackt four planes and went into the world trade center which is in New York City. The world trade center clapst and it is a huge deal espeshially since Bush is calling it like we might start another war.

I'm sooooooo scared.

The fear Zoe expressed in her journal entry hit all of us in different ways. But on the morning of September 11, Indonesia time, it was all still in the future. We wouldn't find out about the terrorist attack on the World Trade Center and the Pentagon until we woke up and turned on the news on September 12. On September 11, still intrepid world travelers without a care, we briefly split up with Tory in Semarang, since our improvisational travel plans dictated that we take different routes from Indonesia to Singapore. Tory found a cheap direct flight from Semarang, but Kolya, Zoe, and I hopped on a short flight to Jakarta in order to use the next leg of our 'round-the-world ticket from Jakarta to Singapore. If all went well, we would meet at Singapore Changi Airport in a few hours.

We watched Tory board first, and although this bifurcation would only last a few hours, it packed an emotional wallop. While in Borneo, Tory had decided not to continue on with us to Vietnam; instead, she would go home after a few days together in Singapore. Kolya and Zoe didn't like the news. Their initial rebellion in Bali had slowly turned into a love fest, and now they begged plaintively for Tory to *please* stay through Vietnam and Cambodia and maybe Nepal, too.

Various factors had conspired to convince Tory it was time to leave the three of us to our own devices. She and I were both pleased with the way our traveling quartet had gelled, and she felt especially touched by how much the kids had warmed to her presence. Between the two of us, however, we both recognized that I was still reluctant to plunge fully into a new relationship. I did want her to continue with us for a while longer, but I also understood that the prolonged uncertainty about where she fit into this roving Glick clan was crazy-making. Better to leave on a high note after our successful Borneo adventures and pick up again under less intense circumstances when we all reconvened in Colorado.

Our Singapore rendezvous went off without a hitch. We caught a plush, air-conditioned cab to a Chinese hotel at the intersection of Singapore's Indian, Chinese, and Arab neighborhoods, where we arrived as night fell on the 11th. Cranky from the heat and the sudden onslaught of Singapore's urban pace, we ate at an outdoor café and retired to our rooms. Because we were beat after our travel day from Java, and because there's a twelve-hour time difference between Singapore and New York, we must have gone to bed at about the same time American Airlines Flight 11 crashed into the north tower of World Trade Center.

The next morning, still unaware of what had happened, we rested in our respective rooms, feeling leaden and disconnected to find ourselves in a modern, bustling, expensive city. Tory prepared to spend the day on the phone with travel agents booking her flight home. We woke up early and used our precious private moments to talk about her decision to leave and our hopes for the future. All in all, we decided, it had been a rich and successful time. A cornerstone had been laid in place: for the two of us, for the four of us.

Meanwhile, Kolya and Zoe were in the next room, watching television:

I had planned to sleep in yesterday morning after a very full day of traveling. Unfortunately, a combination of Zoe walking around and the water from the ceiling air conditioner dripping on me woke me up early, at 9:17. The room was medium priced, but because we were in a more developed city, it was very comfortable. It was about the size of a large modern bathroom. The only furniture was the two beds, and a skinny office file holder which had a very small TV on it.

As soon as I showed signs of waking up, Zoe turned on the TV. The sight of a jet crashing into the Pentagon promptly snapped me out of my morning daze. I was immediately entranced by the morning CNN broadcast which was repeating the events over in a ten-minute cycle. I watched intently until the cycle was renewed.

I had been ignoring Zoe for the beginning part of the broadcast, but it was too much now. She was repeating "Kolyaaaaaa, this is boring, I wanna watch cartoons." When I was sure that she wasn't going to stop, I turned to her and said "Zoe, do you have any idea how important this is?" I think she got the idea a little bit by then. Next we saw the two towers get pelted by jetliner missiles, and a voice talking about the terrorist part of the issue.

As soon as I was sure that I had gotten all the news, I ran across the hall to Tory and Dads room. They were awake, but not moving, I woke them up fully. I think I must have been talking in a little bit of a jumble, because they didn't really get what was happening, and probably thought I had just been watching a disaster movie. I did manage to get them to come into our room to

see, though. Zoe hadn't changed the channel, so I think she was
starting to understand.

I was scared to death because I had no clue what was going
to happen.

Even the kids recognized that the world had changed. I put my
arms around both of them, wishing that they didn't have to see
those indelible images of planes crashing into the World Trade Center, the suicide jumpers, the flames shooting out from the buildings, the collapse of the structures as if they were sand castles hit by
a wave, the onlookers covering their mouths in disbelief and terror.
It was hard to know what to do. Go outside? Stay in our rooms? I
felt small, isolated, wanted somehow to connect to the outside
world, but also felt cocooned inside our travelers' orbit. I wanted the
kids to understand the import of what had happened, but I also felt
an urgent need to make them feel safe.

The shocking images of the twin towers collapsing seemed
incongruous, disembodied—perhaps more so for us than for most
Americans because we'd just emerged from a week in the Borneo
rainforest. The full import of the tragedy, frankly, took a little while
to sink in as we huddled in the kids' room gawking at the slow-
motion replays of footage taken by hand-held video cameras. But
when it did, the impact struck like earthquake aftershocks—random, frightful tremors strong enough to shake the entire world.
Indeed, we quickly realized that even here in Singapore, a bustling
first-world city where finance and trade are a national obsession
and world affairs are measured by how they will affect the markets,
the shock waves would reverberate with unfathomable impact as far
as the eye could see and the heart could feel.

I let Kolya and Zoe eat an early lunch at McDonald's, which, as I
think about it now, might not have been the brightest move. Comfort food for them, but also a potential bull's-eye of a target. At least
we were in Singapore, where an overbearing police presence constitutes an uncomfortable (or in this case comfortable) fact of life.

Before hearing the news, we had already decided to leave the Chinese hotel, which was cheap enough by Singapore standards but at U.S. $60 per night was more than we wanted to pay for our planned three nights in this multicultural city-state. Tory and I scoped out one of the city's low-budget haunts: a basic, mattress-in-a-small-poorly-lit-space, bathroom-down-the-hall travelers' flophouse called Waffle's, with the apostrophe. Even though we had to walk through the kitchen of a cheap eatery to climb the back stairs leading to the rooms, Waffle's was clean enough. It was nice to be around so many travelers, and the kids soon made themselves at home.

Before heading upstairs to our digs, I had picked up a copy of the *Straits Times,* which featured the horrifying image of a man plummeting headfirst from the smoking tower to his death. The stark headline read:

US Rocked by Terrorist Attacks

My years of being a news junkie with *Newsweek* caused me to get the shakes. I needed more news. I bought more papers, including the *International Herald Tribune,* and headed to Waffle's rooftop garden, where a number of travelers from around the globe were gathered around the hotel's lone television, fixated on CNN. Kolya sat next to me, Zoe on my lap, Tory on the other side as we sipped jasmine tea and tried to make sense of what had happened. As the gathered travelers realized we were an American family, one by one they offered condolences with hushed and deferential tones, like well-wishers paying respects at a child's funeral.

The next day, another *Straits Times* headline brought home the seriousness of our situation:

US Makes Plan to Evacuate Overseas Americans

The story made no mention of specific countries where Americans were in danger, and upon closer reading referred more to State

Department employees and oil company ex-pats than it did to dirt-bag travelers like us. But it was clear from the news that President Bush's call to battle and talk of retaliation against Al Qaeda had caused consternation across the Muslim world. Indonesia, the most populous Muslim nation, looked particularly volatile, and I was glad we hadn't bogged down in Jakarta.

It dawned on us after talking to other travelers, however, that we might be bogged down in Singapore. All flights to the United States had been canceled, and Tory couldn't book a flight home for nobody-knew-how-long. I called Vietnam Air and found out that our flight to Ho Chi Minh City (formerly Saigon) on the 14th, however, had not been canceled.

Maybe Tory would continue on with us to Vietnam, after all.

The kids retired into Game-Boy land in their air-conditioned, oversized closet while Tory and I remained fixated on the rooftop TV. From halfway around the world, the significance of what happened seeped in slowly, and I alternated between thinking about how it would affect us and wondering how it would affect my country and our world. I had friends and family in Manhattan; was everybody okay? I wanted to be home; I was glad I was so far away. I wanted to grab a reporter's notebook and go to work on the biggest story in the world; I was enormously relieved to avoid the wrenching job of interviewing victims' relatives.

I wondered if we should call the trip off. It wasn't so much that traveling suddenly seemed more dangerous. In fact, our next stops—Vietnam, Cambodia, and Thailand—were predominantly Buddhist countries posing no imminent threat. In certain aspects, it felt safer being in Asia than we might have felt at home (especially when the anthrax scares hit the news later). Abruptly, though, the trip seemed more frivolous—an act of self-indulgence in the face of so much grief. It struck me that what we needed to do was return home to mourn with our countrymen rather than continue wandering among strangers.

Ultimately, though, remaining part of the world community felt more important than returning early to the United States. Being

Americans abroad took on heightened meaning, and, as always, viewing my native land from across an ocean gave me a different perspective than I would have had at home.

Already, from this distance, we saw a growing rift between how President Bush saw the world and how the rest of the world saw America. The gaffes that displayed Bush's ignorance of the world (such as when, much later, Bush wondered how come Jimmy Carter spoke Cuban so well) were, in this context, hardly funny at all. By day two I was petrified that America was being guided through perilous international waters by a president who had spent less time overseas than my nine-year-old daughter.

Bush's anti-Taliban, anti–Al Qaeda rhetoric acquired distinctly anti-Muslim overtones when heard from a place like Singapore with a significant Muslim population. An editorial in the *Straits Times* warned against lumping all Muslims together even if the evidence against Osama bin Laden was as compelling as the United States claimed it was. Months before the Bush administration began to understand the connection between the Taliban, the Israeli-Palestinian conflict, and public opinion in the Arab world, the papers in Singapore pointed out the relevance.

On a personal level, we were stunned that so many strangers who hailed from countries with terrorism in their backyards offered condolences: an Irish man, an Israeli couple, a taxi driver originally from Kashmir—and later Vietnamese rickshaw drivers and Cambodian storekeepers. Maybe because they knew firsthand the impact of senseless violence, their expressions of sadness and sympathy were heartfelt.

I spent an hour in an Internet café responding to dozens of e-mails asking if we had heard the news, where we were, and if we were safe. Everybody was in shock.

We were in Singapore, I replied. We were safe. Young Singaporean men played intense-looking battle games at banks of computers nearby. The world continued apace.

*

The kids' needs brought me back to the here and now. Bored with their Game Boys, they wanted to shop at the outdoor market or see a movie or something. I felt I should be in mourning somehow, and yet I'd promised Zoe a drink at a fancy hotel called Raffles. We wandered over. We could have been characters in a Somerset Maugham novel, if only I'd been wearing a white linen suit and Zoe a floral print sun dress. Instead, I had on my beat-up travel khakis and she was wearing her stained halter top. Inappropriately attired though we were, I entered with Zoe elegantly on my arm and ordered two lemonades.

It didn't look like the FAA was going to be allowing flights any time soon, so Tory decided to join us in Vietnam. While she negotiated for a ticket home that would allow her to route through Ho Chi Minh City instead of Hong Kong, I splurged on tickets to see *Miss Saigon.*

In the evening, Tory and I escorted the kids to the (almost) Broadway-quality show, a fitting way to introduce the kids to Vietnam. Set in Saigon during the Vietnam War (which Kolya discovered is called the "American War" by the Vietnamese), the story line involves a U.S. soldier who falls in love with a Vietnamese woman as she's about to become a reluctant prostitute after being orphaned at the age of seventeen. During the fall of Saigon in 1975, he reluctantly leaves her behind—pregnant with his child. He flies home, marries, starts a new life. When he returns to Vietnam years later to work on behalf of *Bui-Doi,* American-Vietnamese children conceived during the war, he meets his Vietnamese lover, who has faithfully held a candle for him. He spurns her, she kills herself, and he and his American wife adopt the child.

Kolya disliked the show because it was a musical, and Zoe loved it for the same reason. But despite what Kolya perceived as operatic noise, he seemed to be intellectually stimulated by the historical setting of the show and began an intriguing conversation on the way home with his now-patented "So, Dad."

"So, Dad," he began, "what went wrong with the U.S. and Russia and why?" Before the show, I had tried to explain a little about why the United States had gotten involved militarily in Vietnam in the first place, the "domino theory" about the spread of communism, the origins of the Cold War after World War II. We spent most of the way home on the bus discussing the history of communism, Russian-American relations, and a brief history of Vietnam; the French, the early American involvement, the war.

Something had been unleashed in him and he started extending his questions to the bombing, the Muslim world, Osama bin Laden. Why do they hate America so much, he wondered—the same question everybody was asking. Although he seemed detached much of the time, I realized he doesn't miss much.

He was worried, I could tell. I was, too.

The next morning, with the *Miss Saigon* tune *The Last Night of the World* still running through our heads (well, Zoe's and mine at least), we left Singapore. I watched the kids board the plane, these now well-seasoned travelers with their dirty daypacks and battered earphones, handing over their boarding passes to the gatekeepers as if they were getting on a school bus rather than boarding a plane from Singapore to Ho Chi Minh City. The four of us inched down the gangway in a crowd, and I realized we were the only Caucasians on the flight. The kids didn't seem to notice, and Kolya helped an elderly Vietnamese woman whose rolling suitcase caught on a protruding piece of metal.

I could see them deepening their understanding of the world, even as the world became less comprehensible all the time.

PART 4

SHADOWS

*Having a roadside drink in Tan Phu, Vietnam,
near Nam Cat Tien National Park.*

HO, HO, HO CHI MINH

EVEN THOUGH I had been four years too young to have fretted the draft and fought in Vietnam, no other foreign country held more claim to my imagination. When I was eleven in 1967, my dad had taken Bob and me from our home near Los Angeles to a peace march in San Francisco. I accidentally separated from them outside Kezar Stadium, gaping at the hippies while Dad and Bob marched on by. I'm certainly not the only American whose first experience with Vietnam involved getting lost.

Vietnam, probably more than any other country, felt like a place I had visited many times before I set foot in the country. I'd seen most of Hollywood's biggest war efforts: *Apocalypse Now, The Deer Hunter, Good Morning Vietnam, Born on the Fourth of July, Full Metal Jacket, Coming Home, Platoon.* I'd read Neal Sheehan and Tim O'Brien and Michael Herr. I had friends who had served in Nam, others who had for one reason or another linked themselves to Southeast Asia. Tory had traveled to Vietnam once before, but this was my first trip.

Arriving into downtown Saigon, as most people seem to call Ho Chi Minh City, Kolya and Zoe pressed their noses against the taxi window, mouths actually dropped, amazed at the sheer number of bicycles and motorcycles clogging the oversized roundabouts and undersized streets. Our taxi dropped us off in District 1, headwaters of Saigon's tourist havens, and we settled into two comfortable hotel rooms that, especially after Singapore, were both classy and inexpensive.

My stated reason for coming here was to visit a new national park near the Lao and Cambodian borders, where wildlife biologists had recently documented a remnant population of Javan rhinoceroses long thought to be extinct. International conservation groups and the Vietnamese government had been plotting strategies to preserve these vanishing rhinos' habitat and increase their numbers. I had very little reason to believe that we would actually be able to see rhinos here, but I knew that if we did we'd likely be witnessing the last shadow of a species as it was actually going extinct. This was a sad thought, and I kept it to myself.

At home in Colorado, our favorite restaurant was Vietnamese, and the kids couldn't wait to eat Vietnamese food in Vietnam. Eating is, in fact, their stated reason for being interested in Vietnam. Unfortunately, our first dinner didn't live up to the kids' expectations, but we were happy enough after the tension and uncertainty of our travel day subsided. Kolya wanted to check his e-mail at one of the ubiquitous (but, as we found out, glacially slow) Internet cafés in the neighborhood while Zoe and Tory returned to the hotel.

After Kolya and I spent half an hour trying unsuccessfully to tap into our Hotmail accounts, we gave up and strolled around. Pimps propositioned us with offers of rickshaw rides to "beyoutiful girls," and Kolya wanted to know if he had really heard what it was that he thought he had heard through the clipped accents of Vietnamese pidgin English. I nodded sagely. He smiled sheepishly.

Kolya asked about what Uncle Bob did during the Vietnam War, whether he had served or went to Canada or what. I told him that Bob had a high draft number the year the Vietnam War was winding down. By the early 1970s, it was pretty clear to Bob that the war was a muddled failure, and he probably would have found a way out.

I squeezed Kolya's hand, and in the darkened streets of Saigon we marked our loss again, with memory and story and tears. Whenever the time was right, when I let myself remember and cry, then Kolya could let himself remember and cry.

Back at the hotel, I tucked the kids in and crawled into bed with Tory, touching Bob memories at the tip of my consciousness. Kolya's question had triggered something, and I tried again to wrap my mind around the fact that he was really dead. Tears welled involuntarily down my cheeks and onto my pillow. Then I felt a wave of guilt that I hadn't been thinking about Bob more, hadn't worked to keep my brother alive in my mind every minute. The waves of grief, which came with torrential force and unabated frequency at first, had diminished in power and regularity.

When the waves unexpectedly hit, though, the grief remained ferocious. It was at times like these, insomniac hours in a foreign land, that recollections raced through, frightening and cathartic in their power. Tim O'Brien, in *The Things They Carried* (1990), put it this way:

> But the thing about remembering is that you don't forget. You take your material where you find it, which is in your life, at the intersection of past and present. The memory-traffic feeds into a rotary up in your head, where it goes in circles for a while, then pretty soon imagination flows in and the traffic merges and shoots off down a thousand different streets. As a writer, all you can do is pick a street and go for the ride, putting things down as they come at you. That's the real obsession. All those stories ...
>
> Stories are for eternity, when memory is erased, when there is nothing to remember except the story.

I was suddenly crying again, trying not to wake Tory with muffled sobs of memory feeding into a rotary in my head.

Bob, sporting a black San Francisco Giants cap hiding his hairless skull, shoots me a self-conscious grin when I appear, groggy, and see him busy with the TV. It is not quite seven A.M., but he is already preparing to spend the day engulfed in his enormous brown leather couch, watching sports with me, in a sacred fraternal communion. He checks the on-screen TV guide for the seemingly nonstop listing of Saturday's sports events, brandishing the remote with the enthusiasm of Barry Bonds wagging his bat at a rookie pitcher. "How did anybody ever survive chemo before ESPN?" he asks, without a hint of sarcasm.

It is two days after Bob's second round of chemo, and I've flown to California from my home in Colorado to spell Bob's wife Renda from care-taking duties. Truthfully, I wanted to be alone with him as much as I wanted to give her a break. In the thirty years since we had shared a room during his senior year and my sophomore year in high school, we had never passed a single day together without our wives, our kids, our parents, or our younger brother—much less the three days we now had planned. Why we waited until he was recuperating from breast cancer was one of the first questions we asked each other.

This October weekend is, as it turns out, a perfect time to be incapacitated by Cytoxan and Adriamycin, if such a thing is possible. It is 1999, well into the golden age of cable, with ESPN 1 and 2, Fox Sports, Outdoor Life Network, bowling channels, golf channels, adrenaline channels. The sports gods have colluded to provide us with a confluence of the World Series between the Yankees and Braves, the middle of an engaging pro-football season, bowl-deciding college football games, the beginning of the hockey season, and various lesser sports events that nonetheless fill those awkward hours between kick-offs and face-offs and lead-off batters. Bob has arranged the living room so we can recline a perfect distance from the television set, which is the size and fidelity that any self-respecting sports nut would have if he could afford it—and his wife would let him. He is a doctor and Renda is an exceedingly understanding spouse, which covers both bases.

I watch him fiddle with the TV. He has stayed fit and slim deep into his forties, but today he just looks skinny. Without his hair, his mane, his bushy brown locks that he wore meticulously groomed every day, he appears listless. Delilah must have been an oncologist. His face is thin, just shy of gaunt, and his eyes make him look like he's had the flu for a week.

Bob's intravenous drug cocktail has succeeded in taking him down the way no blitzing linebacker or ruptured Achilles ever could. At six foot, 180 lbs. at his prime, he was a good enough pitcher for the Padres to consider drafting after eleventh grade, and he had a strong enough quarterbacking arm to be recruited by pretty much every Pac–8 and Big–10 school before accepting a football scholarship to Stanford.

"What's it like?" I ask.

"I just feel shitty. I feel like I got the crap kicked out of me. I can't keep food down, besides I have no appetite. The only thing that helps the nausea a little is getting high." *He shows me his medical marijuana stash, given to him by various friends. He thinks it's funny that he suddenly has so much pot. Bob was never quite the stoner I was as a teenager, and smoking dope hasn't been a big part of his adult life. Nor has it been much a part of mine lately. But before the games begin, he asks if I want to get high with him.*

"Nah," I say. "I want to take care of you and don't want to begin rummaging in your pantry for brownie mix and eating it raw. You go ahead."

"I won't do it unless you do," he says.

"I didn't just have chemo, asshole," I retort.

He makes like he's going to heave.

"All right. I'll have a hit."

We light up like two old men with corncob pipes about to discuss the crops and the weather. We tilt the deck chairs back, sit outside on a warm Indian summer day in rural northern California, imbibing the morning sunrays as if they were a healing tonic.

"You know, you can take that hat off. The sun will feel good," *I tell him. He doesn't want to be seen bald, even by me, even now.* "Besides, everybody's shaving their head these days, even the white guys. It's a look. Nobody would even know you had chemo, since you still have your eyebrows. Look at Jason Kidd."

He doffs his hat, lies back in his lounge chair, feels the sun on his pate, and sighs. "This feels soooo good," he says, and I am glad he feels comfortable enough to be hatless for a few precious, unselfconscious moments. We each drink a glass of ice water and soak up the sun.

As the World Series is about to begin, we head to the porch for another hit, plop down on the couch sweaty and newly buzzed. Around the fourth inning, he's ready for food. I make us Dagwood sandwiches, asking him about customized meat and cheese and vegetable combinations. He chews slowly, the cannabis neutralizing the nausea for these brief moments.

The baseball game moves slowly, and he maneuvers the remote to track several games simultaneously the way an air traffic controller tracks approaching planes: The Nebraska game is close, they're in the running for the national championship although they're losing to Texas; the Yankees, the goddamn Yankees, are on their way to sweeping Atlanta, somehow decoding the Braves' awesome pitching staff. We talk, off and on, between innings and periods and plays.

I ask him if he ever regrets not having seen if he could play pro. He was selected first-team all-city high-school quarterback in Los Angeles, went on to start as quarterback and punter on Stanford's freshman team the year after Jim Plunkett led the varsity to a Rose Bowl win in 1970. Unfortunately, he had four concussions that year and hung up the cleats for pre-med.

"You coulda been a contenda," I tell him. "You were good."

"Nah," he says. "I would have been one of those guys who was always injured," he says, something I've never heard him admit. "I never would have played a full season."

"Speaking of injuries, how's the scar?"

He lifts his sleeveless T-shirt up and shows me his nipple-less right breast, which doesn't look grotesque as much as it looks weird. It's healing, the surgeon really did do a bang-up job, but Bob is lopsided, with one sad, deflated pec. He was always so proud of his body, I can't imagine what it's like and can't quite ask. He pulls his shirt down, turns his attention to the television with a resigned shrug.

We drift from watching the games to talking about our family, remi-niscing about him getting kicked out of the house when he was seventeen, my memory of his first shitty apartment where he had a porn book called The Young Librarian, *funny what you recall. How did we become how we are, so different? We are like alter egos. A doctor and a journalist. A convoluted combination of Oscar and Felix. I remind him how I used to make his bed so Mom wouldn't get mad at him.*

He says that it's taken a long time to realize it, but if he had been a kid today, he'd definitely be diagnosed as ADD, attention deficit disorder. It wasn't that he was trying to piss Mom off, he just couldn't remember what it was that he was supposed to do from one end of the hallway to the next.

A Nebraska receiver makes a diving catch in traffic, gets pummeled by the safety.

"Did you see that throw?" *he screams, and I did.*

"Unbelievable," *I chime.*

"That guy's gonna win the Heisman, you watch. But he'll never be a QB in the pros. They're gonna make him into a safety."

"Hunh?"

I've never heard of the Nebraska quarterback he is talking about, Eric Crouch. But Bob goes on. "You know, like John Lynch. Stanford. Quar-terback. Plays safety for Tampa Bay."

"You are fucking unbelievable. Don't you worry that all this useless information might block the medicine from working?"

"Yeah, you try going through chemo. I've watched so much sports lately I know more than Bob Costas."

The afternoon moseys along, punctuated by an occasional pick-me-up to ward off the nausea waves. He insists that I join him at every turn. I have not been this sustainedly stoned since I was seventeen, maybe not even then. I am sure he has never gotten high all day long like this.

We talk, jumping back and forth across years and spanning decades of memories. By now the important ones are honed down to what writer David James Duncan calls "river teeth." River teeth, as I understand what Duncan means, are the essence of experiences, shaped by time and as smooth as a submerged knot from a fallen 200-year-old Douglas fir after white water has burnished it for decades, rendering it as strong as marble.

The late afternoon doldrums hit us and the shadows lengthen. By now, SportsCenter is unwatchable. We've already seen the pregame shows and the games themselves and the postgame interviews and the highlight clips. We stoop to watching the history of wrestling on ESPN Classics, and even Bob is disgusted. Thankfully, the next day, Sunday, is always a good viewing day during NFL season, and we have Monday Night Football to look forward to.

Something to look forward to.

Three asides and a story:

Aside #1: While I was writing this book, Tory gingerly probed me about my relationship with Bob. It seemed to her that we didn't really see each other much as adults, and she was tactfully trying to understand what he represented to me, considering we had so little direct contact. I tried to explain as best I could about our being alter egos, about his being such a solid presence for me even though we didn't live in the same state. When I told her the story that follows aside number three, I think she understood.

Aside #2: Eric Crouch, the Nebraska quarterback, won the Heisman trophy the following year, in 2001. He was drafted by the NFL's St. Louis Rams, and was turned into a wide receiver rather than a safety. Bob was not infallible.

Aside #3: Journalists often use the shorthand "TK" while they are writing an initial draft of a story to indicate a fact they need to fill in later. TK stands for "to come," (don't ask) and also can be easily found with the search function on a computer because there are no words I'm aware of in the English language (the surname "Plotkin" and the Atkins diet notwithstanding) that have the letter "T" followed by a "K". Usage: During the Vietnam War, TK,000 American soldiers and TK,000 Vietnamese lost their lives. (The answer is 58,000 Americans and at least 1.3 million Vietnamese.)

True Story: When I was writing this Vietnam chapter, I jotted down, "Bob had a lucky lottery number and wasn't drafted. His lottery number was . . ." Where I normally would have written TK and then called my parents to ask if they remembered, I wrote down the number 328. And kept writing. My parents, it turns out, didn't remember either. Later, I went on the Selective Service's Web site and looked up the lottery numbers for men born in 1953. That lottery drawing took place on February 2, 1972, my eleventh-grade year, the last draft lottery for the Vietnam War.

Bob's number was 328.

I awoke to the traveler's daily disorientation, sorted dream from reality, last week's bed from last night's bed, and ascertained that I was in the Hanh Hoa Hotel in Ho Chi Minh City feeling incredibly well rested. We descended to a hilarious breakfast served by a fawning and effusive security guard/waiter/concierge/motorcycle parker and electrical repairman, who immediately switched on CNN for us to watch the engrossing and ominous post–9/11 news. In a matter of minutes, the power went out.

We ate fresh-baked mini-baguettes, a salutary remnant of French colonialism, and I savored the best coffee I'd had since leaving the yuppie coffee shops of Boulder. Our new friend scurried to fire up the generator, and just about the time he'd started it, the electricity returned. More news clips flashed by about the aftermath of September 11, and he watched with us and responded, "So terrible, so terrible. Bin Laden bad man." We nodded in agreement.

Tory and I proposed a little cultural sightseeing: the War Museum, maybe, marketplaces, a pilgrimage to the U.S. embassy. The museum idea received a resounding no, so we settled on two out of three. En route to the embassy, we stopped at an indoor market with dozens of clothing merchants, and Zoe purchased another ensemble to add to her international fashion collection. This time it was a traditional Vietnamese *ao dai,* a long silk dress in pastel blue with front and back panels worn over white satin pants, which she bargained for herself in a riotous competitive exchange with two different vendors. She started with one vendor, who couldn't have been more than two or three years older than Zoe, and perused different colors and styles. Then another vendor beckoned, and Zoe went over, looking for a particular combination of buttons and hues. The second vendor took off running to track down what Zoe requested. The first vendor called out, "Good price, good price!" and Zoe went back to hear her offer. I stood back and watched Zoe conduct her fashion business, and when she settled on an outfit she beckoned for me to pay as if she were a princess and I her personal assistant.

We continued on to the embassy as I prattled on about the fall of Saigon, reminding them of the scene from the other night in *Miss Saigon*, the elaborate stage helicopter lifting the last U.S. soldiers from Vietnam on April 29, 1975. We arrived, only to learn that the actual embassy had been torn down, and besides, the embassy had moved to the capital of unified Vietnam, Hanoi. Nearby, however, was the U.S. consulate, where we gazed at the flag flying at half-mast and read a sobering notice warning U.S. citizens to be especially careful and to keep a low profile.

After lunch, I made contact with World Wide Fund for Nature employees working on the rhino issue and arranged to meet the regional director a few days hence at Nam Cat Tien National Park. We decided to visit Dalat in the meantime, a mountain town beautifully situated on a lake, not too far from our ultimate destination.

I bought bus tickets from Kim's travel agency, a classic world traveler business catering impeccably to people like us. The employees were helpful, but I noted with dismay their habit of listing all the trips they offered on a large whiteboard along with the nationalities of the clients who would be on each trip. It occurred to me that, in this post–9/11 world, it would be better not to advertise that a busload of Americans was heading someplace. The warnings at the U.S. consulate drove that home.

I discreetly asked the person behind the counter to please put down a different nationality for us on the whiteboard. She understood immediately and complied with apologies. We were now from the UK.

Dalat is beautiful and surprising, a town that Vietnamese newlyweds choose for their honeymoons. Built around Xuan Huong lake, the tourist town consists of an incongruous mix of faux Paris (with a miniature replica of the Eiffel Tower), kitschy "city of love" attractions such as swan-shaped paddleboats, and a central core of bustling farmers' markets that draws people from dozens of ethnic groups from the surrounding hills. It dawned on me that these were the same ethnic groups collectively known as the *Montagnards* by the French (the word means "mountain people"). They were known as fierce and resourceful fighters who joined with the American forces to fight against the North during the Vietnam War.

Tory and I wanted to take a long, exploratory walk along the lakeshore, but Zoe refused. Kolya, surprisingly, joined us, and we left Zoe happily watching TV in the room. She would be in the comforting hands of the French- and English-speaking hotelier and his wife, who served her room-service lunch as if she were royalty.

It began raining, hard, when we were halfway around our circumnavigation of the huge lake, and we knew we faced a long, soggy return. Kolya chided us about this "pointless walk," but I noticed him engaging more with Tory during our deluge discussion. He actually asked her to tell him more about the work she had done as a National Park Service ranger. He was rapt as she explained how she had trained to use her service revolver by learning to shoot while running through a kind of obstacle course, and he listened intently as she told stories about riding horses all night long to rescue injured people in the backcountry. I'd been cautiously watching my own love for her grow, and I admired how open she was to the kids.

We sloshed past swan-shaped paddleboats and arrived, soaked, back at the hotel. Zoe greeted us, propped up on pillows, with baguette crumbs surrounding her like a moat and empty La Vache Qui Rit cheese wrappers strewn on the bedside table.

We left Dalat by bus, heading south along the same road we had arrived on. We told the driver to drop us off at a town called Tan Phu, about three hours away, where we could catch motorcycle taxis up to the park.

As soon as we disembarked, two dozen young men astride well-worn motorcycles surrounded us, all vying to take us 24 kilometers up a tiny road to the river that served as the border to Nam Cat Tien National Park. As our comfortable, air-conditioned bus pulled away and the heat grabbed at us, the kids squirmed in discomfort. The men shouted and gestured for us to mount their steeds, and I realized that the kids hadn't yet been the center of an Asian mob scene like this.

Tory and I scoped out a roadside café near the bus stop, and I told the kids we'd just calmly saunter over and have a soft drink while we sorted things out. The men followed us like a cloud of dust but backed off while we sipped sodas. Only one man spoke even a few words of English, and I found Vietnamese so damnably difficult that after nearly a week in the country I could still barely say hello and thank you. We negotiated a price for the four of us, and after intense jockeying and bargaining, we settled on four drivers.

Then, frenzy. One young man grabbed Zoe's pack and gestured for her to hop on the back. The scene repeated with Tory, and in a flash the two of them were gone. Kolya looked completely overwhelmed and frightened when two men grabbed his pack as if they would tear it in two. I gestured for him to mount one motorcycle as I hopped on another, wearing my pack. My driver accelerated, and I glanced back at Kolya, who looked bewildered, still the object of a tug-of-war. I tapped on my driver's back but he wouldn't stop. I found out later that the driver I authorized to receive Kolya's fare almost started a fight with another motorcycle driver, who threatened Kolya's would-be chauffeur with a Sprite bottle.

Meanwhile, I whizzed up the road with my driver and didn't know where Zoe or Tory or Kolya were, praying that somehow we would all rendezvous at the same spot. My driver stopped to buy gas, and Zoe, inexplicably, arrived from behind on an ailing motorcycle that was limping along at three miles per hour. Another motorcycle immediately appeared to whisk Zoe up the road.

I motioned to my driver that I wanted to wait until Kolya showed up, which he did, wide-eyed, a few minutes later. He recounted the altercation involving the Sprite bottle with residual fear, accusing me of abandoning him to that frightening scene. I protested that I didn't exactly have control over the situation, but it was a lame excuse. With a few calm breaths and my arm on his shoulders, our heart rates slowed and we started off again, weaving our way through the foot, bicycle, and other motorcycle traffic, trying to beat the afternoon rains. A motorcycle loaded with an enormous live pig in a crate loaded sideways on the back passed in the other direction, leaking urine, and we gaped.

The kids had never ridden on a motorcycle, and I fought off the realistic appraisal that this whole scene, while adventurous, wasn't terrifically safe. The kids' drivers had thrown the backpacks over their gas tanks, rendering the steering about 20 percent effective, and although I wore mine, it felt like the weight could pull me off the back if we hit a rut. And helmets?

I relaxed into the ride, feeling the warm breeze and gesturing for my driver to stay just a little behind Zoe, who grinned wildly as wind flowed through her hair. I involuntarily started to laugh, screamed to Zoe that her Aunt Mel, who is a worrier, would never approve. Zoe laughed uproariously. I shot video footage of Zoe waving her arms like a dancer caressing the jungle air.

Our troupe successfully regrouped at the ranger station on the east side of the river adjacent to Nam Cat Tien National Park. The park is home to a vanishing one-and-a-half-ton beast that once roamed the jungles ranging from northern India through Indochina, south along the Malaysian Peninsula, and across the islands of Sumatra and Java. Victims of poaching, land clearing, human poverty, and almost every conservation challenge facing large mammals, the remaining Javan rhinos now cling to existence in two small enclaves. The more numerous of the two subspecies—*Rhinoceros sondaicus sondaicus*—resides on the western edge of the island of Java in Indonesia in Ujung Kulon National Park. Although they're notoriously difficult to count, it's likely that about fifty individuals still roam that refuge.

On the Southeast Asian mainland, Nam Cat Tien National Park holds the last hope for the related but distinct subspecies *Rhinoceros sondaicus annamiticus*. Their population may have dwindled to the number in our traveling party of four—earning them the dubious distinction of being the most endangered large mammals in Asia, if not the world.

JOHNNY WALKER CONSERVATION

WE FILLED out forms at the ranger station and left our passports as collateral for an undisclosed reason. We gleaned from the kindly ranger, who spoke little English beyond the word "passport," that we could find a ferry to take us across the river by waiting near the water's edge. So we sauntered down to the Dong Nai River, a tributary of the Mekong, which serves as Nam Cat Tien National Park's border, and saw nobody. Waiting in Asia is an art, and even the kids were acquiring the necessary attitude as we set our packs down on the bank and recounted our motorcycle taxi stories in ever more animated detail.

Soon enough, we heard the chug of an outboard from across the river and a boatman arrived. Without a word, he beckoned us aboard the 14-foot metal boat and angled the craft against the current, ferrying across in silence. We expressed our gratitude with our closest approximation of "thank you" *(cám ón)*, which despite our best efforts ("it sounds like 'come on,'" Kolya reminded us), came out as a tone-deaf note of unintelligible sound. The boatman dropped us on the far bank, nodded in response to our thanks, and headed wordlessly across the river.

Cristina Lebre, a Portuguese volunteer through VSO, an international charity that does development work, greeted us from the riverbank. Cristina had been working at the park for more than a year and was its official liaison for tourists, who visited fairly infrequently. Park headquarters resembled a compound of army barracks, which it once was during the war, and Cristina showed us to our rooms.

They were serviceable, with mosquito netting hanging from four-poster beds, several fans (until the power went out, as it did every day during our stay), and Western toilets, to Kolya's everlasting delight. I followed Cristina to the main building to pick up literature and information about the park, which is home to 55 mammal species, more than 300 bird species, and 40 kinds of reptiles, amphibians, and freshwater fishes. It hosts Indochinese tigers, reticulated pythons, wild boar, and sambar deer—as well as a few remaining Javan rhinos.

During the Vietnam War, the United States sprayed Agent Orange on the forests around Cat Tien, which was a stronghold of Viet Cong guerrilla activity as well as a biodiversity hot spot. The forests were deeply wounded, and the rhino was thought to have gone extinct well before the end of the war. In 1988, a local hunter was caught selling a rhino horn and skin from a female he had shot near the Dong Nai River. The find revived interest in searching for other Javan rhinos, and also in the possibility of discovering other forgotten animals in the remote Annamite mountain range.

I retrieved Tory and the kids, who were playing Game Boys under the mosquito netting, and Cristina showed us to the open-air cantina, which serviced the staff of Vietnamese park workers, a few foreign conservationists, and the occasional tourist. We perched under a shaded area overlooking the river as the sun slanted steeply, sipping lukewarm sodas and waiting for our food. A macaque descended from the roof and poked his head out of the awning. It hung nonchalantly on a wooden post ten feet away, appraising our table for gastronomical possibilities. After Bali and Borneo, we were all monkey connoisseurs, and we stared back warily, awaiting his antics.

The food appeared, including our favorite mini-baguettes, and the monkey slyly made his anticipated move to the table. Out of nowhere, a man from another table glided toward the monkey and shooed him away with the menace that I would reserve for a rabid dog. The monkey scampered away, and the man admonished it for our benefit: "Bad monkey. No take food."

We dug in to our noodle plates, and the monkey reappeared like a bounce-up inflated clown. This time Tory imitated a lion tamer, taking her chair and poking it toward the monkey, who didn't take her seriously until Tory almost poked him in the head with the chair legs. The monkey left us alone until we finished. Tory and Kolya sauntered up to the counter to pay, with Kolya clutching a piece of bread he wanted to save for later.

He set the bread down on the counter and looked away for what he swore was a second. The bread disappeared. Across the veranda, the monkey hung from the same post with the baguette in his mouth, gloating. Kolya was seething with a smile.

Darkness swiftly substituted for slanting sunlight. We followed our flashlights to the barrack's mosquito netting, then listened to the otherworldly squawk of geckos in the jungle night as we drifted off. We all slept pretty poorly, with both Tory and me suffering from pretty awful colds thanks to our rain-soaked Dalat walk. As the night wore on, the kids increasingly freaked out at the tropical menaces of mozzies, belligerent monkeys, monster beetles we had seen crawling around the bathroom, intermittent power failures, and the general oppressiveness of the jungle heat. Zoe entered our room in the middle of the night, petrified of the prospect of leeches and scorpions and ominous gecko sounds. I realized the irony—that by showing Zoe the diversity of the natural world, I had inadvertently contributed to making her increasingly fearful of it.

I wondered if Nature's less benevolent sides—poisonous plants and predatory animals, killer earthquakes and destructive hurricanes—forced humans to insulate themselves and, ultimately, to alienate themselves, from their fundamental connections to earth's other creatures.

I hid under the mosquito netting.

Those who labor on the biodiversity front lines rely on another side of human nature—the side that loves adorable critters. To save species, conservation fund-raising campaigns tend to focus on the planet's most visible animal celebrities. Let's face it, humans react more favorably to koalas than they do to slime mold, and Chinese pandas are infinitely more attractive to raise money for than a disappearing coastal wildflower in Ecuador.

As an obvious result of this human bias, international conservation organizations target charismatic megafauna, as large species are wryly known in the environmental world, to be poster children for international conservation. In truth, it was easier to convince Kolya and Zoe to visit places with tigers, orangutans, and rhinos than it would have been to drag them halfway across the world to witness the wonders of the certifiably endangered Furneaux burrowing crayfish, the Kroombit tinker frog, and the pink-tailed worm-lizard of Australia; the Matinan flycatcher, the elegant sunbird, the Javan thick-thumbed bat, and the Bawean hog deer of Indonesia; or even the Collared Laughingthrush, the yellow-headed temple turtle, and the golden dragon fish here in Vietnam. I plead guilty to a certain large mammalian bias myself.

Cynics may complain about fund-raising packets containing cute animal postcards, cute animal calendars, cute stuffed animals, and cute key chains bearing the likeness of an endangered species, but conservation biologists know it's a ruse. A Sumatran tiger is no more intrinsically ecologically worthy than a banana slug, and a leaf cutter ant may arguably be more important to the health of an ecosystem than a zebra or a mountain gorilla.

Despite this ecological egalitarianism, focusing on key species of large, cuddly (or not so cuddly) mammals also makes scientific sense. Big animals require big habitat, and as a particular habitat goes, so goes the rest of the plant and animal kingdoms that reside there. As E. O. Wilson wrote in his book *The Diversity of Life* (1993), "When star species like rhinoceros and eagles are protected, they serve as umbrellas for all the life around them."

That umbrella may be broad, but it's also fragile. The downside of saving large mammals is that their needs so often collide with human needs. Those swaths of undisturbed rainforest, uncultivated lowland forest, pristine alpine valleys, and undrained swamps that animals need to roam are the same swaths where people like to build houses, clear land for crops, mine for minerals, cut timber, and raise their families. Often, as in the case of large predators, an animal pushed to the brink of extinction has proven itself a menace, or perceived menace, to human settlement. Disappearing animals are valued for other purposes—as meat, as medicine, as trophies, as pets.

When these animals decline in numbers, biology often conspires to make conservation and repopulation difficult. Recall the orangutans, who are unusually solitary, mate late in life, only give birth at long intervals, must raise their young for years before they are independent, and have specific habitat needs that are not easily replaced when their homes become palm plantations.

Such is the story of the rhinoceros, an animal of mythic fame that has snorted and trampled the earth for more than 50 million years, since the Eocene era. (*Rhino* means "nose" in Greek, and *ceros* means "horn.") Either the second- or third-largest land animal (after the African elephant and, arguably, the hippopotamus), rhinos once roamed across huge swaths of Africa and Asia in relative abundance. Dozens of different rhino species historically inhabited an area ranging from Bhutan to South Africa, from Bengal to Sumatra, including the largest land animal ever known, the 20-ton hornless *Baluchitherium*, which thundered on the earth throughout the early Miocene era.

Only five species remain today: the African black rhino, which survives largely in South Africa, Namibia, and Kenya; the Sumatran rhino of Indonesia; the white rhino of southern and central Africa; the Indian/Nepalese rhino; and the Javan rhino. All save the white rhino are in serious trouble. The subspecies of Javan rhino found in Vietnam is on the most precarious population tightrope of all.

All of the sadly standard reasons apply: habitat loss, illegal hunting (although rhino meat is bitter and eaten in very few cultures), the animal's own leisurely reproductive biology. But what makes the rhino's story even more compelling is the additional onus of being coveted for its horn, which is believed to have extraordinary healing properties and is utilized in Chinese folk medicine as a male sexual fortifier. Rhino horn is also prized in Yemen to make traditional knife handles.

So it comes down to this: A beast that has survived on this planet since well before humans were still trying to figure out how to light a fire may be lost because of male erectile dysfunction and ornamental daggers.

At Nam Cat Tien, international conservation meets realpolitik. The contradictory pressures of Vietnamese political, social, and economic forces converge here, and Nam Cat Tien proved to be a maddeningly ideal case study of the difficulties of keeping the species umbrella from collapsing.

The park consists of two sections separated by unprotected land that is being populated by refugees from the poorer northern part of Vietnam. In 1992, the government declared more than 30,000 hectares as the Cat Loc Rhino Sanctuary, and in 1998 the southern region, where we were, assumed park status along with the existing sanctuary. The fact that the two park sections are not contiguous poses a monumental obstacle, one of many, for the rhinos and the people who would protect them.

Eric Coull, the World Wide Fund for Nature's regional director based in Hanoi, arrived that afternoon for a quarterly meeting with park personnel, including the director, and WWF employees. Coull, a portly and graying man from Scotland, had come to take the pulse of the WWF's wide-ranging conservation program in the Nam Cat Tien region.

The project, funded by the Dutch government through WWF and the Vietnamese government, is ambitious and difficult. Their goal is to take the two noncontiguous hunks of land that constitute the park and produce a management plan that will, among other things, relocate villages and people who have been in the region for centuries and direct new economic immigrants from the North into less ecologically significant locales.

International conservation work is one part biology, three parts sociology, and ten parts diplomacy. That night, about a dozen park staff, including director Tran Van Mui, feted Coull at an elaborate banquet at the outdoor cantina. Aromatic plates of food appeared in a long stream that made us wish we knew how to order in Vietnamese. Our traveling quartet ate noodles at a nearby table, observing the cross-cultural rituals involved in this brand of international conservation.

Coull had arrived bearing six bottles of Johnny Walker Black Label to act as a lubricant among Vietnamese, Scotch, Dutch, New Zealand, and Portuguese team members. Before the first course appeared, various members at the table stood up and offered toasts: to Eric, to the director, to their cooperative efforts. Each toast was tossed down, "100 percent," and it slowly became apparent that the main "importance" of this meeting was cementing relationships with multicultural inebriation.

Drinking, especially when men are among men, constitutes an inviolate piece of the Asian social compact. Here, despite signs of protestation from the westerners, alcohol served as an intriguing and perhaps undervalued tool for preserving endangered species.

The evening soon devolved as "100 percent" toasts continued and the volume and length of the speeches intensified. Two of the westerners, Kit Howden from New Zealand and Gert Polet from Holland, refrained from draining their glasses with each toast and engaged in a spirited debate with their Vietnamese colleagues about the relative merits of sipping versus chugging Mr. Walker. Kolya, Zoe, Tory, and I sat at the next table, the kids making observations about which men seemed to be getting the drunkest.

Kit, a particularly thoughtful man with a career behind him in the New Zealand park service, was the last man standing. Park Director Tran Van Mui and his lieutenant dragged Eric Coull off to bed, and even the reluctant Gert seemed pretty well lit. Ina, his wife, described with despair how difficult it was to abstain in this culture, since many Vietnamese, including the park officials, were wound so tight from political pressures that alcohol served not just as a social lubricant but as a complete psychic lube job.

Kit told me the next day that I had observed a classic case of two cultures colliding. As long as the Vietnamese drank much less potent rice wine, three-finger chugging toasts were more manageable. But when the same drinking habits applied to 86 proof Western whiskey, the effects were demonstrably more brutal for all concerned.

Coull was sanguine about his performance and let me know the drinking bout was all in a day's work for him, just part of doing conservation work in Southeast Asia. I can't imagine having that level of hangover in the tropical sun the next day. Even if it meant I could save the rhinoceros.

Late the next afternoon, we sat down with the park's leading rhino biologist, Bui Huu Mahn, one of the 100 percenters of the previous night, who seemed to have recovered admirably. He was slight, probably in his mid-thirties, and wore 1960s-style black horned-rimmed glasses as he booted up his computer to show me Geographic Information Survey (GIS) maps of the park and environs. Zoe and Kolya watched the ancient computer blip slowly as the images appeared, and Tory and I peppered Mahn with questions.

Until the poacher had been caught in 1988, Mahn told us, most people believed that the Vietnamese subspecies of Javan rhino had long been extirpated. After that chance discovery, biologists began searching for other rhinos. For years, Mahn and others conducted surveys and saw rhino signs—footprints and scat—but no rhinos. In 1999, a WWF photographer contracted to set up infrared trip wires that activated camera shutters at various points in the jungle. It was a thirty-day contract. On day twenty-nine, there was nothing.

When the photographer retrieved his gear and developed the last film, something extraordinary appeared: a rhinoceros. "We were jumping up and down," said Mahn.

With the discovery, scientists wondered if, despite intensive bombing during the war, parts of this remote mountainous region had become something of a "Lost World." "This is one of the most exciting events in the natural history of Vietnam," exulted director Tran Van Mui in a press release at the time.

Already in 1992, scientists in the region had "discovered" an ungulate (a hooved, ox-like mammal) with long, swept-back horns called the saola, an animal so different from known species that a new genus had to be formed to name it. In 1994, another previously unknown animal was found. Scientists called the deer-like creature the giant muntjac. Clearly, the region was full of possibilities, none more exciting than the prospect of a viable population of Javan rhinos.

Mahn presented a quick overview of Javan rhino 101. The subspecies *Rhinoceros sondaicus inermis,* which used to live in northern India and Myanmar (formerly Burma), was already extinct. The subspecies still found on the island of Java, *Rhinoceros sondaicus sondaicus,* had more than doubled its numbers, from a low of about twenty members in the mid-1960s, thanks to an aggressive antipoaching campaign. That Javan rhino species is still not out of the forest yet, though, since endemic corruption and poverty in Indonesia make any conservation effort an unending struggle.

As for the third subspecies, to which the Nam Cat Tien population belongs, Mahn said that originally he had hoped for a population of as many as ten as a starting point to rebuild the species. After further surveys, he was convinced that the number of surviving rhinos was probably half that. He wasn't even sure if a female was numbered among the survivors.

I was amazed when Zoe asked how old female rhinos had to be before they could have babies (four), and then how long it takes to make (she means gestate) a rhino baby (sixteen months). After our cassowary lessons, she didn't take it for granted that the mothers raised the baby rhinos, but Mahn explained that baby rhinos stay with their mothers for three to four years.

Females, to Zoe's disappointment, have either a very small horn, or no horn at all. The "horn" is not really a horn but a dense clump of hair that is nonetheless treasured for its alleged (and unproven by Western science) pharmacological qualities.

Kolya looked at me knowingly, since I had already explained to him about how Chinese medicine treats rhino horn as Viagra on the hoof.

Tory asked Mahn if he really thought it a possibility that the rhino could come back, since the population had sunk so low. After all, when a reproductive population is depleted, it's likely that a genetic bottleneck will occur even if successful breeding occurs. In other species, biologists have noticed a high likelihood of genetic defects down the line and increased vulnerability to disease when populations sink too low. Are there captive breeding programs? Could Javan rhinos from Indonesia be brought up here to interbreed?

No and no. As far as Mahn knew, not a single member of *Rhinoceros sondaicus annamiticus* existed in captivity. And it would be impossible to interbreed the two species, since they possessed physical characteristics and evolutionary adaptations that were too different for crossbreeding. It was either here or nowhere that the Vietnamese Javan rhino must survive.

Mahn acknowledged that the population was lower than they had originally hoped it would be. "There could be four or five," he says. "I doubt if there are eight." The hurdles ahead were legion, aside from genetic bottlenecks. So far in their surveys, Mahn noted, no footprints of different sizes had been found together. Many of the natural salt licks and watering holes, which normally had served as a kind of rhino singles bar, had been near places where human settlements had taken hold and mulberry or cashew plantations had sprouted. Since rhinos have such immense body mass and live in such torpid climates, they need both salt and water to keep their body temperature low. They spend large portions of the day submerged in mud wallows, and the dried mud serves as a kind of combination sunscreen and insect repellent. The salt licks are also an integral medicine chest, providing a number of essential minerals.

In the middle of this depressing litany of rhino facts, Mahn pointed out one success story: The rhino group had successfully negotiated with locals to stop farming in an area around one important salt lick.

Even if a prospective mating couple met, Mahn said, it would not be a done deal. "The male and female meet and must fight. Only if the male wins do they mate."

We thanked Mahn for his time, wished him luck in his work, and I headed back to talk with Cristina. She offered one hopeful observation about the Vietnamese that could help the rhino in the face of so many challenges: "They are very proud to be the only ones in the world to have this animal," she said.

Kit proposed that I join him and two of his Vietnamese colleagues the next day on an excursion to the northern part of the park where the rhino pictures had been taken. It would be a long drive, a long walk, and a long day, he told me, and he wasn't even sure the authorities would allow it. It would be something of a miracle if we actually saw a rhino, and fabulous good luck if we even saw a sign of one. I told him to ask permission for me to go, anyway.

I wanted to give the kids a sense of this kind of jungle, so we arranged for Cristina to take us on a walk. We first stopped at head-quarters to rent leech socks—knee-high stockings that were sup-posed to keep the little bloodsuckers at bay. We then rubbed what was certainly not an FDA-approved poison around critical areas of our boots and leech socks, and headed off.

Being in the Vietnamese jungle, as any grunt who was there can tell you, is an otherworldly experience. My first thought, once we trekked a hundred yards off the dirt road, was, "How did anybody expect a bunch of nineteen-year-olds from Des Moines and the Bronx to fight in this?" Even without regard for the moral, geopoliti-cal, and patriotic quandaries of the war, it had to have been a colos-sal piece of benighted naïveté that sent 58,000 Americans to die in this jungle, fighting against men who had been raised here and were defending their ancestral land.

We stopped in front of a gigantic banyan tree and posed for a group photo. As I wandered around the back side of the tree, crawl-ing over fins protruding from its trunk like small mountain ridges, I overheard Kolya talking to Cristina. My son, who is forever calling me a "tree-hugger," asked, "Is logging a big problem in the park?"

I didn't say a word.

Tory's cold took a turn for the worse, moving deep into her chest. To make matters worse, some species of tropical insect found her to be a scrumptious delight, and red marks spread across her body like a mild case of chicken pox. To top it off, she was the only one of the four of us whose blood was sucked by a leech. She had plucked off the bloodsucker and examined it sliding along the table with a leech's signature movement, bending almost in half and scooting its body forward like a Slinky, while Zoe looked on, aghast.

Tory's plane was scheduled to depart from Ho Chi Minh City in two days. Given her health, the original plan for her to return solo looked foolish, considering the grueling motorcycle taxi and bus ride that awaited. I felt torn, still hoping for a chance to visit the rhino section of the park, yet wanting to see her safely to the airport. I had decided, after Kit's description of the travel logistics, that it would be too much for the kids to make the trip, especially since we almost certainly wouldn't spot rhinos. I didn't want to leave Kolya and Zoe at the park alone after Tory left, since they were growing increasingly agitated by the jungle milieu. Then, to seal the deal, Kit told me that the park director would not let me go.

I was more relieved than disappointed and decided that we would head back to Ho Chi Minh City with Tory. The kids were delighted not to spend any more time here with the leeches and the mozzies. I told them we would probably have a chance to see rhinos, albeit a different species, in Nepal.

All in all, our jungle experience profoundly moved and disconcerted me. I could feel the population pressures and economic pressures and political pressures all bearing down on these few remaining rhinos. The government and environmental groups are making meaningful and sincere conservation efforts, but for this rhino species, it may already be too late.

ZIPPOS AND AK-47S

BACK IN SAIGON, the hotel staff greeted us like returning relatives when we stepped into the lobby of the Han Hoah Hotel. We had one last celebratory dinner together, even though Tory was still reeling from an upper respiratory infection, several thousand bug bites, and a pair of round, red leech wounds. The next morning, our foursome became a threesome again when we bid a sad adieu to Tory and she started her long journey home with a taxi ride to the airport. We all wondered what it would be like to reunite when we returned.

We are back in Saigon, in the same hotel that we stayed in before. Everyone is just completely flipping out about Tory leaving. Dad and Zoe are just constantly crying, my god. Don't get me wrong at all, I like Tory and enjoyed it a lot when she was with us, she saved my ass from dad a couple times. But we got along perfectly well when Tory wasn't with us as well. She was only with us for like 5 weeks, I just don't get the immense amount of emotion that they are putting into it. Shit, maybe I am just under reacting, but I don't see the big deal in it.

Then again, I might just not have had the same connection with Tory as they do. Because I am mad at them for being such little pussies about it, I don't really have any feelings about it, but I may later.

Dad switched our rooms so that we are all sleeping together. I like the hotel a lot, and this room is even better than the last, and it has a bigger TV. We are mostly just vegging out in front of CNN and seeing how much Bush is pissing off the world. A lot of MTV Asia too though. Dad has a few touristy things that are sorta a must do here. It sounds like it might end up being pretty retarded, but we will see.

Cambodia loomed as our next stop. Via e-mail, I had arranged to meet a friend from high school, Scott Leiper, who lived in Phnom Penh, but he wrote that he wouldn't be free for three more days. With time to kill before we embarked on the long, overland bus ride to Cambodia, we decided to play tourist and visit the Cu Chi tunnels, an underground city of sorts where the Viet Cong lived while they fought the United States and the South Vietnamese army (ARVN) troops. I reserved space for the three of us on a half-day bus tour, again listed as Brits, and we headed off early the next day.

Sanh, our guide to the Cu Chi tunnels, had fought with the South and the Americans during the war, and he was surprisingly frank when it came to what he described as the current regime's bankrupt politics. He talked about his year in a reeducation camp and fifteen years as a cyclo rider (driver of a kind of bicycle taxi), the price he paid for having fought with the United States and come out on the losing end. Despite having been in Denver in about 1973 for air force training, his postwar life remained on the margins of the new Vietnamese society.

The bus ride to Cu Chi was filled with Sanh's version of the war, which provided an intriguing counterpoint to the black-and-white propaganda film from the North's point of view presented to Cu Chi visitors as we arrived. Kolya liked the tunnels.

Vietnam hasn't been the greatest for me. But the Cu Chi tunnels turned out to be at least five times better than I expected. I have studied the Vietnam War in school of course, and it's pretty interesting, and it was great to see it through the eyes of the Vietnamese. We took a pretty painless bus ride to the tourist central of southern Vietnam. We watched a quick movie, which was pretty boring. Then we got a little bit of a lecture from our tour guide, which didn't do anything that the movie hadn't already told us. For some reason, I actually enjoyed the movie and the lecture, which are things that I would have probably fallen asleep during if I was forced to watch it for school. The next part was the tour, it was really short, but I learned a few things. We went into these really cool tunnels that I guess were actually used in the war. It was kinda a thrill to go into them, and really interesting once u got inside them. We got to see a lot of stuff inside the tunnels, mostly remakes of the original, but it was cool.

Even though most of the tour was pretty interesting, the very best part was shooting an AK–47. It is a really really big gun, and is illegal in the United States, I think. I was almost positive that my dad wasn't gonna let me shoot it, I mean this is a father who didn't even let me have nerf guns until I was 8. I didn't even have to beg him though, I just asked if I could, and he said "yes" if I payed for it my self. I was perfectly glad to shell out two dollars for two shots of the gun. The first shot didn't work too well, I had the gun away from my shoulder, and it came back and hit me pretty hard. I didn't even see where the bullet hit.

The next shot just missed the target barely, and I would have shot at least another five bullets, but I still wanted to buy a zippo, so I saved it. It was a huge rush to shoot that gun, and I get it now how people consider shooting a sport. Overall, I am definitely glad we did this thing, I didn't want to go at all at first, but I definitely learned a lot. It was way better than all the other dumb tourist attractions he has dragged us to.

On the bus ride back, Sanh expressed his deep regrets about what had happened in New York City. But he also worried about the tenor of our fledgling antiterrorism campaign. "I hope president Bush will learn from experience in Vietnam and guerrillas," Sanh said. "Not bomb whole village for one terrorist. How can you fight people who hide?" After visiting the Cu Chi tunnels, the rhetorical question didn't sound rhetorical. The comment was prescient, as U.S. troops on several occasions later ended up killing Afghan civilians who were mistaken for Taliban or Al Qaeda fighters.

Back at our hotel, Zoe complained to me that after she peed, it hurt to wipe. She'd heard about yeast infections from Rebecca, and wondered if maybe she had one. As the son of a gynecologist, I'm not exactly squeamish about the subject, but as a male I felt genetically unprepared to diagnose the problem. I wished Tory was still with us. I wished Zoe still had a mother around. In times like these, raising a daughter alone seemed like an impossible task.

Fortunately, however, I actually had planned for such a possibility and had brought along Monistat. But Rebecca had told me that before she used medicine for her own yeast infections, she always tried douching herself with citrus. Besides, it wasn't very likely that Zoe actually had a yeast infection, even though she was uncomfortable. I told Zoe I would go out and buy lemons, and we'd try that first.

I found no lemons in the tourist quarter, so I asked our hotel owner for directions to a fruit market. She offered to go with me, but I told her I'd be fine. She scrawled directions on a piece of paper, and I set the kids in front of the tube and went off strolling through Saigon alone.

In a couple of blocks I found a wide boulevard lined with peasants hawking all manner of fish, fowl, vegetables, and fruit. Since we had a long bus ride ahead of us the next day, I browsed and shopped for snacks while I kept my eyes peeled for lemons. I bought recognizable fruit like pineapples, then more adventurous varieties like rambutans.

But no lemons. I tried asking, unsuccessfully tried miming (you try to mime a lemon), but it was hopeless. Then, in a giant basket, I saw a fruit that looked like citrus, green like a lime and round like an orange. I bought a dozen and returned triumphantly to the hotel, ready to be a consummate father capable of providing my daughter with healing, naturopathic relief.

I squeezed juice from the fruit, which appeared to be some sort of orange or tangerine. I pulled Zoe aside and told her to go to the bathroom and wash herself. She looked at me quizzically, telling me that she thought it was supposed to be *lemon* juice, not orange juice. I told her that I couldn't find any lemons, and citrus was citrus.

Well, it burned. And putting orange juice on a yeast infection, women friends told me later, is like pouring lighter fluid on flaming embers. The treatment stung Zoe horribly, but whether it was because of the orange douche or despite it, the problem went away in a few days. Zoe forgave me, eventually.

After the orange escapade, we ate our last Vietnamese dinner at the Lotus Café. Early the next morning, we ate breakfast with the helpful waiter at the Hanh Hoa Hotel before getting on our bus headed toward Cambodia, the beginning of a long, long travel day. Given the state of the roads after the recent rainy-season floods, we almost ended up swimming to Cambodia.

A Surreal Border Crossing

The bus trip from Ho Chi Minh City to Phnom Penh, as I informed the kids about five hours into it, definitely qualified as "advanced" Lonely Planeteering. With the clear exception of a three-day bus ride Rebecca and I had taken in 1985 from Kashgar in western China over the 16,000-foot Karakoram Pass into northern Pakistan while I was intestinally compromised, this was one of the more challenging overland trips I'd ever taken. I promised the kids extra credit for hanging in there and wondered again why we hadn't decided to fly. It hadn't looked that far on the map.

We loaded onto a bus near our Saigon hotel at a little after 8 o'clock that morning and spent the next hour crawling through Ho Chi Minh traffic to the edge of town. We passed the Cu Chi tunnels again, watched the urban sprawl recede, and in a few hours were unceremoniously dumped at a dusty Vietnamese border town. The bus that would take us on to Phnom Penh, we learned, would meet us on the Cambodian side of the border. We ate lunch at a small restaurant on the Vietnamese side, then headed for the surreal border crossing, a group of block buildings 300 yards away.

We humped our stuff to the Vietnamese border control, where we waited in anarchic lines crowded around a glass window to attract the attention of diffident men in imposing olive-green uniforms. We repeated this process three times: first, to receive an exit stamp, then for an agricultural inspection, then to clear customs. As I patiently stood in lines, the kids began bickering about who would sit where on the bench, threatening a heated altercation. Just as I had tucked away our passports and gathered the increasingly agitated kids to walk across the border into Cambodia, one last man in uniform asked to see our passports with a menacing bark.

Satisfied with our documents, he pointed in the general direction of vacant space adjoining the Vietnamese border booths, across a dozen acres of no-man's land. The muggy, midday heat beat down as we walked slowly through a trash-strewn, barren stretch to be welcomed by a huge Khmer statue and a few bored border guards.

The Cambodian side seemed more like a carnival booth at a school fund-raiser than a sovereign nation's border control. We stood in lines by small wooden shacks as I filled out forms in duplicate for all three of us, wearing my pack and getting hotter by the minute, the kids crouching miserably in a small patch of shade next to the wooden booth. Our visas appeared to be in order, and the uniformed officials waved us into Cambodia with a stamp and a shrug. We still wondered when the next bus would appear.

We walked 300 yards to another border café, where we learned that our new bus, which theoretically *would* pick us up here, hadn't arrived yet from Phnom Penh. Thankfully, we were in good company with four middle-aged Aussie women with good dispositions and a game called *Pass the Pigs*. The kids played *Pass the Pigs* contentedly while we waited, rolling a pair of rubber pigs like dice and counting up points for various configurations, depending on how they landed. (A rare Double Snouter, when both porcine dice land nose up, is worth 60 points, while two pigs lying on their sides is worth only 1.)

Kolya and Zoe both reported that the nearby concrete toilet

building was *disgusting*, a big dipper without even a dipper. The bus arrived, but the driver needed to take a long lunch break before heading back, which we didn't begrudge him. Especially after we saw the state of the road to the capital.

It was one of the worst I'd ever been on in Asia, all the more appalling because it was the main route, National Route 1 in Cambodia, between these two major cities. The potholes were so numerous the bus driver didn't bother trying to avoid them and often took the shoulder rather than trying to brave the macadam crevasses. The rains had filled the holes and often the road itself with brown muddy water. At one point, navigating around a medium-sized town, we drove for at least five kilometers in calf-deep water or deeper, the driver picking his way methodically through side streets.

We drove for hours in our amphibious craft, then the bus stopped to wait for a ferry to cross a river that even our driver couldn't ford. The Aussie women whisked Zoe off to a hole in the ground to pee, and we stared at child vendors proffering plates of fried frogs. The poverty of Cambodia was striking, evident not only in the amphibian snack food and the appalling state of the infrastructure but also in the limited array of goods for sale in the markets we passed. We watched families setting up camp amid shanties others had constructed on the dry ground next to the road. We found out later that large numbers of Cambodians squat on this high ground during the rainy season while their homes were inundated.

For me, it was important that Kolya and Zoe see this. At home, when the kids would whine to me after I refused to buy them a new Nintendo 64 or Sony Playstation, my version of "Clean your plate, there are children starving in China" was this: "In Asia, kids play with rocks and sticks." Then, from the bus window, we saw a group of kids playing by the side of the road. I almost couldn't believe it. They were playing a made-up game—with rocks and sticks. Kolya looked at me, then pointed out the scene to Zoe.

*

One of the more remarkable things Kolya said to me after we were back home was that during the trip, he began to see me as a person in the world rather than just his dad, and his sister as a girl rather than as his sister. I have no idea how all our relationships will evolve as we grow older, but I hope this trip becomes a touchstone of shared experience for all of us. I remind Zoe, when she becomes despondent about Kolya's harsh words to her, that one day she will become his confidante, fashion adviser, and relationship *consigliore.* She isn't convinced.

For the moment, though, I could see how tense it could be for both of them. While Zoe was off to pee, Kolya complained about her again. I told him, with those damned tears welling in my eyes again, that nobody, with the exception of his dad and his mom, would ever love him as unconditionally as his sister did.

"Never forget that, Kolya."

And I was suddenly misty-eyed as we rolled onto the ferry in a fine drizzle, staring out a bus window, again looking backward:

It's the summer after Bob finished four rounds of chemo, and he's bouncing back strong. He's back at work, his hair has grown in, the prognosis is excellent, in the mind-numbing way they put it: a better than 90 percent chance of a five-year survival rate.

Out of a deep, life-affirming wisdom we had gleaned from the cancer scare rather than morbid fear, the three brothers and their families decide to go on a vacation together. It's the first time we've done this, and our families have long been reconfigured; Bob has remarried, his daughter is in high school, and his son is off to college. Renda has two kids from her first marriage, whom Bob has adopted—the eldest, a daughter, is a teacher, and the son is in college. I am into my first full summer as a single dad. Stevie alone has remained fully nuclear, with his wife Melanie and two boys. The eldest is just slightly younger than Kolya, and the youngest is Zoe's age.

Bob and Steve each have huge Ford pickups they use to pull monstrously comfortable Winnebagos, something that I never thought any of us would ever possess. Bob rents a smaller, self-contained RV unit for me and the kids, which is still about four times the size of the camper van we eventually drove around Australia. The three families pile into our respective rolling homes and head north to the Oregon coast. When we arrive, the three brothers play guitars together as the sun sets and the barbecue coals turn the color of the sun.

One misty day, Renda and Melanie send us off for a kidless and wife-less walk. In the light rain, the three of us, alone for the first time in years, follow an amazing trail along the cliffs and down to a deserted beach. There we pause, form a circle of brotherly embrace, loving each other and knowing, not knowing, that something is special about this moment, irreplaceable, necessary. An affirmation of everything, every game of catch and basketball, every slugfest, the secrets we kept from our parents, our love. We didn't play with rocks and sticks, but we did pretty well with a ball and not much else.

"I love you like a brother." Isn't that the deepest vow in our language, far surpassing "til death do us part" in depth and permanence?

"I love you guys," Bob tells us.

"Ditto."

"Ditto."

Two months later he receives a death sentence from the oncologist. Steve and I both wonder if Bob knew then, deep down, that he was dying.

We finally arrived in Phnom Penh after traveling for eleven hours. My friend Scott's wife Sochua arrived and took us to a gleaming new fast-food burger restaurant, which the kids loved. After seeing the state of the road and the roadside poverty for so long, Kolya and Zoe had their doubts about what Phnom Penh was going to be like—and certainly weren't expecting a strawberry milkshake at the end of the trail. To be picked up in an air-conditioned Land Cruiser with a driver and whisked away to a fast-food joint was immensely reassuring. Sochua paid in dollars, which had the kids' eyes bug-

ging out, and told us that most of her day-to-day commerce tran-
spired in U.S. currency.

Scott greeted us at home and we met his two youngest daughters, Thida and Malika, who were almost exactly Kolya's and Zoe's
ages, respectively. Their eldest daughter, Devi, was in Jakarta at a
boarding school where Scott's brother was the headmaster, since a
similar school in Phnom Penh had very few high school–aged students. In the post–9/11 world, however, Indonesia was no longer
such a great place to be, and a year after we returned reports sur-
faced that foreign students living in Jakarta had been the target of
an aborted Al Qaeda attack. The reverberations keep expanding.

Scott and I had gone to Berkeley High School together, had
scooped ice cream for $2.10 an hour together, and had spent my
seventeenth birthday backpacking together in the Sierra Nevada
mountains. He left California for college at Amherst in Massachu-
setts, came back in the summer, and introduced me to his friend
Keith, who became Scott's traveling partner after college. The two of
them left home to see the world, and neither came back. Keith,
whom we'll visit in Kathmandu, married a Nepali woman and
works for Save the Children. Scott had met his soon-to-be-wife
Sochua working with Cambodian refugees on the Thai border just
before Rebecca and I passed through to visit in 1984. Sochua was a
Cambodian exile who left the country to go to school in Paris just
before Pol Pot's murderous regime took complete control. Her parents stayed behind, were forced to toil in the countryside in labor
brigades, and didn't survive the regime.

During the long bus ride here, I had briefed Kolya on the place
we were about to visit and its context in history. Like Vietnam, Cambodia had been a French colony until the mid-1950s. The CIA and
several U.S. presidents tried to influence Cambodian politics by
supporting pro-Western political leaders, and in 1970 a U.S.-backed
Cambodian general named Lon Nol took control in a coup. Toward
the end of the Vietnam War, when I was Kolya's age, the United
States "secretly" bombed Cambodia, killing more than 100,000

civilians. Depending on whom you believe, I told Kolya, our bombing and support for Lon Nol helped pave the way for the disaster that followed—or prevented Cambodia from becoming one of the famed Communist "dominos."

Even in these patriotic, post–9/11 times, I wanted Kolya to understand how the United States might have generated such murderous venom from other cultures. Our country had acted badly in many parts of the world, I told him, and many people think the United States has been a bully on the world stage, projecting its power with tragic, unintended consequences.

After the war ended, what happened in Cambodia was infinitely complicated. A number of different Cambodian political factions joined together for a short while to oppose Lon Nol. One of those factions, the Khmer Rouge, was led by a man named Pol Pot, who ultimately ousted Lon Nol and turned Cambodia into what was infamously called "the Killing Fields." Between 1975 and 1978, about 20 percent of Cambodia's population—1.7 million people— were killed in an orgy of ideological murder, starvation, and disease brought on by Pol Pot's dream of a Communist agrarian utopia. Intellectuals and city-dwellers of all stripes were moved to the countryside. Many educated people were summarily executed, families were torn apart, and the country's infrastructure disintegrated.

To give Kolya a frame of reference for this nearly ungraspable idea, I told him it was as if somebody had come in and killed or starved every person who lived in Denver *and* Boulder and everywhere in between, just because they thought they were overeducated and needed to be farmers. Kolya knew the word "genocide" from studying the Holocaust, but he had no idea of what had happened in Cambodia. I told him that one reason we couldn't take a direct bus there from Vietnam was because in 1978, the Vietnamese had invaded Cambodia. Thirteen years of political violence, anarchy, and guerrilla activity in the countryside followed the Vietnamese occupation. It was only in the late 1980s, when Kolya was born, that the Vietnamese agreed to leave. Cambodia began a period of relative peace after a framework for elections was agreed upon in 1991. I promised to watch the movie *The Killing Fields* (1984) with him at home as part of a Vietnam War movie marathon.

Scott started his first international aid job on the Thai-Cambodian border in the early 1980s to help Cambodian refugees during the Vietnamese occupation and the Khmer Rouge resistance. Over the years, his expertise and responsibility grew as he worked for various United Nations organizations, harnessing international aid to help Cambodia recover from decades of colonial rule, mass murder, political insanity, and a dysfunctional economy.

As soon as Scott and Sochua deemed it safe, which is a relative term in Cambodia, they moved to Phnom Penh. It was 1989, during the last stages of the Vietnamese occupation and two years before the Peace Accords that paved the way for elections. Sochua, after nearly two decades in exile, worked in and out of government on women's issues. When we visited, she had been the minister for women's and veterans' affairs for three years as a member of a minority party in the ruling coalition. She had become a leading advocate for women and children, a monumental job in a country where about 40 percent of the population is younger than fifteen.

They had a rambling, colonial home in Phnom Penh with, we learned, its own private lake in the rainy season where the driveway should be. Scott and Sochua had taken in the few surviving relatives on Sochua's side, plus two orphaned girls. Their house was a welcome refuge after our jungle days in Vietnam and the long bus ride.

I wished that Tory could be with us and felt alone even though we were among old friends. I missed her, but I also knew that the decision for her to go home was probably the right thing. Being out of contact so suddenly was difficult. I didn't even know if she had made it back, and I worried because she had been so sick when she left. I felt that Zoe missed Tory's enveloping love, and tucked her in with extra kisses.

Scott and Sochua both had full workweeks ahead with unavoidable meetings, so we decided on a three-day trip by ourselves to see the great temples of Angkor Wat. A six-hour "fast" boat ride would take us up the Tonle Sap River and across Tonle Sap Lake, the largest freshwater lake in southeast Asia. Tonle Sap swells to six times its dry-season size during the monsoons, and it was pretty vast this time of year. The boat drops tourists off a few miles away from Siem Reap, the staging area for tourist expeditions to the thousand-year-old temples surrounding the town.

Scott promised to call a friend in Siem Reap to arrange for someone to pick us up at the boat dock and drive us into town. He warned us about the mob scene when the boat arrives, from touts and taxi drivers and tour operators, but that I should look for a man holding a sign saying "Glick."

TOMB RAIDERS

BEFORE WE BOARDED the boat in Phnom Penh, a man at the dock asked if we had anybody meeting us to take us to Siem Reap. I told him we had a ride, thanks. He asked my name, and I thought he was being friendly so I told him: Dan.

We climbed onto an open-air platform as soon as the boat began moving, settling in with dozens of other world traveler types for the long ride ahead. Scott and Sochua had seen to it that we were properly provisioned with a picnic lunch, and we passed the six hours relatively comfortably despite deafening diesel engine noise.

When we arrived, we saw nobody with a sign saying "Glick" among the predicted throngs, but we did see a young man with a sign saying "Mr. Dan." I waved him off, looking for Scott's man. Then the Mr. Dan man came up and told me that he was the guy I was looking for, that my friends in Phnom Penh had arranged this. I was completely confused. Ultimately, no "Glick" sign appeared, so we hopped in with our new friend, Sam'oun.

He steered us to a hotel and we settled in for a rest before beginning our afternoon temple tour. From Scott, I had heard about

Angkor Wat for years. He had driven Rebecca and I to nearby Khmer ruins when we had visited him on the Thai border back in 1984, hurrying back in time for curfew in those volatile times. Until relatively recently, however, Angkor Wat was still a place that only the most adventurous tourists could visit, given the political instability, the banditry, and the land mines.

I launched into tour guide mode as the three of us strolled down the long approach on the stone causeway to the main temple, since I was the only one who had any interest at all in the tourist brochures and books Scott had loaned us. The temple complex encompasses almost an entire square mile, a vastness filled with ghosts. In the eleventh century, when Europeans were still leeching blood and living in drafty stone castles, the Khmer civilization was in full flower, leading Southeast Asia, if not the world, in art, culture, architecture, and governance. Only hints of that former glory remain in these magnificent structures scattered around Siem Reap, which were rediscovered by accident in 1860 by a French botanist. Every civilization has its day, I told the kids, and for the time being, America was reveling in its moment in the sun. Kolya and Zoe liked the stone serpent balustrades and the huge pyramid temples.

A man in a police uniform approached us and tagged along. He recounted a few of the stories depicted on the stone-carved bas reliefs, which were interesting enough. Ran, our policeman/tour guide, told us he had signed on with the Khmer Rouge army at fifteen, then switched sides at seventeen. His parents had been killed, his sister committed suicide, and his brother was blown up by a land mine, he said, matter of factly.

I didn't know what to say. I immediately felt compassion for his perfectly plausible story about his brother and the land mine. At the same time, a wary feeling came over me as I wondered if we were being reeled in by the policeman's sob-story tourist schtick.

Kolya, increasingly discomfited, blurted out, "I'm sorry." Ran shrugged.

Ran bounded up the steep steps without fear, then stood above us and told Kolya about Khmer Rouge "monkey school," where Ran had trained for jungle warfare. Kolya couldn't climb the same steep steps here unless he went to "monkey school," too.

Our guide pointed out bullet holes in the carvings and referred obliquely to the genocide of the Pol Pot era. I muttered something that let him know I had a rudimentary grasp of Cambodian affairs. "Then you know a little of the sad history of my country," he replied. Indeed, I could almost feel the human suffering exuding from the walls.

The next morning, I awoke before dawn to have Sam'oun drive me to another temple, Bayon, for some quiet time. It's an incredible place, with 200 stone carvings of the Khmer god-king Avelokitesvara, smiling like the Bodhisattva he said he was, glowing in the dawn light. I found myself musing about the concept of karma in this Buddhist land, privately asking the unaskable question about whether 9/11 represented a huge karmic debt being repaid—for what we did in El Salvador, Chile, Iran, Angola, Zaire, the Philippines, Vietnam. And here in Cambodia.

I couldn't help but wonder what kind of karmic payback I might be experiencing myself, losing a brother and a marriage in the span of a year.

When I returned to the hotel, the kids were watching a cartoon called "Johnny Bravo," which I had caught snippets of in the past and had declared to be the stupidest cartoon in the world. The kids, in fact, did not dispute this fact. I sat down to write in my journal when I realized that Johnny Bravo was being broadcast in Thai, and the kids were *still* absorbed in it. It was time to take them outside.

Sam'oun drove us to Ta Phrom, an unrenovated temple whose contemporary claim to fame is that the film *Tomb Raider* (2001) was filmed there. The fact that Scott had told us about meeting Angelina

Jolie during the filming made it even more tangible for the kids. On the way, we stopped to hear a group of musicians, disabled war veterans. Zoe, spellbound by the unfamiliar quarter-tone music and stirred by their disabilities, gave them some of her own spending money, and some of mine.

At Ta Phrom, tree roots melded into stone, the centuries' neglect demonstrating how man's works will eventually become overgrown. Kolya and Zoe actually seemed to enjoy it, even as it started raining. We goofed off and strolled around. The kids' new thing is a line from *Dr. Dolittle 2* (2001) one of the pirated DVDs they had seen at Scott's. In the movie, Dr. Dolittle (Eddie Murphy) can of course talk to animals and understand them. He is taken by a tough-talking Bronx-accented raccoon to visit "the beaver," a Mafia don type. The beaver is a gracious host and asks Murphy if he'd like a fish. He politely but firmly declines, which outrages the bodyguard raccoon.

"When the beaver offers you a fish," he menaces, "you take da fish."

The line caught on and became a tool that I could use to persuade the kids every now and then. At Ta Phrom, when I said, "Hey, why don't we go to the top of the temple?," Zoe demurred. Kolya turned to her and said, "Hey, if the beava offas you a fish . . ." We were lucky. Zoe responded: "You take da fish." And off we went.

That evening, Kolya wasn't feeling well, so Zoe and I went out to fetch dinner and shop at the market. The day's grace continued. We walked hand-in-hand, chattering about everything and nothing. Zoe stopped to buy a beautiful woven pouch to give to Rebecca.

"Do you think Mama will like it?" she asked anxiously.

"She'll love anything that comes from you," I told her, wondering how hollow those words must sound sometimes. I was heartbroken that my daughter must feel such anxiety about pleasing her absent mother. We sat down at an Italian-ish restaurant and ordered a pizza to take back to Kolya. Zoe and I held hands while we waited, sipping sodas and enjoying our "magical" and exotic father-daughter date.

Mr. K didn't get sick, thank goodness, because we had to awaken early the next day for the return boat. Sam'oun's car leaked all the brake fluid on the way, and we drove without brakes, inching slowly on the crowded, potholed road as we took in the rainy-season life of people and pigs and ducks and boats and floating houses. We thanked him, having thoroughly enjoyed his company for the past three days. Only when we returned to Phnom Penh did we learn that Scott had never reached his friend in Siem Reap.

Back in Phnom Penh, we left the kids with Scott's daughters, the housekeeper, and a pile of DVDs. Scott and I headed across town to meet Sochua for dinner. Driving with Scott across the pockmarked streets of Phnom Penh, I watched him weave through the cyclos and the motos, talking all the time, knowing when to continue inching forward and when to make a bold move. He avowed that he worked long hours and people accused him of being too caught up in his job. "I don't think I'm a workaholic," he told me. "It's just that there's too much work to do."

We met Sochua, who tackles the role of minister with passion. She is an advocate for the most disadvantaged women and children in the country, many of whom are sold into sexual slavery or rented to beggar women in Vietnam. Sochua created international head-lines when she called for the deportation of Gary Glitter, an English rocker who had been accused of child pornography in Britain and was found suspiciously in the company of a ten-year-old girl in Phnom Penh. Sochua used the incident to raise awareness of the child sex trade in Cambodia. At one point she told Zoe and Kolya that, in all likelihood, the women we saw begging on the streets of Saigon with what appeared to be their children in tow had actually rented Cambodian children to increase the compassion factor.

I was never sure how much Kolya and Zoe were taking in, but apparently this lesson stuck, at least for Zoe:

We were walking along the street in Vietnam one day and we saw a mother and her baby begging. We felt so bad for them. I wanted to give them all the money I had and all the money I would ever earn. But we kept on walking.

Later when we were in Cambodia, Sochua told us that mostly all the women that you see on the streets don't actally own the babies. They go to other mothers to rent the babies. People actualy rent kids. Sad isn't it? As soon as I heard it I wanted to throw up. Babies are humans and they deserve more respect than they get.

"Family Rate" at Pat Pong

OUR ARRIVAL into Bangkok went flawlessly—such a contrast to the local bus that Rebecca and I had taken into town from the airport seventeen years previously through crowded back streets, getting lost and wandering aimlessly as we looked for our guest house. In the intervening years, Bangkok had transformed itself into an almost gleaming Southeast Asian capital—which is all the more striking when contrasted with Ho Chi Minh City and Phnom Penh. At Tory's recommendation, we called the Peachy Guest House from the airport, climbed into an air-conditioned, metered taxi, and took the expressway into the tourist ghetto of Banglampu without a hitch. Now certified world-traveling veterans, the kids are barely daunted by the modest guest-house accommodations, even though the bathroom is down the hall. At least there are no big dippers.

Before leaving home, I had tentatively decided that we would fly from Bangkok up to Chengdu, in China's Sichuan Province, to visit the giant panda preserves of Wolong and Wanglang. Now, however, after three months on the road, the logistics of a spontaneous China excursion felt overwhelming. The panda's plight was certainly worthy of our attention. But as I had already realized, I could conduct research on alarming ecological case studies in every country in the world. Including my own.

As I wrestled with the idea of eliminating China from our itinerary, I received an e-mail from my sister-in-law Renda. The hospital where Bob had worked had announced it would rename the emergency department after him and had scheduled a dedication ceremony for December 1. Could we return by then, and would I be the master of ceremonies?

Up until that moment, Christmas had been our drop-dead return date, for no other reason than that I had promised Kolya and Zoe we'd be home by then. Now, all signs pointed to an earlier return. If we chose to be home by December 1, we could easily plan to arrive the last week of November and join Tory and her family for Thanksgiving in Puerto Vallarta, as we had the previous year. We would still have time to explore Nepal, spend the better part of a month in Europe, go to Mexico, and be in California in time for the dedication. It seemed a fitting endnote to our travels, and I e-mailed Renda that we would be there.

As soon as I made the decision I felt relieved, especially about eschewing the Middle Kingdom. I felt the kids were losing steam, and they increasingly looked forward to having been to these places rather than actually *going* to them. I sat the kids down for a powwow and explained the recent turn of events. Kolya shrugged and said no worries, and Zoe didn't put up much resistance either—especially after I mentioned an option that was now available to us to spend a week on an island here in Thailand. They were fine with going to California for Bob's dedication, and they loved the idea of going to Puerto Vallarta for the second year running.

I called a friend of a friend with whom I had corresponded before we began the trip. Julia Gajcek was the PR director for the Regent Hotel, and our mutual friend had told her about us. She kindly invited us to lunch the next day at one of the hotel's upscale restaurants. Who were we to refuse?

With that set of decisions completed, we set off on foot to explore our neighborhood. Despite its modernization, Bangkok still amazed me. Its pace isn't really fast, but the motion is continuous. Traffic loud and furious, diesel fumes, and honking horns: The noise is deafening, a tribal pulse infiltrating the streets and everything in them. When the sun sets the tropical heat slowly recedes. Life abounds, honking and gyrating and pulsing, street corner stalls and teeming Asian night. The formerly ubiquitous unmuffled *tuk-tuks* (three-wheeled motorized rickshaws) have been largely phased out in favor of Japanese taxis and motorcycles.

We roamed the streets, smelling, inhaling, captivated: flower markets, chicken on a stick, fruit hawkers, bicycle vendors with sticky rice desserts on sidecar platters, urchins on wheels with their sisters on the handlebars. An assault on the senses, eardrums bombarded with Thai sing-song and cars and buses and taxis and motorcycles and noise and decibel overload. Foods frying and stewing and barbecuing, squid and intestines and undifferentiated pig parts. Shops blaring rap and techno music, antiques and bolts of cloth and pens and shoes and tiny restaurants dotting the street, enlivened by the strollers, the snackers, the women shoppers, the hanger-outers. People weaving impossible paths through relentless traffic, motorcycles picking their way through blocked and baying packs of vehicles.

The next day Julia escorted us to an Italian lunch served on white tablecloths, complete with Tuscan wine and fawning waiters. The kids, thankfully, knew more or less which fork to use and behaved themselves. It was interesting to hear Julia's take on the effects of 9/11 on the tourist business—which of course had been profound but perhaps not as devastating as she and her colleagues might have predicted. Americans were staying home more, she said, but other nationalities continued their business—and pleasure.

I asked Julia's opinion about our Thai beach options, whether we should go to the southern islands of Ko Phi Phi, Ko Phangan, Phuket—or else stay closer to Bangkok and hang out at Ko Samet. She said that she was actually pretty new here in Thailand and hadn't gotten out much, and then offered us more than a fish: When we returned from the beach, she'd see if she could put us up for a night at the hotel. The kids lit up as if they had just been offered a small principality to govern, and I thanked her for her generosity. She said if it worked out, we could maybe take a tour of nearby Pat Pong, the notorious red-light district that has been made a little more family-friendly by the proliferation of souvenir shops and a great night market.

I decided that with trekking season fast approaching in Nepal, it would probably be a good idea to make reservations for our onward leg from Bangkok to Kathmandu, now that our plans were firming up. I excused myself and called Royal Thai Airlines to make reservations for ten days hence. The reservation agent informed me that I could either have confirmed seats for three days from now, on October 5, or else book tickets for after Thanksgiving. I weighed the uncertainty of flying standby against a few restful beach days. I took the fifth.

Even if we had wanted to go to China, it wouldn't have worked out. Serendipity rules.

I returned to the table and informed the kids of the new situation. I was immediately excited about the prospect of spending more time in Nepal, where I had been three times previously and which held a strong allure for me. It meant, however, that we would only have two more nights in Thailand.

Julia said she would see if she could sneak us into the hotel for our last night in Thailand; when I phoned that evening from our low-rent digs at the Peachy Guest House, she had good news. Would we like to spend a night in the Regent tomorrow? The kids stood next to me, watching my face for clues to this fateful conversation. I smiled, gave them a big thumbs up, and we quietly slapped each other high fives while I was still on the phone.

We would like, I told Julia, with pleasure.

In the morning we bid goodbye to our $8 a night room before hopping into a cab and walking, *avec* backpacks and skateboard, into the lobby of one of the finest hotels in Asia. We felt like gilded impostors, strolling under the hand-painted silk ceilings and the expansive lobby filled with hand-crafted Thai teak furniture and what appear to be genuine antiques. A string quartet played classical Western music from the balcony, and patrons sipped tea from exquisite china. We were back in Somerset Maugham land, for real.

The kids jumped on, then burrowed, into the large beds. They watched a giant TV with a zillion channels, and I partook of the elegant health club. When I returned after a workout and a sauna, Kolya asked why we couldn't stay in places like this every night. We did the math. One night here would cost at least as much as a month at the Peachy. I told him that even if I was a millionaire, I wouldn't want to stay in places like this every night. (Well, maybe every now and then. It was pretty nice.) Admittedly, our room at the Peachy was a little moldy and the bathroom was down the hall, but the clientele was a little more interesting, wasn't it?

We joined Julia for a drink and Japanese food before the three of us headed out to Pat Pong. I reminded the kids about the scenes in *Miss Saigon*, which took place here after the war, when Bangkok became the sex capital of Asia. Bars featuring barely clad women who had been plucked from impoverished northern villages lined the streets, with doors tantalizingly open for glimpses of women gyrating on and around stainless steel poles. Kolya, his blue eyes bulging beneath his brimmed hat, looked over a "menu" of the acts that awaited him inside, and he asked me if we could go in for a "soda." I told him these particular delights could continue to await him until he was old enough to come here by himself. He looked at the menu and could only fantasize about the "pussy shooting banana" and "smoking pussy" show.

I trailed behind the three of them, trying to keep track of Kolya peeking at the girlie shows and Zoe flitting from jewelry stand to wood-carving bazaar, when a barker signaled to me to come see his club's unique *divertissements*. I pointed to the kids and Julia and smiled, which he took to mean, "I'd like to, but . . ."; without missing a beat, he grinned and said, "Family rate!"

Needless to say, we have a new family joke.

We were walking around in Pat Pong, the red-light distrik and there were open doors to clubs. Obviously there were prostitutes and stripers in there. It disgusted me. I couldn't see how women could sell their bodies to strangers. But also I have to hear their side of the story too. I bet the only reason that they are prostitutes is because they're so poor that they need money I guess. You can buy some things in the world with money but you can't buy love.

We joked around and shopped and gawked until about midnight, then headed back to the hotel, shopped out and tired. Walking up to the huge, columned entry to have doors opened by liveried doormen, we all felt like we had entered a movie set. We bid Julia goodnight, went to our room, and giggled at our good fortune.

And then. Something snapped. While we were gone, the hotel staff had wheeled a third bed into the room. After eating our mints, we began negotiations for who would sleep in the slightly smaller rollaway, marginally less comfortable than the two main beds. I proposed they flip a 1 baht coin to see which of them would have the rollaway. They both agreed to the game of chance. I flipped the coin, Zoe called it in the air, and I could see before they could that Kolya had won. Neither of them could see the result, and my immediate instinct was to lie and tell Kolya that he had to sleep on the rollaway, since I suspected that Zoe would not go gently into that good night.

I should have followed my instincts, as unfair as that would have been to Kolya. Zoe immediately broke down into howls of complaint, screaming at midnight in the hotel room, completely unable to listen, be comforted, or in any way modify her thoroughly spoiled behavior. I wanted to appeal to a higher power but there was none. I dug in my heels, although part of me wanted to simply sleep in the rollaway myself. But I couldn't give in, even as she was screaming and crying and inconsolable.

It took a long time for her to quiet down, during which time I confess that the impulse to put a pillow over her mouth was almost too strong to resist. Kolya of course was both smug and angry, asking me to give Zoe "consequences" for being such a poor sport and for screaming at midnight in a luxury hotel.

What consequences, I asked myself, could possibly do any good?

The kids finally drifted off to sleep, with Zoe in her inferior roll-out bed. I was suddenly spent, tired, despondent. I wished my brother wasn't dead. I missed Rebecca. I missed my family of four. I missed having a partner in raising the kids. I wondered why it was all coming on so strong right now, and I realized that Bangkok was the first place on this trip that Rebecca and I had also visited together. Marriage memories washed over me as I watched the kids sleep: our three-day wedding party; the adventures of our three-year Asian honeymoon; our excitement when we found out she was pregnant with Kolya, then with Zoe; the first words and first steps and first days of kindergarten and long years of confident, loving camaraderie. I wondered again how we all ended up so far apart, how it came to this.

In the sleepless depths of this Thai night, I beat myself up, blaming my own inattentiveness and self-absorption and fear. Contrary to my own self-image of being a hang-loose, go-with-the-flow Berkeley boy, I am as reactionary as Kolya with his diagonally-cut French toast when he was four. As Rebecca began to grow and change, I wasn't able to respond and support her search for an identity that extended beyond the boundaries that she knew.

Would it have mattered if I had acted differently?

Ironically, in that luxurious hotel room, comfortable beyond desire, I spent one of the saddest and most sleepless nights of our whole trip. When I finally drifted off, I had a dream where the details were lost, but the meaning was clear:

I *hadn't* done anything differently.

I *couldn't* do anything to change what happened.

And it was time to move on.

As usual, Zoe woke up the next morning as if nothing had happened. We exited the Regent looking like an incongruous traveling menagerie among the matching luggage sets of the Hong Kong and Singaporean businessmen. The doorman hailed us a cab, and we entered like royalty.

The driver dropped us off at the Royal Thai Airlines terminal, and like a surprise it hit me that we were en route to Kathmandu, one of the most evocative city names on the planet, like Timbuktu or Cairo or Mandalay or Istanbul. The kids and I had snapped out of our funk and we talked excitedly about seeing my friend Keith and his family, about going trekking and tracking rhinos and tigers in the jungle. I remembered to ask for seats on the right side of the plane in order to catch our first Himalayan views, but everybody had read the same guidebook. We were seated on the left, but it didn't matter. The day was cloudy, and nobody saw Mt. Everest eye-to-eye at 29,000 feet.

PART 5

STALKING SERENDIPITY

Zoe rhinoceros-viewing from atop an elephant near
Chitwan National Park in Nepal.

KE GARNE?

THOUGH THE high peaks of the Himalaya were shrouded in late-monsoon cloud, the kids and I stared, captivated, at the view of Kathmandu Valley, which stretched out below us like a detailed aerial map. As we descended, we picked out smoky, dusty villages ringing the capital city, the countryside green from the season of rains, the gray haze of exhaust fumes floating above the valley floor like a shroud. You could sense the clash of millennia below; the tendrils of the twenty-first century expanded like a strangler fig growing alongside its host tree, inevitably destined to suffocate it. In the city, bony Nepali men born into an age before foreigners were allowed into this Hindu kingdom sauntered past Western trekkers hunched over terminals in Internet cafés fretting about their stock portfolios. Simply flying into Kathmandu struck me as an act of sacrilege.

Despite its evocatively named capital and its reputation in the West as home of Everest and Buddhist retreat centers led by exiled Tibetan rinpoches, Nepal remains one of the world's political and economic basket cases. A month before we started our trip, this remote Himalayan country was stunned by a regicide that further destabilized a tenuous political situation. On June 1, 2001, Crown Prince Dipendra, heir apparent to the throne, shot his parents— King Birendra and Queen Aishwarya—in a drunken argument over the prince's choice of bride. While the royal family and entourage engaged in a royal cocktail hour, the prince entered wearing combat fatigues and brandishing a submachine gun, then opened fire in the palace. The prince took successful aim at seven other members of the royal family before turning the automatic weapon on himself. The royal massacre flattened Nepal's collective psyche and made way for Maoist insurgents to continue their violent offensive against the constitutional monarchy.

"I fear for this tiny country," wrote my friend Keith Leslie in an e-mail I received in Australia. I started wondering aloud if Nepal would be stable enough for us to visit. During his eighteen years in the country working for Save the Children, Keith had certainly seen political instability before, including a historic shift from an autocratic king and his government by nepotism to a parliamentary democracy of sorts in the early 1990s. He had witnessed the accelerated growing pains of a country that was under cultural siege from an annual onslaught of half a million Western trekkers, wanderers, stoners, seekers, sightseers, mountaineers, pilgrims, tourists, artists, hippies, ne'er-do-wells, investors, traders, merchants, aid workers, and millions upon millions of dollars in international assistance. (In 1962, the number of tourists totaled about 6,000.) Yet Nepal steadfastly remains one of the poorest countries in the world, one where distances between villages are still mostly measured in walking days and where babies still die by the thousands from diarrhea.

We touched down at Tribhuvan International Airport and entered a terminal that had been upgraded since my last visit but was still fittingly basic. We disembarked directly to the tarmac and walked into the terminal to be processed. The guidebooks say that tourists can simply pick up visas on the spot, which is technically true. It just takes a little while. The Nepali bureaucracy, reassuringly, remained timelessly and cheerfully inept.

Although I tried to hurry Zoe off the plane to the long customs line, she had lost something of immense value under her seat (a packet of gum, I think). We were among the last to deplane, then found our place nearly at the end of imposingly long immigration and customs lines. A semi-official-looking man walked down the line "inspecting" everybody's documents. When he got to us, he found fault with the stash of passport photos I had been carrying around for this very purpose. I admit that the digital pictures I had taken and printed on a cheap color printer were not of the highest quality, but they resembled us and that had been good enough so far. The man signaled that with a little *baksheesh* he could ensure that the photos would clear the customs officials, but I decided he was bluffing and waved him off. He shrugged and went up the line to inspect other travelers' documents.

Zoe was out of sorts because I had tried to hurry her off the plane, and threw herself down on our packs in the middle of the dirty floor, refusing to move when the line inched forward. I had tried to explain to the kids that customs lines were about the last place I wanted to have scenes, but the lesson, if it had ever penetrated, was forgotten now. Kolya proclaimed his mortification because of his sister's behavior, and it's safe to say that the hour and a half we spent in that line was the low point of our Nepal visit. Which, in retrospect, was actually pretty good news. At the time, however, I wondered if I could put her on the next plane to Dhaka, Bangladesh. By herself.

We were the next to last people to clear customs, but thankfully nobody else tried to shake me down because of low-quality visa photos. We blinked into the gorgeous sunlight of the Kathmandu Valley, searching for Keith, and peered around at the taxi drivers and hotel touts who were fishing for tourists. Then I spotted him, calmly reading the *Kathmandu Post* and leaning against his car. He peeked up, smiled, and greeted me with a bear hug, his hair grayer than it was the last time I'd seen him but his impish smile the same.

I had not been to Nepal since the mid-1980s, around the time Pico Iyer was writing *Video Night in Kathmandu* (1988) and Jeff Greenwald was researching *Shopping for Buddhas* (1990). Keith had lived here the whole time and had found a comfortable niche, speaking idiomatic Nepali with an incongruous New York accent. I apologized for being the last out of customs, and he shrugged. *Ke garne?* he said, "what to do?" He reminded me of this most indispensable Nepali phrase: when a bridge is out, when a government office is inexplicably closed, when a flight is canceled. Ke garne? He had waited in Nepal before.

Uncharacteristically, the kids rode in silence as we wove our way up the Ring Road, passing a brand new golf course as we exited the airport. Like Bangkok, Kathmandu had received a few face-lifts over the past decade and a half, but the pace of the change was slower and the starting point less modern. The roads were still cratered, the three-wheeled *tempos* still belched black smoke, and bicycle rickshaws still peddled the roads on wobbly wheels. It felt remarkably familiar to be back.

Keith and his wife Shakun had recently moved into a new house they had built on the north end of the Kathmandu Valley above the village of Budhanilkantha. We rose out of the valley on increasingly rutted roads, Keith weaving around the potholes, motorcycles, and pedestrians with the horn honking. I smiled broadly, glad to see Keith, glad to be there, relieved to have a safe haven for the kids to orient themselves to the subcontinent.

We arrived at a gated compound and Keith's *chowkida-or*, watchman, opened the gate to reveal a magnificent house and courtyard. We dropped our stuff at the cozy, detached guest house and climbed the steps to the main house. His two boys, Josh and Ezra, were still at school, and Shakun wouldn't be back until dinner. But the baby, Leah, was there with the *didi* who looked after her. The *didi* served us a round of *chiya*, sweet milk tea, accompanied by biscuits, and immediately adopted Zoe, who seemed to take to her, too. Keith returned to work for afternoon meetings.

I walked outside, breathed deep, looked down at the valley floor below, and smiled again.

*

Keith's sons, both baseball nuts, were then absorbed in Barry Bonds's pursuit of Mark McGuire's new single season home-run record. When they returned from school, they checked the Internet for updates and box scores in the *International Herald Tribune.* Josh and Ezra are sandwiched in between Kolya and Zoe in age, and the four of them disappeared outside to play catch as if they'd had a play date arranged for days. Shakun arrived home from her boutique, where she designs and sells clothing to Western buyers, and soon Keith joined us in time for dinner.

Shakun soon retired with Leah while Keith checked up on the kids' homework and schedules for the next day. We finally put all the kids to bed, and I broke out a bottle of duty-free single malt scotch so we could settle down in the living room for serious catching up.

The last time I'd been here, I was with Rebecca, on the upward trajectory of our marriage. We had passed through three times during our "honeymoon." The first time was in 1984, just after Keith had met Shakun. Rebecca and I had trekked up to Everest base camp in the Solo-Khumbu region, spending seven weeks on the trail. Later, Keith engineered a "motorcycle trek" for the three of us to Pokhara and Chitwan, where we would visit on this trip as well. Rebecca and I had also passed through on our way to and from Tibet in 1986, the last time we were here. Another life.

Keith expressed the same disbelief that most of Rebecca's and my mutual friends had expressed: We seemed like a couple who had figured it out. What happened?

I shook my head and said I was no longer even trying to decipher Rebecca's motivation, then told him about my dream and epiphany in Bangkok exhorting me to stop rehashing what had happened.

He asked how I was coping with Bob's death. Keith empathized —about brothers, family, loss. Somehow, his years in that Hindu kingdom had given him an Eastern sensibility toward these things—sadness as an inextricable part of life, to be mourned and marked with ceremony. He recalled meeting Bob during a trip to California once. We drank in silence and headed for our beds well after midnight.

I retreated to the guest room, half-drunk, and the kids were snoring. Almost exactly a year ago, Bob had phoned with the worst news I've ever heard.

There was nothing left to do, Bob told me on the phone. He was dying. He seemed resigned, subdued, but it felt like he was telling me something less daunting, less final, like he had to have another round of chemo or surgery. The cancer had metastasized into his bones. He didn't know if he'd live to see his forty-eighth birthday on January 2.

He'd lost weight, 15 pounds, in the past month or so, and he felt lethargic. He had chalked it up to overwork at the hospital, to the chemotherapy's lingering effects, to his working overtime starting up a new clinic, to anything but what he probably knew deep inside. Finally he relented, told his oncologist friend that there was something wrong and that maybe they should do a bone scan.

The news was about as bad as it could be, but his oncologist still offered more chemo, more radiation, a small hope they could at least pro-long his life. Bob knew, he told me, that he couldn't do that, there was nothing to do. It was a damned shame, he said, but he was dying. Stark as that. I just cried.

I wanted to catch the next plane out, but Bob said he and Renda were heading off in the Winnebago to the Southwest for a little while. They needed to make a pilgrimage down there, seeking the desert land-scape of consolation and despair.

I hung up. Kolya saw that I had been crying and I called him into my arms. "Uncle Bob is dying," I told him, and we held each other and cried. Suddenly I was sad not for Bob, but for Kolya. He and Bob had something special, and now Kolya would lose his uncle, too. It all seemed so insufferably unfair, wrong, screwed up. We sat immobilized on the couch, our tears mingling on each other's cheeks and rolling down until our T-shirts were wet.

For the next few weeks, my parents and I, Stevie and I, called each other, begging for news. Bob and Renda were in Arizona, they were in Utah. Bob was sinking fast, they said. He fell down in the RV's shower; he couldn't focus with both eyes and had to wear a patch. We fretted that the two of them would drive the F–350 off a mesa top. I tried to imagine what it would be like if I never saw him again. It was unthinkable.

It is still unthinkable.

After two weeks, Bob and Renda decided it was too hard; they would head home. On the way, the Winnebago broke down. They lost a wheel while driving on the highway and could have easily died that way. Renda had to do all the driving toward the end because Bob couldn't function well with one eye. They bought him a cane, and he had taken short walks in the red rock canyon country he had always wanted to visit. The picture that the kids and I gathered around before the trip had been taken in Canyonlands. He was leaning against his wooden staff and staring at death with a grim smile.

When they called to say they were coming home, I immediately made arrangements to go out there with the kids, taking them out of school to be with their uncle, with their extended family. Ever since the divorce, I had reinforced for them the depth of their connection to my family, our Russian-Jewish immigrant clan that only survived in the New World because they stuck together. My paternal grandmother Genia, the oldest of five orphaned siblings at fourteen, had brought her brothers and sisters to New York by the graces of an uncle who had already emigrated. Family was everything; support, survival, succor.

Damn Rebecca for throwing that away.

In a residual fit of anger that swept over me in a Kathmandu bed, I blamed her for Bob's cancer, for beginning to unravel my life, our children's lives. Then I laughed through my tears. So much for my beautiful Bangkok dream about moving on, I chided myself. Then again, nobody ever said healing was a linear process.

*

The main Hindu holiday of Desain would begin soon, and Nepal, the only officially Hindu nation in the world, takes the holiday very seriously. Keith and Shakun planned to travel to Cambodia to meet Scott in Siem Reap and visit Angkor Wat. Before they left, baby Leah had a red-letter date in the Nepali life calendar to commemorate. According to the Hindu *Dharma-satra*, every individual must pass through many *samskaras*, or ritual passages—beginning the moment of conception *(garbha-dhana)* and continuing until death *(antyesti)*.

Leah, approaching her six-month mark, was about to mark her *annaprasana*, her rice-feeding ceremony, her first solid food. Shakun consulted with monks and chose an auspicious day for the ritual. On that day, Leah would be fed *khir,* rice boiled with milk, with a golden ring or silver spoon. Keith and Shakun, who is Thakali, an ethnic group from the mountains of central Nepal, like to joke that they may have the only Jewish-Thakali children in the history of mankind. *Jewkalis,* they joke. It is possible.

Keith and I headed down to the Buddhist temple (called a *stupa*) of Bodinath to have lunch, catching up and assessing world affairs while Buddha's painted eyes stared knowingly from the four sides of the stupa. We sat at an outdoor terrace overlooking the prayer flags and the pilgrims, the souvenir shoppers and the Tibetan merchants. Tory had once lived near Bodinath, studying Buddhism, just before her marriage disintegrated. She had asked me to say hello to the temple on this trip, and I did, pressing my hands together and bowing slightly to the flapping prayer flags. As I made this simple gesture, I imagined her blue-green-eyed smile and missed her.

I purchased bus tickets that would take us on a triangle through several of Nepal's top tourist highlights. First stop would be the lakeside city of Pokhara 120 miles west of Kathmandu in the shadow of the Annapurna Range. Then we'd head to Chitwan National Park in the south, where we would conclude our quartet of environmental case studies with a look at how the Bengal tiger was faring after decades of concerted tiger conservation efforts—and more than a century of even more concerted tiger killing.

RAKSHI ON THE ROYAL TREK

LEAVING KATHMANDU, the bus inched along the choked main artery that links the capital with Nepal's most popular trekking region. Unfazed by the slow pace, the kids settled into the mere six-hour bus ride as if we were driving 45 minutes to downtown Denver. The road had been improved markedly since Keith, Rebecca, and I rode motorcycles along this same route to Pokhara, and I recounted the story of our "motorcycle trek." I wondered if it was difficult for them to hear about happier times for their mama and papa. I intuitively felt it was better to talk about her than to pretend I didn't think about her. At certain times, like at that moment when I was literally retracing a path Rebecca and I had taken together during our extended honeymoon, it would have been hard to pretend. It was important to allow the memories to wash over me, to let the kids know they were born into a union of love, no matter how incongruous that notion may have seemed since their mom moved away.

After a few hours, we stopped for a snack at a roadside hotel. Lunch, part of the bus ticket package, consisted of stale egg salad sandwiches and cold fried potatoes, which elicited memorable grimaces of disgust from Kolya. I sagely advised the kids that this was the kind of day when you eat when you can eat, and we choked down the uninspired fare.

The bus driver announced, in fractured English, that we should meet at the bus in 45 minutes; people going to Pokhara should stay on the same bus, and people going to Chitwan should change to another bus. A Japanese woman at the next table looked completely lost after the announcement. I asked if she had understood. *Wakarimashita-ka?*

Zen-zen wakaranai, she replied—not a word. So I explained in pidgin Japanese what the driver had said, and she thanked me without the obligatory astonishment that most Japanese people display when a foreigner speaks their language. Kolya and Zoe, who had never heard me speak Japanese, looked more shocked than the woman. I have noticed that the kids actually take pride in their dad when he speaks other languages, which is touching since most of the time they think I'm a complete dweeb.

During my years on the road, I had learned, in descending order of fluency, a number of languages: French, Spanish, Japanese, Dutch, German—and a smattering of Nepali, Italian, Russian, and Chinese. For the most part, we're talking about survival linguistics: Where is the train station, the bathroom, how much is it, thank you, etc. But I can still tell our basic story in a few different tongues, and on the trip I had conversations in various languages that certainly must have sounded more fluent to the kids than they did to the people I was conversing with.

To my joy and surprise, the two of them had taken an interest in languages along the way, and we continued with the rudiments of Nepali there on the bus: *Namaste,* easy, hello and goodbye, coupled with placing the palms together, the nicest greeting in the world, "I salute the God within you." They've learned "thank you," "my name is," "this is delicious," nouns like *chiya* (milk tea), *pani* (water), and *chini* (sugar).

On the bus we were working on a bonus addition to Namaste. In Nepali, I explain, it is customary to greet people with a word that shows respect for your age difference. If a man is older than you, you call him older brother, or *dhai*. If he is younger you call him *bhai*. The words for older and younger sister are *didi* and *bahini*, respectively. And for much older men and women, *ji* and *aama* are grandfather and grandmother. I knew that if the kids had these greetings memorized, their tiny effort would be repaid with appreciative smiles.

We arrived in Pokhara in the late afternoon, and the bus summarily dumped us off in a vacant lot a few miles from the closest hotel. Predictably, we found ourselves surrounded by touts and taxi drivers, and since I had no guidebook and didn't remember much from the last time I was here, we had to wing it. We listened nonchalantly to the touts and found one with a low-key spiel we liked: "I will take you to my hotel, and if you do not like it, I will take you anywhere you like." We climbed into his battered Toyota, he drove us to his guest house, we liked. After we chose our room, he served us chiya and proposed treks for us.

When Rebecca and I had trekked before in the Everest region, we headed off for seven weeks without guides or porters. Now, since the kids had proven their mettle at Mt. Agung and on the Hinchinbrook backpack, I figured we could do a short trek on our own here as well. The Annapurna region is the most trekked part of Nepal, and since we only had about four days we wouldn't be getting into the high country of the Annapurna Sanctuary. But hiring a porter to help lighten Zoe's load could be a good idea, and we would widen our options by taking a guide.

The hotel owner said that if we wanted to go on what he called "the apple pie" trek, where everybody went, we might not need porters or a guide. Whatever the apple pie trek was, Kolya immediately liked the sound of it. What it meant was the most well-worn tourist path, with rows of teashops and little lodges catering to trekkers. It also meant being with other foreigners along the trail. The "apple pie" appellation derived from the fact that this was an apple-growing region, and every lodge had learned to cater to Western palates with passable pastries.

Despite Kolya's sudden enthusiasm for pie, I was much less keen on the idea. Instead, I perked up when the hotel owner offered the possibility of a much-less-traveled trek. Dubbed the "Royal Trek" because Prince Charles had once walked the four-day loop (with an entourage of ninety), it promised the classic middle hills scenery, stays in small villages, and great views of the Annapurna and the Manaslu-Himalchuli peaks, if the clouds ever parted—without requiring us to climb above 7,000 feet ourselves.

Zoe thought it sounded great, especially the royal part.

Kolya stuck to the apple pie trek.

Ultimately, I decided to follow Prince Charles's (and, apparently, Mick Jagger's) footsteps. Neither of these famous trekkers impressed Kolya sufficiently to keep him from a virulent sulk when I informed him that I had engaged the services of a porter and a guide (the latter was the hotelier's brother) for the Royal Trek. The prospect of hiking with very little weight on his back did not assuage him, and he remained adamant that the apple pie trek would be infinitely better.

Late that evening we met the two young men with whom we would share the next four days. Since our hotelier spoke impeccable English, we were a little taken aback to realize that our porter spoke very little and our guide only a bit more. We planned to leave the next morning for a short jeep ride to the end of the road and the beginning of the trail.

We followed a ridge east through villages and farmlands and started the trek by fording a river and climbing steeply out of the river valley. We passed villagers working the terraced rice fields near harvest time, the men carrying huge loads on their backs in traditional *doko,* or carrying baskets. Despite the muggy day and the initial steep climb, Zoe was in good spirits, chattering away.

Kolya sulked, although he was cheered a little by the stash of *mitai*, or Nepali sweets, that we had purchased for the trek. As we passed through small Gurung and Chettri villages and were swarmed by the local children obviously intrigued by their Western counterparts, I heard Kolya responding to a little girl's greetings of "hello" with his own: *Namaste, bahini*. Greetings, little Nepali sister.

We arrived at the Shanti Maidan Guest House in the village of Kalikastan. Two dirt floor rooms awaited us on the second story, up a rickety and uneven wooden stairway. Inside each room we found two reasonably comfortable twin beds. Though the lighting consisted of single bare light bulbs, the kids announced that the rooms compared favorably to our accommodations at the Crack Hotel of Kumai, until they saw the toilet, or *charpi*. It was located down the wooden stairs, down a dank mud-packed hallway, down stone stairs, and in a small outhouse that was no more than a hole in a dirt floor with a jug of water next to it. A big dipper.

Zoe visited the toilet first, then reported breathlessly to Kolya. He vowed that he hadn't used a big dipper yet, wasn't planning on starting now, and patted his pocket, which he had filled with toilet paper.

An accommodating couple with three young children ran the guest house, and the woman prepared lunch for us as we lounged around a wooden table drinking well-deserved sodas. We saw no menu and no apple pie, but we were soon served an enormous silver platter full of *dahl-baat*, rice and lentils, the ubiquitous Nepali national food. I showed the kids how to scoop up handfuls of rice and lentils with their right hands.

Thankfully, blessedly, the kids not only ate it but *loved* it. Each place we would eat along the way prepared its own version of curried potatoes or spinach and pickled vegetables as a side dish, and the Nepali tradition is that dahl-baat is all-you-can-eat. As soon as our plates were empty, the didi brought more—and after a full day of hiking we were fully prepared to clean a second plate.

Zoe disappeared into the kitchen with the didi to help make

chiya, and the four of us boys hung out and exchanged pleasantries with a few of the local men. Just before sunset, Kolya and I walked up to a little overlook, where we caught sight of Machhapuchhare, a diamond-cut 22,940-foot peak. Its imposing presence reassured us of our exquisite insignificance, and I stood behind my son with my arms draped over his shoulders and planted a kiss on his ear.

We walked through rhododendron and sal forests, rising and falling with the trails. I honestly hadn't known what to expect from the kids, but they seemed impressed with the fact that we hadn't seen another westerner since we'd left Pokhara and that we were having a pretty authentic Nepali experience. Even Kolya allowed that this was turning out to be okay, and the two of them added *kasto chha?* (how are you?) and *ramro chha* (very well!) to their Nepali vocabulary, exchanging greetings on the trail as we passed through villages. After about six hours of walking, we came to a village called Lipyani. Our guest quarters were similar to the previous night's, as was the big dipper and the dahl-baat.

The next morning we awoke to the hubbub of a gathering just below our balcony. The rumor was that four buses had been burned near Pokhara, possibly lit by Maoist rebels. Our guides worried that we wouldn't be able to return to Pokhara on the local bus at the end of the trail, and the kids looked to me to see how worried we should be. It was hard to know, and in any case we couldn't do anything about it. Ke garne? We'll see.

We fell into a comfortable routine on our third day, and I wished we could go on like this for weeks. Kolya and I hit a side-by-side stride, touching hands occasionally, and he started a conversation with the familiar, "So, Dad...." This time he wanted to know about China and Tibet, Mao Tse Tung and the Nepali Maoists. What did they want, exactly?

I gave him a broad-brush explanation of how in Nepal, the royal family has controlled much of the foreign aid and tourist dollars through a system of patronage and corruption. The Maoists want to overthrow the monarchy, attempt a redistribution of wealth, and establish a central government controlled by "the people." Although it sounded altruistic, I reminded him that we'd talked a little about what had happened in Cambodia during the Pol Pot era and the excesses of the Communist Party in China during the Cultural Revolution. The Nepali Maoists displayed the same myopic revolutionary fervor and violence. Still, as he had heard me rail before, the gap between the rich and the poor, even in our own country, aches like an embedded splinter infecting human societies.

He changed the subject. Was I worried about getting back to Pokhara?

I told him I didn't think it was in anybody's best interest to harm tourists. I thought we'd be okay.

We walked and talked, telling stories of our past, of me and Momma, of Grandma and Grandpa, of Uncle Bob and Uncle Steve. It occurred to me, as I thought about how the news of the bus burnings in Pokhara had arrived at Lipyani, that Nepal was still a culture where the oral tradition survived, where until very recently, news traveled from mouth to ear. Sure, we heard crackly battery-powered radios along the way, but rural Nepal is barely inching into the twentieth century, much less the twenty-first. How different it all was for Kolya, born into an age of Instant Messaging and Napster and Kazaa and a thousand cable television networks.

We stopped to rest under a shady tree. Zoe headed off to the side of the trail to pee. In less than a minute, she emerged screaming, pulling her pants up and scurrying toward us.

"What's up, Zoe?" I asked, rising in fear that she'd been bitten by a snake or something. It turned out to be something a little less life threatening.

In Nepal we went on a trek it was very fun but there were leechise. I went to go pee in the bush one day and I got a leech on me. I said holy shit get this slimy blood sucking viper off me.

My dad and brother looked at me like I was a goldfish that was breathing air. I said get it of get it off then my dad said you just flick it off. My brother started giggling then I finally flicked it of and jumped back into the trail scraming.

We arrived in mid-afternoon in the village of Chisopani, which means "cold water." The lodge here was much nicer; there was even a shower. In the courtyard, a man made *rakshi,* rice wine, by boiling a large pot full of rice, and he promised that in the evening we'd have a tasting. Zoe disappeared into the kitchen to help with the cooking.

Kolya and Zoe later spotted an eight-foot-high marijuana plant growing in the courtyard by the guest house and giggled over their discovery for awhile. Zoe walked me to a sign at the edge of the property warning visitors in English not to wander away from the compound at night, since tigers were known to roam the area.

It's not a joke, I told her.

She nodded vigorously to show me she understood.

As we ate our evening dahl-baat, a vessel filled with rakshi appeared on the table as promised, along with *chang,* Tibetan-style beer made out of barley. I much preferred the rakshi, our Nepali friends preferred chang, and we each proceeded to elevate our spirits with our spirit of choice. Rakshi and chang are both low-octane beverages, but after a few glasses we were singing and the kids looked on curiously as their dad and the two Nepali men who had been our constant companions for three days became increasingly lit. The warm night filled with moonlight and Zoe flitted back and forth to the kitchen, helping the didi. We brought Kolya to the outskirts of manhood with sips of rakshi. Zoe returned to sit on my lap as we embraced this perfect moment, candles flickering in the night breeze and illuminating our smiles.

As we hiked out the next day, we breathed relief when we came to the road and saw buses waiting. We hopped on, and after a brief conversation with the bus driver, our guide reassured us that in less than an hour, we would be back "home" again in our Pokhara hotel. Kolya, in an act of graciousness, allowed that he actually had a great trek despite the paucity of apple pie, and Zoe concurred.

The next morning we boarded a bus for Chitwan, changed buses at the same place with the stale egg salad sandwiches, and descended in a southerly direction toward the Terai, the Gangeatic plains of southern Nepal. Our destination was the town of Sauraha on the border of Chitwan National Park, where the kids would, among other things, have their first elephant bath, see their first rhinoceros, and trek through the jungle in search of tigers.

DEMISE OF THE TIGER?

IN THE PANTHEON of earth's creatures, *Panthera tigris* holds a particularly strong hold on the human psyche. "The historical record overwhelmingly favors the view that the tiger was mankind's most implacable enemy," wrote the Dutch scholar Peter Boomgaard in his book *Frontiers of Fear: Tigers and People in the Malay World, 1600–1950* (2001). From a tiger's point of view, I'd imagine the feeling is entirely mutual.

If humans fear tigers, we have also revered, worshiped, and admired them for their stealth, beauty, and astounding strength. Tigers are the largest of the cat family Felidae, and until just 100 years ago there may have been as many as 100,000 of them roaming over much of Asia—from Siberia to the tip of India and from eastern Turkey to southern China. Since 1900, the number of tigers, and, not coincidentally, the amount of tiger habitat, has declined by nearly 95 percent worldwide, and the number of surviving tiger species has dropped from eight to five. With few exceptions, the tiger's trend lines point in a desperately downward direction.

Because of the majesty implied in their singular place atop the food chain—nothing eats the tiger—these large cats have been prized for centuries for the supposed medicinal properties of their bones and internal organs. To this day, tiger bones are crushed and sold for exorbitant prices and are treasured, especially in Chinese medicine, as an ingredient of tonics or wine taken as a hedge against lagging male potency and energy. Tiger pelts adorn the floors and walls of the wealthy and powerful, perhaps an even more totemic statement of authority these days than in the past, since trade in tiger parts is illegal across much of the globe.

Like most top predators, tigers need something that modern civilization holds at a premium: large tracts of undeveloped land, ecosystems as varied as the northern Russian forests, or *taiga,* and the jungles of the subcontinent, where tigers furtively make their living like ghosts. A single male tiger may lay claim to up to 40 square miles of terrain, and females up to 15 square miles, preying primarily on ungulates such as wild deer; wild cattle such as gaur or water buffalo; or wild boar. And occasionally, a human as well.

The Bengal tiger, which can grow to nearly 10 feet long from head to tail and weigh more than 450 pounds, has long been the preferred target of Indian royalty and Western trophy hunters as well as black-market trappers for the lucrative Chinese medicine trade. Once estimated to roam much of the subcontinent in the tens of thousands, in this century the Bengal tiger's numbers and range have dropped precipitously. There are probably between 3,000 and 5,000 wild Bengal tigers, most of them in India, with a smattering remaining in Nepal, Bangladesh, Bhutan, and Myanmar. The Bali, Caspian, and Javan tigers are true ghost hunters—each of these species became extinct, respectively, in the 1940s, 1970s, and 1980s.

In the late 1960s and early 1970s, world conservation groups began sounding the alarm that additional tiger species were on their way to an accelerated extinction, even as the Caspian and Javan tigers were about to disappear. Since that time, a number of conservation programs have emerged that have enjoyed marginal success at restoring tiger populations.

One place where these programs have shown moderate success is in the Terai, or southern plains of Nepal. A glimmer of hope remains for these magnificent beasts and for the other animals that share this place on earth with them.

The bus dropped the three of us off in an empty field, and we once again picked the young man with the best sales pitch: a free ride to the town of Sauraha in his open-air jeep as long as we looked at his hotel first. The proffered accommodations were more than acceptable, and we settled in to our large room overlooking the Rapti River that constituted the border between the town and Chitwan National Park.

What a difference a decade and a half makes. The last time I was here with Rebecca, to celebrate Christmas in 1984, Sauraha's tourist amenities were at their most basic: a smattering of travelers' hotels; two or three curio shops, and scattered come-ons in bad English to go for elephant rides or to stay in the vaunted (and expensive) Tiger Tops Lodge inside the park. In 2001, Sauraha was packed with upgraded versions of all of the above. Every storefront advertised jungle tours, elephant rides, and river trips. The dirt streets offered the unusual sight of an elephant rush hour, with and without tourists aboard. Ecotourism in all its promise and disturbing hues.

The area now called Royal Chitwan National Park had long been treated as a well-guarded hunting preserve for the Nepali Rana rulers, off-limits to the people the way English forests were closed to the hoi polloi in the times when English lords hired surly gamekeepers to keep them away. In classic raj-era fashion, huge hunting parties consisting of Nepali and foreign royalty were invited to Chitwan for what amounted to exotic target practice. Low-caste "beat-ers" would flush the game into the sights of the shooters. King George V came to Nepal in 1911 and, with his entourage, killed 39 tigers. In 1939, the tradition ended after the British viceroy took part in an enormous hunting party that killed 120 tigers, 38 rhinos, 27 leopards, and 15 sloth bears. Described as the last great Chitwan hunt, it's unclear whether people grew disgusted with the sheer excess of the viceroy's party, or if the advent of World War II and disillusionment with the British raj contributed to the end of such profligate killing.

In any case, Chitwan became the Mahendra Deer Park in 1959, a private hunting reserve of the late King Mahendra and his friends. Four years later, in 1963, the area south of the Rapti River was set aside as a national rhinoceros sanctuary.

In 1973, His Majesty's Government of Nepal declared the land as Royal Chitwan National Park. The park served to diversify the draw of tourist dollars into the Kingdom of Nepal as well as nomi-nally protecting the species-rich area from development. Instead of merely appealing to hippies headed for Kathmandu's Freak Street and the throngs of trekkers bound for the high peaks of Everest, Nepal could now boast the prospect of seeing tigers and rhinos in the wild. Eleven years later, UNESCO declared the park a World Heritage Site.

The region known as the Terai sits on the northern edge of the Gangeatic plains, and its lushness provided a magnet for popula-tion growth in the country after massive government-sponsored DDT spraying in the 1960s eliminated malaria from the region. Bordering populous India to the south, the Terai was quickly being stripped of its forests as population soared and newcomers cleared the forests for mustard plantations and scoured the woods for firewood and other sources of income—such as rhino horn and tiger bones. Chitwan National Park, though nominally a sanctuary, was routinely overrun by poachers and poor villagers who (like their Vietnamese counterparts surrounding Nam Cat Tien National

Park) saw the protected area more as a convenience store than a conservation showcase. The fact that His Majesty's government, meaning the royal family and entourage, reaped virtually all the profits from Chitwan's tourist trade didn't exactly endear the idea of the park to the locals.

In the 1980s, conservation biologists warned that if the park and surrounding areas weren't better protected, the tiger wouldn't survive. In response, the Nepali government, in concert with international aid organizations, began what came to be known as the community forest movement.

In areas around the park that had been virtually denuded, the Nepali government paid for local communities to replant and manage their own forests of native rosewood and acacia. In 1996, the government created a 750-square-kilometer buffer zone around the park—about two-thirds the size of the park itself. It contained both private land and government-owned forests. The idea was to allow local communities to manage the lands and to reap the benefits—and profits. In turn, wildlife habitat would expand and the park itself would be better protected.

Over time, the replanted forests grew enough to be selectively harvested and managed by local councils. Villages surrounding the forests identified individuals who were allowed to gather firewood, livestock fodder, and thatch for housing, to hunt, and to create tourist enterprises on these community forests. The income was to be recycled back into the communities. Despite predictable problems such as corruption and nepotism, the community forest system represented an improvement. Locals saw that the additional income resulted in tangible results, including health clinics and new schools.

Miraculously, the habitat range for animals like the rhino increased, and so did their numbers. Locals began giving their own "jungle tours" away from the government-held monopoly inside the park, and the tourist dollars poured in. The rhinoceros population increased to the point where government biologists actually transplanted Chitwan rhinos to the Bardia National Park west of Chitwan in order to augment shrinking populations there. Tiger populations suffered from a rash of poaching in the early 1990s, but by most accounts, tiger populations have held relatively steady since then, especially compared to nonprotected areas around Asia, where their numbers continue to decline precipitously.

The program began gaining supporters, especially when the locals could begin exercising their exclusive rights to take forage and fuel from the forests. This conservation program reached into the surrounding communities, providing villagers with alternative fuels, such as kerosene, and offering small loans to local women to help them start their own businesses—bee-keeping, for example, to sell honey to tourists. The government agreed to give 30 percent of the income from Chitwan back to the local communities. Whether the officials kept their word is unclear, but there's no doubt that local programs for the Tharu ethnic group helped to ease the strain on the park's resources.

Here, more than in many places, the promise of ecotourism is evident as the economic largesse strewn in its wake is used to restore and sustain natural systems.

The last item on the kids' pretrip wish list was to ride on an elephant, topping the list of scuba diving, surfing, letting Kolya drive, and eating Vietnamese food in Vietnam. This was certainly the place to do it. We arranged with our hotel manager for an elephant to pick us up for a dusk walk as easily as if I had asked the concierge at the Regent Hotel to have a cab ready to take us to the airport.

As we ate lunch, we saw a curious and amazing sight from our perch on the hotel deck overlooking the Rapti River from the edge of the floodplain. A half-dozen *mahouts,* or elephant-trainers, led their charges to the river. Our hotel manager told us that if we went down with a few rupees, the mahouts would let the kids climb on for an elephant bath.

Kolya was reluctant; Zoe couldn't wait. The mahout smiled and invited them aboard, commanding his *haathi* to kneel in the secret language known only to a mahout and his lifelong elephant partner. The kids climbed on, and the mahout commanded the elephant to fill his trunk with water and spray the kids, which the elephant did.

They squealed with laughter and I snapped a picture: Zoe, in her purple sarong, is sitting behind Kolya on the elephant, grasping his waist with both hands, her legs tucked behind her. They have just been sprayed by the elephant's trunk and are soaking wet and belly-laughing with pleasure. Kolya's head is tilted toward the camera. He is shirtless, his hands on the elephant's back and face in a broad grin. It is the most endearing, revealing, and indelible image of the entire trip.

Late that afternoon, "our" mahout, a dark-skinned Tharu man who spoke perhaps three or four words of English, arrived for our jungle walk. We mounted the haathi from a platform and stepped onto the wooden elephant saddle. With an outburst of grunts, the mahout convinced the elephant to trudge through the village and into the bush. The wooden saddle chafed our legs, and the elephant's plodding gait exacerbated the discomfort.

We passed the border of the Baghmara Community Forest after about half an hour and paid our entry fee, which would in theory support the village's health and welfare programs. Then we plodded toward the river and through the tall grass in the slanting afternoon light. Suddenly we heard a rustling in the grass and the mahout turned us toward the noise. We saw our quarry entering a mud wallow: two rhinos, a male and a female, looking perfectly prehistoric in this southern Nepali jungle. There they were, wallowing, and there we were, gawking. And smiling. Make that impulsively, irrepressibly grinning.

Humans have always had a complicated relationship with animals like tigers that treat *Homo sapiens* as prey. Large predators bring out a curious savagery in humans that is understandably born of an instinct for self-preservation. Over time, however, that well-placed instinct transformed into something more complex and even perverse. Comprehending the reasons for that transformation may be the key to these animals' continued survival.

Throughout human history, humans have tracked, pursued, and hunted nonhuman "beasts," sometimes for self-preservation or sustenance but more often for the medicinal or symbolic usefulness of these carnivores' pelts, teeth, claws, and even internal organs. Animal predators have captured the human imagination with legends in every culture that hosts an animal capable of killing humans. (How *did* the tiger get its stripes, which are, by the way, as unique as human fingerprints?) In certain cultures, adolescent boys must successfully hunt a large predator to finish the rite of passage into manhood. Conversely, being killed by a lion, tiger, wolf, or bear remains a source of timeless, mythic fear to this day in every culture that coexists with these predators.

In modern times, certainly since the invention of accurate firearms, it's clear that these "beasts" have evoked something even more mysterious and complicated and even paradoxical in us. As the need to kill for self-protection or for winter coats declined as humans urbanized, other, more perplexing motives came to the fore. Greed, of course, is hardly an enigmatic motive, and many of these animals have huge prices on their heads. But killing for sport or with the avowed goal of wiping an animal out with extreme prejudice—therein we unleash our darker shadows. Large predators, in particular—big cats such as lions and tigers, wolves, sharks, grizzly bears—have learned how cunning and violent humans can be. Like soldiers who have faced each other in battle, they seem to understand that humans can be unfathomably vicious.

Just ask the wolf. It is not merely the fear of our children or our livestock being carried away by a *Canis lupus* that prompted the wholesale eradication of that species from many parts of the American West—through techniques that can only be described as torture. The brutality and single-mindedness unleashed on the wolf (and the grizzly bear and the cougar) in our own history suggests that the power to *tame* the wild, once we thought we could do it, became an obsession.

We're now discovering, at least some of us are, that there is something archetypal and *necessary* about wildness. In the time it has taken us to exterminate 95 percent of the tigers on this planet, we have shifted from a predominantly rural and agrarian society to one that is urban and mechanized. In the emerging field of evolutionary psychology, it's becoming clear that the shift happened too fast; we are reeling from the unintended consequences of insulating ourselves so quickly from the cycles of the natural world. For tens of thousands of years, the seasons and the lunar orbit charted our lives and our psyches; we now live in climate-controlled comfort in cities whose light drowns out the stars and the moon. We work night shifts under fluorescent lights, travel casually across time zones, and defiantly treat the rhythms of the millennia as if they really didn't matter.

As these carnivores have been exterminated, whether in the name of commerce or for public safety, some humans have sounded the alarm. For biological as well as psychological reasons, we run a fantastic risk if we eliminate all the other animals that share the top of the food chain with us. Conservation biologists warn about losing "indicator species" that hold large ecosystems intact in ways we can only begin to explain. Social scientists insist that it is not simply bunny-hugging sentimentality that pushed us to bring back the wolf in a government-sponsored reintroduction program to places like Yellowstone National Park. Perhaps, they argue, these animals remind us humans of our predator selves, lost in the aisles of grocery markets and digitized existence. We may *need* to have tigers and grizzly bears walking the earth with us to maintain our collective sanity. As we reexamine our relationship to the wild, which was such a huge influence on developing our collective psyches, how we treat our most fearsome bestial foes may hold the key to how—or whether—we ourselves survive as a species.

If these stalked creatures know a collective fear, these days it is for their very existence. From the Bengal tiger's haunts in the mangrove swamps of the Sunderbans in India to the grizzly country amidst the ponderosa pine forests in the Bitterroot Valley of Montana, large carnivores cling to a precarious ledge of existence. It is possible that we need them more than we know, if only to remind us of the humble lessons we learned when we understood that we, too, were considered prey.

Interestingly, it may be the people who live among the tiger, even in fear of it, who may supply the key to the tiger's survival. *Smithsonian* magazine reported that after several "man-eating" tiger attacks outside Chitwan that must have occurred just after our visit, field workers from the King Mahendra Trust for Nature Conservation interviewed people who live in the area about whether the tiger in question should have been killed or "rehabilitated." The tiger had fatally mauled somebody who had strayed from their village. Nearby resident Surya Prasad told the interviewers: "If the tiger had come to our home and killed us, it would be appropriate to kill the tiger, but since that's not the case, it would not be appropriate."

I arranged for a daylong jungle walk inside Chitwan National Park, a chance to possibly see a tiger as well as more rhinos and other animals. We engaged the services of Akash and Baba Ram, two slight young men of gentle disposition and eagle eyes. Akash grew up in an area inside the park and seemed to know every sound, every paw print, every piece of life in the area. We left before dawn for an hour-long jeep ride through the morning fog to where we would begin our trek.

On the way, Akash pointed out eagles, herons, storks, parakeets, crocodiles, a mongoose, orioles, sparrows, and more as we clung to the bars of the open-air jeep. We arrived at the park entrance, crossed the river in a deep, dugout canoe, and began walking as the day warmed. I asked Akash what he thought about the community forest program. He had a generally good impression but knew that it wouldn't stop poaching. "If you kill a rhino and sell the horn," Akash says, "it's enough to live for one lifetime."

As we walked, Akash pointed out sloth bear tracks, discoursed on how recent the rhino spoor was, and picked out camouflaged animals from thickets of brush. The tracks were of minor interest to the kids, who became a little restless.

"Tell us about the time you and Mama got chased by a rhino," Zoe prodded, trying to distract herself. The kids know this story, it's practically a fable. "When Mama ran away and tried to climb a tree."

It's a favorite story of mine as well. Rebecca and I were six months into our Asian honeymoon. We had met up with old friends and new ones in Chitwan to celebrate Christmas. Rebecca and I, joined by our friend Sophie on a "jungle walk," hired a five-foot-tall Nepali man to guide us along the dangerous footpaths. We were armed only with a telephoto lens (in my case) and a stout walking stick from a tropical hardwood tree (the guide's).

Suddenly we heard the crashing of an enormous animal, and in a moment we glimpsed a rhino thundering down the path straight for us. Our guide thwacked his stick against a tree, screaming at the rhino a loud "Ha!" The rhino didn't slow and I stood directly behind our guide holding my camera in my hands, too paralyzed either to take a picture or to run. He repeated his thwack and his "Ha!" and the rhino charged to within 25 yards of us, then suddenly veered off the trail into the thick underbrush. Our guide turned to me with a satisfied grin, knowing he had earned a monstrous tip. I turned to Rebecca and Sophie, but they were nowhere to be seen. They had run back along the trail looking for a tree to climb.

"Mama was just gone, huh?" observed Kolya.

"Like I shoulda been," I replied.

"I would run and hide behind a tree because I don't think I could climb one," Zoe said.

"You'd probably just stand there and get run over," Kolya chided.

"You may have a chance to see for yourself, Mr. Brave Guy," I added. And we continued trekking.

We were probably walking a path similar to the one that their mom and I had padded down a lifetime ago. "They say that a tiger is one hundred times more likely to spot you than you are to lay eyes on a tiger," I mentioned casually, playing up the tension. "So keep your wits sharp, you two. And if anything happens, listen to Akash." Akash led the way and Baba Ram brought up the rear. Kolya and Zoe suddenly began paying attention to every rustle in the bush.

I began wondering, meanwhile, about the protocol for dealing with a tiger that you run into on foot. I knew from my backcountry wanderings that if you cross paths with a mountain lion, you're supposed to make noise and appear very big and threatening. But I had no idea what to do with a tiger. Except pray that they won't attack five humans at once.

We passed another sloth bear track, mounds of steaming rhino shit, and very fresh rhino prints, which were much bigger here on the ground than they seemed from the back of an elephant.

The kids became a little more interested.

Ahead, Akash bent over and beckoned to us. In the mud, we observed a tiger pug mark, a footprint almost as long as Zoe's, and we huddled around it. Then we cautiously peered in all directions, a little bit spooked. If a tiger were there, Akash said, it probably wouldn't bother us, but none of us should wander off alone.

We continued, a little more closely bunched now, and I was satisfied with the pug mark sighting, taking a lesson from Peter Matthiessen's *The Snow Leopard* (1978). In the book, Matthiessen spends months trekking through remote mountain terrain in Nepal in order to glimpse the elusive snow leopard, but he never sees one. He decides in the end that *not* seeing the cat may have been the point.

For us, here in Chitwan, simply feeling the hair-on-the-back-of-the-head sensation of momentarily being prey was lesson enough.

After the paw print sighting, the shadows had already lengthened and we still had a long walk back to the river and the jeep. I put Zoe on my shoulders and she chattered away, until Akash interrupted our conversation with a gesture to be quiet. He heard, as did we, a rustling in the tall grass that was probably a rhino. Thrill matched fear as I once again realized we were on foot in the middle of a jungle, with nothing but our guide's stout walking stick to protect us.

Two elephants appeared with tourists aboard, stalking the same rhino. Akash signaled the mahouts to circle around and flush out the rhinos. We all ran back and forth—half in pursuit of and half in flight from the thundering noises emanating from the tall grass.

We heard the crashing of the rhinos before we saw two of them appear 25 yards ahead of us. Thankfully, the mother and baby crossed the path and headed directly into the thicket on the other side of the trail. Kolya, Zoe, and I, our hearts beating, looked at each other with unabashed wonder.

We arrived back at the river as the sun set, crossed in a dugout canoe, chugged a soda, liberated our feet from our sandy shoes, and hopped in the jeep. On the way home at deep dusk, Akash spotted a silhouette by the riverbank, stopped the jeep, and beckoned for us to step out. With no time to don our shoes, we scrambled over to the riverbank and took in the sight of a dark rhino as big as a baby elephant, grazing. We stood there gaping until the rhino must have smelled us and thundered away into the underbrush.

Only then did Kolya point out that we were standing, ankle deep, in rhino droppings. And we were very happy to be there. Zoe memorialized the event:

One day in Nepal we went on sort of a safari trip. After the day was over we saw 7 crocodils, 1 mongus, 10 eagles, 3 rhinos and a spotted deer. We took a jeep in to the jungle we walked for about 3 hours then as we were driving home our driver said STOP. We all jumped out of the jeep and over on the other side was the biggest rhino in the world. It looked prehistoric. We stared at it for a minit or 2 then it ran away.

Then Kolya sad oh yesh gross.

What? I said.

Do you know what we are standing in he said?

No.

We are barfeet in rhino shit.

I look down then screamed and ran back to the jeep.

Shopping for Ganeshes

We arrived back in Kathmandu to a much less harried scene than what we'd found at our recent bus terminals: Keith met us and took us home without any negotiations. His family was leaving the next day for Cambodia, so we all shared a last dinner together. Keith and I put the kids to bed before sidling off to the living room to polish off the Glenlivet and solve the worlds' problems.

His take on environmental crises reminded me of something I'd thought about for many years: At the source of nearly every environmental crisis, if you look deep enough, are the dual demons of poverty and overpopulation.

So much of Keith's work there revolved around children's issues, but it's a short step to women's issues. Especially in the developing world, the correlation between educational attainment for women and lower birthrates, lower infant mortality, and increased economic activity is astoundingly clear. We won't be saving many tigers, he remarked, until we solve other problems. Women and children first, I guess.

The kids and I planned to go to India for a week before flying to

Europe, and I asked Keith for advice on travel options. He informed me that my notion to go overland to New Delhi via Varanasi and Agra would involve epic, bone-wearying hours in super air-conditioned buses blaring Hindi disco music. After all the bus riding we'd already done in Nepal, I made the executive decision to fly to Delhi. From there we could take a train to Agra and visit the Taj Mahal, then continue on to Varanasi if we wanted. The kids displayed uncharacteristic enthusiasm; Zoe had heard that Delhi was a clothes-shopper's paradise, and Keith recommended the Taj so highly that even Kolya wanted to see it.

It was well after midnight when I descended the brick stairs to the guest house. On the way in the dark, I tripped, fell, and heard a sickening "crack." I was certain that I'd broken my ankle and could feel it swelling immediately. Everybody was already in bed, so I figured there was nothing to do but chomp ibuprofen and wait until morning.

I slept fitfully and awakened to feel a ghoulish balloon of inflamed tissue where my ankle used to be. I could put pressure on it, however, which was encouraging. Keith offered to take me to his friend who is a doctor, but I decided to wait a few days to see how it went. He and Shakun offered the house for me to convalesce while they were away, but since they lived so far away from town we chose the convenience, if not the ambiance, of a cheap guest house in the tourist ghetto of Thamel.

As soon as we settled into our room at the Sherpa Guest House, I sent the kids to ask the Tibetan desk clerk for ice. I wrapped a bundle of it around my ankle, gobbled a Vicodin that I'd carried halfway around the world for just such an occasion, and moped. The kids worried about my sudden infirmity but manifested their concern by fighting. The three of us in our room, without their beloved MTV Asia, promised to devolve into a World Wrestling Foundation match, or maybe even the Ultimate Fighting Championships. I came up with the brilliant idea of sending the two of them into the streets of Kathmandu to shop. I asked them to scout

out a statue of the Hindu elephant god Ganesh for me and to buy Christmas presents for our family.

Ganesh is revered as the destroyer of obstacles. Just before Zoe was born, I bought Rebecca a beautiful bronze Ganesh to help her through childbirth. After Kolya's birth, Rebecca had a difficult time recovering, and I knew she fretted as Zoe's delivery grew imminent. Her Ganesh sat plumply and happily on our dresser for years until it moved to the coast after the divorce. I missed having a Ganesh around, and there in Kathmandu I decided it was time to have one around the house again.

I grilled the kids on the usual procedures: What was the name of our hotel, take the phone number, make sure they had copies of their passports, never lose sight of each other, what would you do if such and such happened. I outlined the parameters of their shopping universe—up and down the street where our hotel was, down one perpendicular street to the corner. No further. I gave them spending money and told them to go forth and shop well.

They were excited to head out on their own and seemed to enter into a rare spirit of cooperation. Zoe headed out the door at a trot, and Kolya hung back for a second, saying, "Wait for me in the lobby, Toots."

I knew what was coming. Ever since Australia, when Kolya had walked by a head shop in the laid-back surfing town of Byron Bay, he had been badgering me for permission to buy hash pipes as presents for his friends. He said he had promised to buy a friend a glass pipe, and after initially saying no I relented. Thankfully, the Australian pipe he wanted was too expensive, and I took the occasion to tick off a number of reasons why it was a bad idea—including the fact that I did not want to go through international customs in half a dozen countries toting drug paraphernalia.

Everywhere we went he kept pestering, and everywhere we went there were pipes to pester me over. We saw rows of carved wooden hash pipes for sale in Bali. Ornate opium pipes for sale in Vietnam and Cambodia. And now, Kathmandu, the mother of all counterculture curios, lay before Kolya like a no-holds-barred, no ID-required stoner heaven.

"Dad, can I *please* buy some pipes for my friends?"

"Haven't we had this discussion?"

"C'mon, Dad, if my friends are going to smoke dope, they're going to smoke dope whether or not I buy them a pipe."

It was fair enough logic, and I almost caved. But a very sane voice tried to hold the line somewhere. "Kolya, if you really want to buy a pipe for yourself and promise not to use it for its intended purpose until you're eighteen, I'll say okay to one."

He was happy but not satisfied. "Thanks. But I really want to get some for the guys. It'd be cool."

"It won't be cool if their parents find out," I shuddered.

"They won't find out." (There's an original line.)

"Let's say they do."

"My friends won't tell where they got it."

"I doubt that, Kolya."

"But nobody will find them."

"They'll find them, trust me. Buddy, don't you see that then I'm in trouble?"

"I'll tell them that I snuck it, that you didn't know."

"I couldn't lie about that, Kolya." The fact that I knew his friends' parents made discovery a distinctly uncomfortable prospect.

He resorted to begging. "Pleeeeease?"

I don't know what came over me, I really don't. But I relented with a single word. "Okay."

He actually kissed me, then he headed quickly for the door before I could change my mind. "Take care of your sister," I said, trying in a half-hearted way to link this pipe purchasing privilege with him taking more responsibility.

"I will, Pop," he replied, running down the hall.

I sighed back into my bed, ankle throbbing, and wondered about this rash and reckless way to get them out of my hair. What parent in their right mind would let a thirteen-year-old boy and a nine-year-old girl loose in Kathmandu to buy carvings of benevolent Hindu gods and soon-to-be-malevolent hash pipes?

A bad one, I told myself.

Not necessarily, I responded in my own defense. These kids can handle it. They are savvy, the place is crawling with tourists and tourist police. It's safe.

What about the hash pipe thing? How do you expect him to get the message that you really don't want him to start smoking dope yet? You already screwed things up in Australia.

Yeah, I know, I know. But hell. How often is he going to be in Kathmandu?

The two of them returned quite safe, several hours later, toting plastic bags full of small wooden carvings, prayer wheels, cheap paintings, and a bunch of hash pipes that somehow Kolya had convinced Zoe were not what they really were.

He was as happy as I'd seen him. But somewhere, I knew that letting him buy these pipes was a very bad idea that would come back at me snarling.

Despite my bad ankle, I hadn't given up on India. The next morning I limped out of bed and hailed a bicycle rickshaw to the Indian embassy, leaving the kids to their Game Boys and with permission to ply the same shopping streets.

The Indian visa process in the Nepali embassy is like a bad caricature of post-raj subcontinental bureaucracy. I spent the better part of the morning and the following morning in a succession of long lines with fellow westerners before finally emerging with the requisite passport stamps. On the way back to the Sherpa Guest House, I checked my e-mail to find a note from our friends in Switzerland whom we were planning to visit after India. Could we arrive earlier than planned? If so, they would have a long weekend free. They proposed driving together to the Italian part of Switzerland, Tessin, where a friend had offered them a house.

Italian Switzerland sounded pretty appealing after two days at the Indian embassy in Kathmandu.

I updated the kids. We put our heads together and decided to join K. C. and Kathleen and their sons Rowan and Quin a few days early. The Taj Mahal would have to wait for another trip, and I made new plans: In two days, we'd fly from Kathmandu to New Delhi to Vienna to Zurich, all part of our 'round-the-world ticket extravaganza.

The next day, our last full day in Asia, the kids showed me the shops where they'd scouted interesting Ganeshes. Kolya and Zoe had softened up the various merchants with their repeated visits, and at the first store the owner greeted me as if I were a buyer for the National Museum.

"You are their father? They are beautiful children! How is your ankle? You have been so many places! Please, have some tea."

We wheeled and dealed, purchased Ganeshes in both wood and bronze, and Kolya remembered one more kid who needed a hash pipe back home. We spent the evening with our booty scattered around our room before I figured out how to stuff it all into our backpacks and rehearsed telling the Swiss customs agents why I needed so many hash pipes. Which, thankfully, I never had to do.

That evening at sunset, I limped solo into the Kathmandu night while the kids watched *Dr. Dolittle 2* (again) on the laptop. The transformation of Thamel over the past seventeen years was jarring, especially the neon signs, which are switched on by dusk. I tried to find the little guest house where Rebecca and I had stayed, one with an enormous garden behind walls, a sanctuary in the middle of the tourist madness—but it was gone. It seemed fitting.

I gimped up to the terrace of Helena's restaurant across the street from our hotel, nursing a Singapore Sling I had picked up at the bar on the way. We'd eaten breakfast at Helena's every morning, and the staff asked me where the children were. "They're resting," I replied, and the waiters nodded sagely.

From the empty rooftop terrace, I surveyed the lights of Kathmandu. I took in the famous monkey temple Swayambunath, mystically lit on a hill to the west, where Kolya and I had climbed early in our stay. In a 360-degree circle, the lights of the Kathmandu valley glittered as gently as the lights of Thamel did garishly.

I sensed the end of the trail looming, with relief, sadness, and a profound sense that we had done something extraordinary. I allowed myself another self-congratulatory moment, reflecting on this unbelievable trip: well-paced, adventurous, exciting, warm, loving, difficult, eye-opening, educational, unforgettable. The kids and I had developed such a strong bond, despite all the bickering and fighting; we had private jokes to last forever.

Just before going out, I'd snuggled up with both of them and told them what amazing and adventurous children they'd been. I think they knew this already, sensed how this trip would change their lives, how it would change our lives together and their view of the world. Kolya remarked that before this trip, he hadn't even really known that Nepal was a country, or Indonesia for that matter. So much for the world geography unit he'd missed in school. And although it may be years before they recognize the importance of this trip, I was certain in that moment that it had opened their hearts and minds in incalculable ways.

I wondered which memories would come to the fore as we each rehashed the trip over time. I suspected that Kolya's perception of our trip would be weighted by his memories of Zoe commanding the emotional scene.

And yet, I often returned from a solo errand to find them playing a made-up game together, or surveying their loot from a shopping spree, or caught them giving each other a mutually secretive glance, hand gesture, or verbal phrase that confirmed their closeness. The trip's many wonders.

As the trip went by I feel my feelings towerd my brother are much deeper than before. I feel for the 1st time I really love him and I think it brang us closer forever. Ya sure sometimes I hate him but

I still feel really close. I know he does not feel the same way. But I just wish he would.

Zoe will always be Zoe, a human roller coaster ride inspiring me (and others) to fantastic highs. She brings a lot of everything to my life. I grinned as I thought about her parading around Kathmandu or Saigon or Ubud in her native dress, drawing smiles and invitations to sit and talk and hugs and cheek-squeezing. When she hopped in my lap and threw her arms around me and called me "my snookums," it was hard to stay mad at her. A perfectly honed survival mechanism, no doubt.

As I etched the Kathmandu skyline in my mind, I invariably, inexorably, returned to touch the deep, deep sadness about my marriage and family breaking up, about Rebecca's fateful decision to leave. When I thought about how much she would enjoy seeing the kids here, I felt so damned sad.

Then, like a twin tower of personal loss and grief, Bob's death hit me again and I realized that the end of the road, and the dedication ceremony, would bring me face to face with the reality of Bob's passing. I missed him terribly, even though for most of the years since he left home for college we had rarely seen each other more than once a year. Before he got sick, not seeing Bob for half a year felt normal, but of course nothing was normal about it now—and I was afraid to go back for the holidays and be confronted by the stark reality of his permanent absence.

With a second Singapore Sling as company, I allowed myself to be overtaken with a gin-soaked sadness, evoking Bob's memory on purpose and trying to face again the fact that when I went back, he wouldn't be there. It was still so hard to believe.

After Bob's surgery and chemotherapy but many months before he's diagnosed as terminal, we're invited to go to Puerto Vallarta with Tory's family for Thanksgiving. This is an annual ritual for her father, stepmom, siblings, niece, and nephews, so it's a big step for Tory to invite the three of us to be part of her extended family for this family holiday.

The Mexico trip is scheduled for ten days around Thanksgiving. But six weeks before the holiday, Bob receives the news he is dying and leaves on his southwestern pilgrimage with Renda. We don't know when they'll be back, if they'll be back, how long he has to live. As the Puerto Vallarta departure date approaches, I am paralyzed and don't know if we should go. It's hard to ask Bob, "Hey, do you think you're going to die soon, or can I go to Puerto Vallarta?" But he does return home and gets treatment after a harrowing trip. On the phone, he preempts the unaskable question. "Go on. Drink a margarita for me. I'll still be alive when you get back."

We compromise and go down for five days and fly back to San Francisco on Thanksgiving Day. On a whim the kids goad me to rent a red convertible Camaro. We career over the Bay Bridge in late November with the top down and the heater cranked up to full, eating corn dogs and slushies for Thanksgiving dinner at a mini-mart and blasting Kolya's CDs on the sound system so loud that people can hear us in the next lanes.

We arrive late, stay at my parents' house, and the next day I go up by myself to visit Bob, who is not up for commotion. Bob greets me at his door, admires the convertible, and tells me that he's never actually ridden in one.

The change even in the past few weeks is noticeable. He has lost weight, is still wearing an eye patch because a tumor is messing with his sight center, and is a little more unsteady on his feet.

He can still take walks, and we follow his routine of walking a mile up and a mile back on a trail that leaves from his front yard. It's a fine November day, and although he uses a walking stick there's a bizarre air of normalcy to our conversation on the way to the halfway mark, one mile away.

On the way back, Bob says that he always knew that he would die young, but he didn't figure it would be this young. He has already had so many near-misses. A few years back, he discovered he had a rare genetic blood disorder that made his cholesterol level exceedingly high; after diagnosis, he had to watch his diet and take drugs to maintain a tolerable level. About the same time, he was pricked by a nurse with a needle from an HIV-positive patient, and we all had to wait nearly a year before the AIDS scare was lifted. He had even survived a near-fatal car crash when, returning from an all-night shift at the ER, he fell asleep less than a mile from his home, only to career his car into a tree. It was amazing, in a way, that he hadn't found a more abrupt way of dying along the way.

The next day we celebrate Thanksgiving as a family at Steve's house, but Bob isn't up for the half-hour drive and all the stimulation. So we gather for what we all know will be our last Thanksgiving dinner while Bob's alive, and it is so melancholy an affair, Ingmar Bergman could have directed it. We try to keep things from getting too morose, but it's impossible. We don't know how to sit together without it being so strange.

I realize how much time we spend making plans, talking about upcoming events and vacations and holiday planning. Each time somebody mentions something that might happen in the future, the unanswered question is whether Bob will be around to witness it. Bob's pregnant daughter is there with her husband and is beginning to show, a budding reminder in her belly that Bob will not live to meet his first granddaughter.

On Helena's rooftop terrace, yet another wave of sadness washed over me—sadness because the trip was coming to a close, because I didn't know what the future held, because we were leaving Nepal and Asia and the biggest part of our adventure. I didn't know what work I would do, whether or not I would write a book about this trip, how I would make a living. I wondered what the post–9/11 world would look like at home, especially since the economy was tanking and journalism always seems to take one of the first hits when corporate advertising budgets dry up and magazine editorial content shrinks proportionally.

I was also just plain tired. These past few days in particular had been difficult, partly because of my injured ankle, but also because the kids had been sedentary and needy at the same time. I'd spent waaaaay too much time in Internet cafés arranging onward passage, contacting our European friends, our New York cousins, Tory, my parents, asking Rebecca about Christmas plans. Although I could send the kids out for mineral water or to pick up snacks, all the niggling (and huge) details and choices and decisions fell to me.

I returned to the Sherpa Guest House as the kids finished up the DVD, and we sortied for our last Kathmandu dinner. I tried to convince them that we should have a final Nepali meal of dahl-baat, but I was outvoted two-to-one in favor of an Italian-run pizzeria called *Fire and Ice,* where we have already eaten twice. I started to rail against their lack of culinary adventurousness, then recalled that these were the same children who had trudged through numerous jungles, endured many long bus rides, and slept in crack hotels from Singapore to Kalimantan. Pizza would be fine.

After dinner, we had one last errand to run. We walked over to a store where we had purchased a Tibetan thangka the day before. The painting depicted the life of Buddha, and the kids were enthralled as the woman who ran the shop explained the intricate symbolism of the painting. She had promised the day before to mount the painting on a traditional silk background, and with pride she now unfurled the result, which was breathtaking. We shared a soda with the shopkeeper and her son as she wrapped it in a cardboard tube for us to hand-carry all the way to our living room.

I felt palpable relief to have gotten through Asia without any of us getting sick or lost or misplacing a backpack or having my laptop stolen or any other major mishap. It was appealing to realize that we still had more than a month of traveling before we hit routine again, especially since so many wonderful stops awaited us. I was looking forward to all of them, a combination of seeing long-lost friends in Switzerland, France, and Belgium, then visiting my sister-in-law and nieces in Holland.

We weren't done adventuring yet—and still had the whips and handcuffs of Amsterdam's red-light district to explain to Zoe . . .

PART 6

RENAISSANCE MAN

Kolya, Zoe, and the author in the Swiss-Italian Alps.

EUROS AND ESCARGOTS

THE CONTRAST between Kathmandu and Zurich must be one of the most intense urban juxtapositions on the planet. Suddenly, instead of wandering among the sari-clad throngs and animated street vendors selling Tibetan prayer wheels near Durbar Square, I was strolling on the Bahnhofstrasse past Bruno Magli, Chanel, Louis Vitton, Cartier, BVLGARI, Salvatore Ferragamo, Hugo Boss, Yves Saint Laurent, Rolex, and Bucherer stores alongside somber, gray-clad Swiss-German window shoppers.

While flying west over Afghanistan en route to Austria, I had the growing sense that one journey had nearly ended, and a new one—one for which I had no itinerary, and no Internet reservations—had begun. As we passed through Europe over the next few weeks, however, it seemed as though each country still had one lesson to impart.

In Switzerland, we met with old friends who are codirectors of the American program at the Ecole d'Humanité, an international boarding school perched in a high Alpen valley. We had lived a block and a half away from K. C. and Kathleen in Takoma Park,

Maryland, when I worked in Washington, D.C. Their boys, Rowan and Quin, straddle Kolya in age and had been his closest friends. Their family had moved to Switzerland a year before we moved to Colorado, but the connection among all of us remained strong and we arranged visits on one continent or another every other year. As a bonus, another mutual friend of ours from Takoma Park days, Melinda, was there with her younger son Jesse, who is Zoe's age.

It was incredibly reassuring to be among old friends, to feel I was finally able to let down after being responsible for everything for so long. We jammed everybody into two cars and drove to Berzone, a tiny medieval village in the valley of Onsernonne, a skip from the Italian border. As the kids played, the grown-ups took turns catching up. My friends knew the outlines of what had happened—Rebecca, Bob, the trip—but the details needed filling in.

Even as I felt myself moving on, here among these old friends I realized that my life with Rebecca would never be completely behind me. Rebecca had been our family's social coordinator and had nurtured the connections with our friends much more than I had. Kathleen and Melinda had been two of Rebecca's closest friends, and those three moms had coordinated most of our gatherings. As Kathleen, Melinda, and I talked and cooked and walked over our few days together, I slowly realized that Rebecca had curtailed her contact with even these old friends, and they were almost as baffled as I at the turn of events. I also realized that even though Rebecca's ghost remained in the background, I knew I could no longer rely on her to maintain my connections to our old friends; I had to forge new connections myself.

Talking about the events of the past few years reminded me again of what a wild ride I'd been on. Yet I felt something different happening as I told our story, a little distance and perspective, as if I'd sailed through a violent storm but had somehow crossed into a protected harbor. Kathleen, bless her heart, took me aside and told me what a wonderful job I was doing with the kids. I had really showed up when it counted, she said. Kolya and Zoe were very, very lucky.

I hugged her and sobbed, filled with relief and gratitude and sadness.

Three days passed in recuperative bliss and we headed back to the school. The following day, we said our good-byes, drove to Zurich, and caught a plane to Paris.

As a parting gift, Kolya bequeathed his battered skateboard to Rowan and Quin, knowing that I had promised him a new one upon our return.

Twenty-seven years previously, when I was at the height of my "sardine eater" stage, floating on the wings of serendipity around Europe, a couple named Daniel and Bénédicte had picked me up hitchhiking at dusk outside of Limoges, France. They were Parisian but had been living in central France. When Daniel heard I hailed from Berkeley, he told me he had been a student leader during the student protests at the Sorbonne in 1968 but was now an English teacher. Bénédicte wondered where I was planning on sleeping that evening.

Since the answer was *je n'ai aucune idée,* I haven't a clue, they invited me to spend the night. And another. And another, embroiled in intensely French discussions about politics and the state of the world. We parted, reluctantly, with each other's addresses scrawled in our respective books.

Over the years, we'd exchanged postcards and letters. Once, Daniel visited me in the States, and once Rebecca and Kolya and I visited the two of them in Paris before Zoe was born, in the same place where they now lived. I had told them that the kids and I might be passing through Paris on our trip and had taken them up on an open invitation to visit.

They met us at the airport and drove us back through rush hour to their beautiful little apartment in the fifth *arrondissement,* le Marais. They were about to take a mini-vacation in Normandy, so they introduced me to the concierge, handed over the keys to the flat, and left. The kids, who had seemed nonplussed over the fact that I had friends like Scott and Keith in far-flung places, couldn't quite believe that these strangers had just handed over the keys to an apartment in Paris. Then we went into the bedroom and noticed a picture of Kolya, aged three, sitting on Daniel's motorcycle with a gigantic metallic blue helmet on his head and Daniel standing by his side.

Kolya and Zoe were even more amazed to see a picture of Kolya in a Parisian bedroom.

The kids' appetite for sightseeing at this point was about equal to their appetite for stewed tripe, but they stated a willingness to be dragged to the Eiffel Tower, Notre Dame, and the Louvre. Those cultural obligations fulfilled, we returned to the apartment and the kids settled in to make phone calls home and watch TV.

I roamed the streets searching for a perfect café for a Pastis. The temperature had dropped, hardly Pastis weather, but after wandering for an hour I ducked into a smoky Bar Tabac and hunkered over a small round marble table. I ordered one anyway and indulged myself in what have become periodic solitary communions with Bob, making peace with myself for being, if not always a perfect brother, at least one who came through toward the end.

In early December, I ask Rebecca if she can fly to Colorado to be with the kids for ten days so I can be with Bob and my family before the kids are free for Christmas vacation. She graciously agrees.

I stay with my folks, who live half an hour from Bob and a mile from Steve. Bob and Renda are not receiving many visitors these days, a source of immense frustration for everybody. Our family dynamic gets intense as we debate who gets to see Bob, and when. Nobody is sure if Renda is being protective of Bob or Bob is being protective of Renda, or what. We learn from Renda that Bob is beginning to suffer from a kind of dementia at times, getting unreasonably angry, asking about things getting lost, complaining about us.

Since I came from out of town, I'm allowed to visit most days but can't stay very long. He's declining pretty fast at this point. We go on walks almost every day, but by this time he needs a portable oxygen machine and a cane to make his ritual two-mile hike. Even so, he won't use the oxygen on the first half of the walk, to the one-mile turnaround point. Once he makes it halfway, he places the breathing tube under his nose and I carry the machine and keep close enough to grab his elbow if he stumbles. He walks slowly, deliberately. It seems to take tremendous concentration for him to stay upright on the uneven dirt path. If he doesn't time the pain meds right, it hurts like hell.

One afternoon I'm there when the hospice nurse drops by. He's a gentle man, matter-of-fact in the shadow of death, asking about Bob's pain, about the weird mouth infection Bob has, thrush, a by-product of one of the meds he's taking, about his appetite. He talks about what to expect next and tells Bob he should probably double his dose of OxyContin, the little blue painkillers. Bob doesn't like them much—they make him foggy—but the pain is consuming if he doesn't. He agrees to up the dose a little.

As the nurse is leaving, Bob walks him to the door and almost takes a tumble going down the two low steps back to the sunken living room. Because he was wearing an eye patch, his depth perception was shot. Every time I see Bob careening around the house I'm afraid he's going to fall.

I discreetly ask Renda if maybe I can install a ramp or a handrail or something to help him negotiate the two steps, and she thinks it's a great idea. I go to Steve's house and we're both seized by a plan to do something useful for Bob. Both former woodworkers, we mill up redwood handrails and mount them on brass hardware. Bob is pleased, and Steve and I feel like we've accomplished something. He walks up and down the two steps gripping the well-sanded rail.

One afternoon Bob takes a nap and I go for a long run. As I head up a hill nearing his home, I find myself involuntarily crying, then running faster, then crying harder. With every sob I gasp more air and run faster, as if I could outrace Bob's death demon, as if I could will him to heal by the sheer force of my vitality. At the end of my run I stand in the yard, face his house, and sob uncontrollably, fighting the growing sense that

Bob will soon be dead, feeling as if I were abandoning him by even allowing the thought to enter my brain.

The next day I arrange to bring dinner for him and Renda, offering
to make anything he wants. He is finicky about what he can stomach
but tells me to pick up a really good steak. I buy filet mignon, potatoes to
bake, an extravagant bottle of French Burgundy. I try not to have it feel
like a condemned man's last meal by talking about other culinary
delights he might want me to bring up tomorrow.

We take a walk before dinner and talk bluntly about the process of
dying as the slow metronome thwwwup of compressed air shoots oxygen
into his nose, counterpoint to the thunk of the cane. He doesn't rail or
complain about how unfair it all is, somehow accepting it more than I
would. I guess not surprisingly, since he's a doc, Bob can see the clinical
stages of his own dying in unflinching detail. When he could no longer
see with both eyes, it meant that one of the tumors was pressing up
against his optic center. Another tumor is pressing against his hip, so it's
getting painful to walk. He has fallen several times already and thinks he
might have cracked a vertebra in his neck. Pretty soon, he figures, he
won't be able to swallow. Then it will get really ugly.

He says he has been under pressure from his medical friends to do
palliative therapy, and he's already had a second dose of radiation to
shrink the tumors temporarily. Could he buy a few more weeks or
months with another? Would it be worth it?

"I think I'm done. No mas," he says, parroting the immortal boxing
words of Roberto Duran when he threw in the towel against Sugar Ray
Leonard.

He knows that the last stages of cancer will be unbearable, and I realize he's not as worried about himself as he is about Renda and his kids
and everybody else. He doesn't really want to go to the bitter end, but it's
difficult even for him as a doc to find a legal and gracious way to check
out. Maybe when he can no longer wipe himself, he says. It's as good a
line as any.

He sure is enjoying the walks, though.

We head back, stop under a huge pine.

"I'm sure going to miss you," I tell him, tears suddenly welling, unbearable.

"I love you, Danny," he responds. I hug him, his oxygen machine nearly flopping off my shoulder. My tears against his unshaven cheek.

For now, blessed moment, we can be together, he can take in the cirrus sky and smell the pine needles in the warm afternoon and absorb the orange glow of the madrones in the slanting sun. I can still hug him.

He reminds me that three nights before his wedding to his high school girlfriend, a marriage that lasted seventeen years and ended in disastrous divorce, we stayed up all night on a beach with a bottle of Jose Cuervo. I had told him, "It's not too late. You don't have to do this."

He turns to me now. "You were right."

I leave on December 15, with plans to return on the 21st with the kids to spend Christmas and New Year's together. He smiles wanly and tells me he sure as hell wasn't going to die around Christmas, that'd spoil it for everyone. And with the Vikings and the Oakland Raiders destined to meet in the Super Bowl in late January, he'd do his best to stick around at least that long.

I was brought back to the incongruous present by a French waiter wearing a bow tie.

Autre chose, monsieur?

Non, merci, I replied. I didn't need anything else right now.

Before I met Daniel and Bénédicte outside Limoges in 1976, I began my first solo European travels by meeting an old girlfriend who had been studying in England. We met up in Luxembourg, home of a school friend of hers and the destination of the cheapest flight to Europe on Icelandic Airlines. Carolyn's school friend Jim lived outside Luxembourg City. We became fast friends, and the three of us traveled to Greece together. After Carolyn went home, Jim and I hitchhiked back to Luxembourg, where his father found me a job picking grapes.

After I returned to the States, Jim married a French woman, Véronique, whom he had just met during the time I had been living in Europe. As with Daniel and Bénédicte, we stayed in touch over the years with letters and the occasional visit. Now both Jim and Véronique were Eurocrats with the European Commission, living in Brussels with their two kids.

We arrived at their elegant home, another safe haven. Jim and I sat over a bottle of Bordeaux and caught up after the kids went to sleep.

I had another moment of discovery, talking with my Luxembourgish friend: There was something incredibly reassuring for me to connect with people I knew *before* I met Rebecca. Jim and I rehashed memories of the flirtatious Irish girls we had met on the Greek island of Poros, and the renegade Turkish tourist bus that took us from Thessoloniki to Skopje, in Yugoslavia. Over the past few years it was as if I couldn't remember my life before I married. Here in Brussels, switching back and forth between French and English with my old friend, I felt my footing in the present grounded much more solidly to the many footsteps I had crossed to get here.

The next day we headed to Holland. The taxi driver who took us from Jim and Véronique's house to the train station provided more than just a ride, however. Originally from Morocco, he had lived in Brussels for thirty years, but he clearly traveled in circles of Arabic ex-pats. We spoke in French, and when he learned I was *américain* he launched on his theory of what *really* happened on September 11.

Did I realize, he asked, that Afghanistan just happened to be strategically located in the middle of America's biggest enemies and potential enemies? With Iraq, Iran, China, Pakistan, the breakaway Soviet Republics, and Russia all within convenient earshot (or missile shot), it made perfect sense that the U.S. government would create any pretext it could to invade Afghanistan. After all, occupying Kabul was a piece of cake compared with trying to take Hanoi. "You watch, they'll be there for the duration, just like Vietnam," he wagged at me.

I had read that many Arabs thought that the whole 9/11 disaster was a conspiracy, but here was the first person I had met who *believed* it. He said that Americans set up the whole thing in conjunction with the Israeli Mossad in order to crack down on the Muslim diaspora. To prove his point, he noted that the death toll seemed to be getting smaller every day—and was down to a few thousand rather than the initial estimates of more than 5,000. He wondered aloud how it could have been possible for the terrorists to have pulled off such a massive strike without help from Americans, and he repeated the theory that there were few Jews among the dead because they had been warned not to go to work that morning.

"Vous voyez ce que je veux dire?" "Do you get what I'm saying?" he said, sincere as a man on his death bed. The whole thing was a ruse, he was sure, and just wait to see if he wasn't right.

I translated for the kids as we boarded the train to Amsterdam. Kolya wanted to know if maybe I had misunderstood the cabdriver. He didn't really think that the U.S. government had set up the whole thing, did he? I told him that, unfortunately, the U.S. government had not always done things in the past that would inspire confidence in people like our driver. I hated to break news that wasn't likely to be covered in his American history classes, but the United States had arranged coups and funded covert operations all over the globe. It had fomented unrest, had its own puppets elected, and manipulated systems and governments by any means at its disposal.

I ranted a little as the suburbs of Brussels flashed by, wondering if Kolya wished he didn't have a journalist as a dad. I explained to him that America had been wildly effective at making its citizens believe in the omniscience of its military apparatus, projecting its strength across movie screens and satellite television, promoting it until we believed we could manipulate world events with impunity.

The cabdriver's tirade was evidence of the backlash. Even after the horrors of September 11, America's motives were *always* suspect. "How could this have happened?" remained a good question without a simple answer. One part of the answer, though, was that America had proven to the world that it had the capability and the hubris to try almost anything. It was not a surprise, I told Kolya, that people believed such outlandish stories.

Why else, then, would a Moroccan cabdriver in Brussels believe that the Americans had perpetrated this crime on themselves in a Machiavellian plan to take over a geopolitical centerpiece of the post–Cold War world? The taxi driver believed not only that we *would* do such a thing, but that we *could*. I wasn't sure which was harder to understand.

WHAT ARE THOSE WHIPS
AND HANDCUFFS FOR?

As we clickety-clacked our way to Amsterdam, I finished my world-according-to-Dad lecture. As I ran out of rant, we watched the earth flatten and entered what the French call *le bays pays,* the low country, where Kolya and Zoe's maternal grandparents were born and where Rebecca lived until she was eight. The kids were excited to see their aunt and cousins, and I was, too.

Kolya had pushed me for permission to visit one of Amsterdam's infamous "coffee shops," which are basically hashish cafés, and I was torn about whether to allow it. I knew I'd muddled my "Just Say Not Yet" message with the episode in Australia, not to mention giving him permission to buy pipes in Kathmandu. On the one hand, it felt inevitable that he was going to experiment soon, and I figured it was a plus for him to do it where it was legal. On the other hand, I thought he was still too young.

For the moment, I put him off with a "we'll see," and he knew better than to argue the point.

I observed him on the train, listening to his music, sliding over politely when somebody got on and sat next to him. I'd witnessed him maturing before my eyes during the trip—literally growing up and coming into his own as a person. I felt certain that he had sprouted at least three inches in the past four months, and he was now complaining that my extra pair of size 11 $^1/_2$ shoes—which he had appropriated—were too small for him. I had grown to have much more confidence in his decision-making ability, in his sense of self, in his ability to be influenced but not driven by peer pressure. I worried that as soon as we arrived home, however, the provincial milieu of wealthy, white-bread Boulder would act quickly to narrow his world, to close his perspective, to make him less introspective and thoughtful and more vulnerable to teen taunts and dumb dares.

Aunt Corrie met us at the train station with her two grown-up daughters, Sanne and Nien. Corrie is the eldest of four children in Rebecca's family, eleven years older than her baby sister with two boys in between. I'd last seen Corrie's daughters ten years previously, when they were twelve and seventeen, respectively, and they had grown into beautiful and vibrant young women.

In an uncanny precedent, Corrie had left her long-term marriage and begun a relationship with a woman many years before Rebecca did the same. Unlike Rebecca, Corrie waited until her girls were out of the house to ask for a divorce. She had been living with the same woman ever since. Sanne and Nien seemed to have a great relationship with both their mom and their dad, as well as with their mom's partner and their dad's new wife. It was nice to see and hear about how they had done with the situation.

We all converged on Corrie's home with her partner, Thea, and proceeded with our raucous family reunion, talking about our trip, their lives, Rebecca, Bob, everything. Zoe snuggled into her aunt's lap, and Kolya was captivated by, if not in love with, his gorgeous grown-up cousins.

Rebecca called early the next morning, waking the three of us sleepyheads for an early morning chat. Zoe crawled into bed with me and I could listen while she chatted to her mom about Aunt Corrie, about the *Mona Lisa*, about conversations she'd had with her friends back home. Zoe worried about reentry, whether her friends had changed or if she had changed. She couldn't wait to see her mom and was disappointed to hear that it wouldn't be until after Christmas.

The next day we toured around Amsterdam, ending up in the evening at the famous red-light district known as the Walletjes. Kolya couldn't believe what he was seeing, scantily clad women in different costumes, a veritable smorgasbord of fantasy, theatrically lit in picture windows lining the streets. Zoe was also transfixed but couldn't figure out what certain shops were selling, or why. We passed an S&M shop, and Zoe stopped.

"What are all those whips and handcuffs for?" she asked her cousins.

They didn't know exactly what to say.

"They're sex toys, Zoe," I explained.

She didn't ask a follow-up question.

A cousin of mine who was an international aid worker also lived in Amsterdam, so the next night, Kolya, Kenny, and I headed out for a boys' night on the town, leaving Zoe with her aunt and "girl cousins." I had discreetly asked my nieces about the coffee-house scene. To Kolya's deep disappointment, Sanne informed me that even in Amsterdam, you had to be eighteen to purchase anything smokable. Kolya refused to believe it and talked about it all through dinner at the very trendy Brasserie de Luxembourg, where I did allow him to order his very first beer, a cherry-flavored brew called a *kriek*.

As we strolled after dinner, Kolya stood like a puppy outside a coffee shop begging to go inside. I reminded him of what Sanne had said, and he begged me to please try anyway. We went in.

Alright, we did it, legally.

Amsterdam is the greatest place in the world. It was one of the best days in Holland. We spent the day sleeping, and touring a little bit with Corrie, Sonne, and Neinke. It's a cool city, even without the hookers in the windows, the head shops, the coffee shops, and the sex shops. The whole structure and the canals are pretty rad. Plus, I like being with my family, especially the ones that I haven't seen in a while.

So all that was a plus, but the highlight of the day was in the night. We met up with Kenny, my second cousin once removed or something like that. He is a guy who has gone through a lot in his life, like a whole damn lot. Just a little while ago, he got held hostage for three weeks in Chechnya (Russia). He works for Doctors Without Borders and right now is working out of Amsterdam.

Anyways, we met up with him and strolled around for a little bit, with me asking my dad to take me into a "coffee shop" every now and then. The "coffee shops" in Amsterdam are pretty legendary, it's basically a place where you can sit down, order a joint from a list of flavors, strength . . . etc, and smoke it right there. He kept telling me "we'll see." I just kept my fingers crossed. We stopped in at the "Luxemberg Café" where I tried my very first hamburger since I made the mistake of ordering one in Australia. It was sheer bliss. This along with the very first beer that my dad bought me to myself was the perfect meal for the night, and that day. It just fit my mood like no other.

I would've been pretty happy if we hadn't done anything else that night, but because I'm a greedy little kid, I kept asking for a stop in a coffee shop. The very first coffee shop we saw, my dad stopped in for me, and asked the question that you would obviously get a no to, like "you wouldn't let an underage kid buy a joint, would you?" And of course they said no.

I was kinda mad, because as long as you are gonna go half way, you might as well go all out. So I made a deal with him: we go into the next shop just as customers, no questions asked, and try to buy me a joint, then I will stop bugging him. We did, and the guy let me have it, I was sooo stoked, just having a joint makes you feel like a complete badass. I don't even know why, but it did. I was so happy with my dad. The whole 4 inch thing cost the US equivalent of 4 dollars.

I smoked it and didn't feel anything, I was pissed. As it turns out, they mix their weed with tobacco over there, so I ended up just going out of there just feeling a little sick. I was still really happy for my dad taking me though, but I knew he was gonna tighten up a whole lot after we got back, he made that clear to me.

Damn straight, Kolya.

Our last night in Amsterdam, we had dinner at Nien's apartment. Kolya wanted one more shopping tour of the area around the train station, and Nien agreed to accompany him then put him on the right bus to Corrie's. I warned them both not to visit a "coffee shop." They swore they wouldn't, and the rest of us went home.

Nien called right after she put Kolya on the bus. She had realized that the bus route had recently changed because of a construction detour, and she was pretty sure she had told Kolya to get off at the wrong stop.

Corrie and I put our heads together and tried to figure out a plan. I didn't even think Kolya had Corrie's phone number. I was pretty sure he had the address written down somewhere, but I couldn't be sure. We decided that if he followed Nien's instructions, he would be getting off at a stop about a kilometer away. I took off at a run to see if I could head him off.

No luck. I didn't see a soul at the bus stop. It was a rather desolate section of town, and I stood there, heart in my throat, wondering what I would do if I was a thirteen-year-old boy who thought he was getting off at the right stop but nothing looked familiar. I couldn't believe that I had gotten the kids through Ubud, Pangkalan Bun, Saigon, Phnom Penh, and Kathmandu and now had lost my son in Amsterdam.

I ran back and forth along the street, trying to anticipate where he might have gone. I went into a restaurant near the bus stop to see if he had been inside, and the woman said he had. I ran outside and glimpsed a familiar silhouette emerging from a side street.

He didn't seem panicked but was pretty confounded. He hadn't figured out that he had been given bad directions and wondered why nothing looked familiar. I was decidedly more flipped out than he was. I put my arm around his broadening shoulder, and we walked home in step. Flush from his Amsterdam adventures and with the prospect of returning home soon, Kolya confirmed what I had already decided was true for myself.

"This has been a pretty amazing trip, D," he said.

The next morning, we were on a plane to New York, to a changed country from the one we had left.

SUNRISE WHERE THE TOWERS WERE

OVER THE PAST few years, I had impressed upon my kids that our family was bedrock even as our nuclear family was falling apart. During and after the divorce, both my family and Rebecca's had continued to support all of us. As Bob was dying, the kids had witnessed how our extended family could pull together. Now we were arriving into the bosom of an entirely different part of the family, our infamous East Coast cousins.

I was born in the mid-1950s in *Leave It to Beaver* times, had been reared in the heart of the suburban dream, and came of age in the bulge of the Baby Boomers' do-your-own-thing self-absorption. So it had been something of a revelation to realize how old-fashioned I could be at times when it came to family matters. As I was coming to grips with the fact that I was going to be raising my kids in what was quaintly once called a "broken home," I grieved so many things: One of them was my inbred sense of a mom-dad-and-the-kids family. Family, for my grandparents' generation, meant survival and gave meaning to the trivial affairs of the outside world.

Kolya and Zoe immediately warmed to our extended East Coast family the next day at my cousin Jenny's home in Chappaqua. We were enveloped, treated like prodigal sons and daughters after our trip. Jenny and her sister Tina voted me "father of the year."

The afternoon melded into evening and the family filed out. Jenny and I settled in for a long talk, Kolya hung out with Jenny's two high-school-age sons, and Zoe curled up in front of the telly. Jen is a single mom, and we exchanged notes on teenage sons, absent partners, new relationships, and the whole overwhelming, rewarding, and challenging prospect of raising kids solo.

We planned to visit another cousin and do some sightseeing in Manhattan the next day, and Jen offered to drive us in from Westchester County. She informed us that the "Statute of Liberty," as Zoe called it, was still closed to visitors, as were other tourist attractions. Still, I had hoped to take the kids to Ground Zero, the newest and most macabre New York tourist site. As we approached the Henry Hudson Bridge that links the Bronx to Manhattan, Jen casually turned on the radio searching for music. Instead, we heard breaking news about a plane crash, an American Airlines flight that went down while leaving John F. Kennedy International Airport. Nobody knew what had happened, but the first reaction, of course, was that it had to be more terrorism.

Until the authorities figured it out (authorities later said it was almost certainly an accident caused by engine failure), all the bridges into and out of Manhattan were immediately closed. Jenny pulled over and asked what we wanted to do. We had the option of taking the train in, but Kolya and Zoe both adamantly made their wishes clear: Manhattan felt too scary.

I told Jenny to take us back to her house, and she happily obliged.

The next day, I left the kids with their cousins and took the train into the city for some face time with various editors. I met a friend downtown and she took me to the area around Ground Zero, a jumble of yellow police tape and uniformed men. Even though she had been there since 9/11, she became disoriented. Everybody in the city, she said, had used the World Trade Center buildings as navigational tools when downtown.

It was difficult to weave past the phalanx of uniforms to see the pit, but it didn't matter. I stood there behind the yellow tape, taking in the monumental anguish that I had first heard about halfway around the world in Singapore. And I cried, waves of grief stirring up waves of grief, uncertain where one ended and the next began.

Kolya, Zoe, and I show up in California four days before Christmas, renting another red Camaro convertible to offset the grimness of the visit. Since Bob had told me that he had never been in a convertible before, I get it in my head that he would like that. The next day I drive up and load him and his oxygen into the car and drive into the foothills.

It is a mild December day, and we are comfortable with the top down. He directs me to back roads, climbing through forests of digger pines and scrub oaks, winding through the sun-dappled Sierra foothills, going nowhere in particular. He has deteriorated in the past week and is sadder than I've seen him, regretting out loud that he spent so much of his adult life in a first marriage that didn't make him happy. He's so happy with Renda, happy to have had this last decade together.

I have a difficult subject to bring up, at least it seems difficult to me because it's about the future, about what happens after he's dead. I tell him that I've been thinking about taking the kids around the world. Sort of in honor of him. Because it's scary to see somebody so healthy and strong just get sick and die.

He tells me that he had his first insight into mortality when his best friend in medical school, Bob Grassburger, dropped dead on a basketball court. "You never know how long you've got, Danny," he says, and coming from him, here, now, it doesn't sound like a cliché at all. "I think you should do it."

We drive to a little roadside burger joint, pick up chocolate malts, then drive some more. I watch him staring out of the car, and I wonder what you think about when you're dying, when you know that you won't see another season. We ride in silence and I turn the car homeward. He thanks me for his first convertible ride.

He later tells Renda that I made him do it, that he didn't even want to drive in the convertible at all. He tells her that I stole his skis from him and that he's really pissed off. Renda tells me all this and I'm crushed. I try to gently remind Bob that I never did borrow his skis. I had my own. Bob cannot be convinced, seems really pissed off at me.

Renda pulls me aside in tears. "See," she says. "He gets so angry." His dementia is getting worse, which is hard to take because it's intermittent and we don't understand the dance between lucidity and cancer-fog.

I come back the next day and tell Bob that I brought his skis back, they're in the downstairs closet. I apologize for taking them.

He's okay with that. No problem.

Each day is more difficult for him. Christmas is maudlin, but Bob makes a gift of his mandolin to me. "I never learned how to play this," he says. "Maybe you can."

I have a gift for him, too, and am praying that it will arrive on time. My first book is literally hot off the presses but won't be in the bookstores until after the first of the year. I had asked my publisher to hurry copies to Bob's house because I wanted him to see the book's dedication:

To my big brother, Bob
Go long

It's an inside joke. When we were kids, Bob and Steve and I would play our own made-up football game called "off-deef," short for "offense-defense." It was simple: Steve and I would take turns as receivers and cornerbacks, guarding each other, and Bob would be quarterback.

Sometimes, toward the end of the game, he would coax one of us to "go long," run as hard as we could as far as we could. After sprinting 60 or 70 yards, we'd stop, saying, "You can't throw it this far." Often enough, he could. But sometimes, he'd simply tuck the ball under his arm and start for home, saying, "You're right." Like Charlie and Lucy.

Go long, Bob.

The books arrive and I show him the inscription, although by now he can barely read. But he reaches over, puts his hand around the back of my neck, and pulls me to him for a kiss.

He makes New Year's, makes his forty-eighth birthday on the 2nd of January. He gets more incoherent daily. By the 7th, I have to go home, bring the kids back to school, but it's almost impossible to leave. My parents tell me that life goes on, the kids need their routine, I have been a good brother and son being here, there isn't much I can do. There's no way of knowing if Bob will last a week or three months, and I should go home.

It's a week.

The Sunday night after I leave, after the NFL conference playoffs, I speak to him for the last time. I ask him if he saw me on 60 Minutes after the game, since I had been interviewed about the subject of my book. Bob babbles something, but I'm not convinced that he knows he saw me on TV, although Renda said they all watched.

Suddenly, he becomes lucid and tells me that since the Raiders lost and so did the Vikings, there isn't much use in sticking around for the Super Bowl, since it'll probably be a stinker. That night, trying to go to the bathroom by himself, he falls and knocks his head. He dies in his sleep, probably from internal bleeding that saves him from a coma.

In a perverse cosmic joke, Bob died on the one-year anniversary of the formal death of my marriage.

We spent one more day at Jen's, and the following morning we awoke before dawn to catch our plane, which took off from Newark. We wound our way from Westchester and onto the New Jersey Turnpike. We watched the first hints of sunrise appear, long since passing over the jungles, mountains, friends, and oceans of the past months' wanderings.

Across the Hudson River we took in the Manhattan skyline etched on the eastern sky. The kids and I stared in desperate wonder when, at the moment when we crossed their ghostly path, the sun appeared perfectly round and orange, filling the void where the twin towers once stood.

PART 7

FULL CIRCLE . . . AND BEYOND

Robert Paul Glick (1953–2001).

THE ROBERT P. GLICK EMERGENCY
SERVICES DEPARTMENT

IT WAS TORTURE for the kids to pass through the Denver airport and not see their friends, but we still had more stops before we'd be home to stay. After a painfully long delay on Concourse B, punctuated by the kids' desperate pay phone calls to friends, we boarded a plane to San Francisco for a joyful reunion with my folks, who had driven down to the city and gotten us all a hotel in Japantown.

Despite the fact that we were not at home, it felt very grounding to see my parents, and for the kids to see their grandparents. Several cousins were also in town, and we gathered with family and old Bay Area friends for an impromptu party, narrating our stories while showing digital photos on my laptop.

Since I was always the itinerant son, under normal circumstances my parents would have taken my extended travels with patient acceptance. But I had realized that after Bob's death, I now wore the mantle of eldest son. Even in our family, where there was no kingdom to inherit, I suddenly felt the weight of that mantle. I saw my parents in the process of aging and realized that I needed somehow to step into that role, which Bob had filled so naturally. I wasn't sure exactly what it would mean, but just as I stepped into the role of single parent, I knew that I faced more transitions in my family.

Tory met us for a joyous reunion, and we headed off for a last foreign excursion: our second annual Puerto Vallarta extravaganza. Kolya, Zoe, and I got along so well with Tory's nieces, nephews, sisters, brothers, father, and step-mother that our sense of extended family extended further. The week passed in sunshine, margarita fests, poker nights, body surfing, and forays into town.

I realized upon seeing Tory how important it was that she had joined us during the trip, and the kids really responded to seeing her again. I also realized that she and I had yet another gulf to try to bridge—sharing our inner lives of the past two and a half months since she'd left us in Vietnam. Tory and I tried to find time to reconnect, but we were on a family vacation and there was always something to negotiate or plan. We danced lightly with each other, wondering what our lives would be like when we arrived home, knowing that we had so many transitions ahead.

I preoccupied myself with my return to California, since the dedication ceremony to rename the hospital's emergency department after Bob would take place two days after we arrived. I wasn't sure if I was supposed to give a speech or a eulogy, like I did at his memorial service. That was one of the hardest things I'd ever done, standing up in front of 400 people and trying to sum up the life of somebody I loved.

I remembered saying that I felt it was small consolation that, as a doctor who melded his physician's skills with a fundamental humanity, Bob most certainly did more good than harm in the world. I looked around the packed room and knew that there were probably dozens of people who were sitting there because Bob had literally saved their lives.

I knew for certain that he had saved his son's life once, after he had fallen out of a tree while Bob was at work. My nephew had been taken to another emergency room and was given a clean bill of health. When Bob returned from work, he took one look at his son and rushed him to the ER, where they treated his ruptured spleen and saved his life. Another time, after my father had received a stint to open a blocked heart valve, Bob happened to be visiting the hospital when my father began bleeding from the femoral artery where they had inserted the stint. If Bob had not been there to staunch the flow, my father would have certainly bled to death before someone noticed.

I guess it's easy to glorify the dead, especially from the vantage point of an adoring younger brother. But as I looked around the room, I felt a deep pride that Bob had left a legacy of those who loved him, and the many more whom he had helped. The high standard he had reached for living one's life was something to be much admired and emulated.

We flew back to California in time to see the finishing touches on the memorial garden they had built in Bob's honor. Steve had worked very hard on the memorial, designing and landscaping it. Many people had volunteered their time to bring it together, and the workmen were ready to lift into place the granite slab that had been laser-engraved with Bob's likeness.

I arrived with Renda as a man was maneuvering a crane to place the huge slab, which was still wrapped in canvas. It was raining, and after the stone was placed, Renda temporarily lifted the covering so I could see it. There he was, a frightening likeness of his face etched on the stone, and I immediately and unexpectedly broke into sobs.

The rain continued through the next day, and the ceremony had to be moved to a nearby athletic club, which I joked was fairly appropriate given Bob's sports-mad life. I dressed up in Bob's suit, which I also had worn to his memorial service, and held it together for my role of introducing the speakers.

The room was filled with family, friends, well-wishers. After it was over, I sought out Kolya and Zoe, gathered them in my arms, and reminded them that Bob was still with us, in our memories. And I privately thanked him for our trip.

On the memorial is engraved a favorite saying of Bob's, by Mahatma Gandhi:

Whatever you do will be insignificant
But it is most important
That you do it

Back in Our Cages

Home sweet home

Holy shit we are driving in to Nyland! I'm finaly home, I said to every one when the car was still moving. I jump out of my car and ran to my close friends house hoping with all my hope she would be there. She was in the kichen stuffing some tomatos in her mouth. Her name is Ana and we ran to each other and hugged for 30 min about. Saying stuff like, "ho I missed you," "never go agin." It was a very touching moment.

As we drove west from the airport on a clear December day, the Rocky Mountains loomed before us with the first snows already blanketing the Continental Divide. We crossed the South Platte River, low at this time of year, and sensed the prairie grasses hunkering down for the long winter that lay ahead, brown and bent in the chill afternoon breeze.

Zoe leaped out of the car before it even stopped moving, and Kolya spied his neighborhood buddies right away. He mounted a friend's skateboard after a few high fives, and almost immediately it felt as if we'd never left.

The man who rented our house had left it spotless, almost too clean for us to recognize. We quickly ended the fleeting appearance of order by strewing our bags and backpacks all over the living room. One by one the neighbors stopped by to inquire about how the trip went.

It was hard to sum up in a sentence or two, and I muttered words about it being an incredible adventure, a wholly insufficient sound bite. The stories will eke out over time, over coffee, over beers.

The kids only had one day at home before they were scheduled to go back to school. They knew they only had two weeks before Christmas vacation, so they actually exhibited signs of being excited about school.

Their classmates treated them as if they were each a combination of Amelia Earhart and Marco Polo back from the dead. Kolya downplayed the attention while secretly appreciating it, but Zoe openly reveled in the fawning attentiveness of her classmates.

For both of them, scholastic reentry proceeded fairly effortlessly. Kolya actually finished the fourth chapter of his algebra book on the plane back from Denver, and his class started Chapter 5 the first day back. Zoe's class had been working on a semester-long science project that she was too late to join. Instead, her teachers asked her to create a poster display about her trip, which she completed with journal entries, photos, and show-and-tell souvenirs from Bali and Nepal. It was a hit at the science fair.

I knew from my many previous trips that the excitement of coming home lasts a precious few moments, so I tried to enjoy them. It was hard, though, not to feel like I'd awakened from a coma and was trying to catch up on a million details that piled up while I was incoherent. I spent hours on hold with phone companies, insurance companies, newspaper carriers, and assorted services that needed attending to. The moment I found myself saddled with a cell phone, a set of keys, and my all-too-familiar role as a chauffeur, staff sergeant, and maid, I was ready to quit. One week after arriving home, I wanted to board a plane and head somewhere else. *Irgund wohin. N'importe ou.*

"Hey kids," I asked at dinner one night. "How'd you like to go to Africa and South America next?"

Kolya: "Not a chance in hell."

Zoe: "Sure. When?"

Routine chores quickly insinuated their own, uncompromising demands. Zoe's class held a potluck party, and I baked brownies for the occasion. I realized with satisfaction that I knew many of the kids in Zoe's class, her teachers of course, the school janitor, and also many of the parents. That had been less the case when I was married to Rebecca.

A mother tasted my brownies approvingly. "You didn't *bake* these, did you?" she asked, with too much incredulity in her voice.

No, I had my maid do it, I snidely replied to myself, hopefully without opening my mouth.

"Why yes, I did. It was a mix, but I added a few things to it."

"They're delicious."

"Thank you." I am developing an affectionate relationship with my inner Betty Crocker.

At home, however, I suffered the slings and arrows shared by housewives across the nation when I tried to prepare something more interesting than Kraft macaroni and cheese for dinner.

"Nasty! You put anchovies in it!"

"They're not anchovies, they're capers."

"Nasty! I hate them."

"Have you ever actually tried them?" I said to Kolya, making him a little green offering.

"Yeah, they were nasty."

Me, sighing, "Just pick them out."

I felt contrite for my past sins, thinking of all the times my brothers and I would look at a plate of *something* unrecognizable that

Mom had made and said, "Yecch," the 1960s equivalent of "nasty" to her. But although a single generation has shifted us from *Ozzie and Harriet* to *Ozzie Osbourne*, I will not succumb to the temptation of feeding them a diet of hamburgers and microwave dinners.

We decorated our living room with new treasures from the Orient: a Balinese mask, our Tibetan thangka, the Ganeshes we hand-carried back from Kathmandu. The kids' rooms filled with their own souvenirs, each one accompanied by a story, a bargaining session, the memory of a shopkeeper's face.

Before we could even catch our back-to-school rhythm, the holidays came around. Rebecca had planned to come out to spend the time between Christmas until just after New Year's with the kids, and I had arranged to go up to a mountain cabin with Tory and write the proposal for this book. Rebecca would stay in the house with the kids.

We had already begun something of a new family ritual on the first night that Rebecca came out to stay with the kids—as strange as it seemed at times, the four of us would go out to dinner. This time we went in honor of Zoe's tenth birthday on December 27. We regaled Rebecca with tales of our travels, and she pulled me aside and thanked me for doing this for and with the kids.

When I returned from my short working vacation, trouble awaited. Kolya had given his Nepali "gifts" to his friends, and as I had predicted, one of the parents found a pipe lying around. As I had also predicted, the friend quickly identified Kolya as the source of said pipe, and a second kid also came clean to *his* parents.

Kolya told me the story, head hanging. "I know, I know, you told me so."

"What can I say, Kolya? I'm screwed."

"I'm sorry. I mean it," he said, and I believe he did. It didn't help.

I called up the parents, trying to blunt the inevitable accusations about my singularly poor judgment with preemptive abject apologies. At one point, I thought of trying Kolya's logic that their kids would smoke dope whether or not Kolya gave them a pipe, but I decided that an unequivocal expression of regret was preferable.

Then, as Kolya had surmised in his journal, I let him know bluntly that what had happened in Australia and Amsterdam was an anomaly. We were back to "Just Say Not Yet."

As part of Kolya's agreement with his teachers, he had to do a presentation on his trip before his entire school. He put together a slide show and acquitted himself admirably. I sat there quietly, hitting the button to bring on the next slide, listening to him, marveling at the contrast between his nonchalance when he mentioned the trip to me and his sense of accomplishment and pride when he talked about the trip to the audience.

Even, to my surprise, when the subject was me.

One kid asked Kolya how we dealt with the language issues, noting that it must have been weird being in a place where nobody spoke English. Kolya answered, exaggerating extravagantly, "My Dad spoke pretty much every language in every place we went." A teacher asked him to name one of the things that he remembered most vividly, and he replied that seeing the poverty in Cambodia really made an impression on him. Kids there played with nothing but rocks and sticks.

At dinner that night, I complimented him on his presentation and joked again about going to Africa and South America next. He looked at me like I was completely crazy.

Then, a few months later, the three of us were interviewed on a National Public Radio show about our trip, and Kolya surprised me when he was asked about his willingness to go someplace else.

"So where to next?" the interviewer asked. "Would you do this again?"

"In a long time, and for not as long a time," Kolya replied. "I could see a month in Africa or something. That's about my max for time."

As far as I'm concerned, that could make for a pretty interesting adventure. I know that mountain gorillas in Rwanda are in deep trouble . . .

EPILOGUE

The Glue that holds humanity together

*The author, Kolya, and Zoe
at Ta Phrom ruins, Siem Reap, Cambodia.*

MORE THAN a year after our return, the kids and I continue to reinvent ourselves as a new, if idiosyncratic, family unit. The other evening, I prepared a pork roast, mashed potatoes, gravy, and green beans after picking Kolya up from basketball practice and Zoe from gymnastics. With my best June Cleaver voice, I cheerfully called the kids to the table. Zoe took a look and exclaimed, "This looks just like a *real* family dinner!"

I am an imperfect Dad, as both Kolya and Zoe tell me frequently: quick to anger, demanding in my expectations, frustrated at my inability to be in three places at the same time. Zoe feels acutely that she has been slighted because I, of all people, am her only day-to-day parent. When she recently recounted an interaction with her school friends and I made some *obviously* bone-headed remark, she calmly took my hand in hers and pretended to use sign language in my palm. When I still didn't get her point, she sighed. "Dad you're clueless. You're like Helen Keller." She continued to sign into my palm, hoping that she might lift me from my sheltered, drab world into the radiance of her insight and beauty.

Kolya has now started high school, and I'm elated that we went on the trip when we did. We traveled through a perfect window of opportunity, as I'm certain he wouldn't go on a similar adventure willingly if I proposed it today. He is a mass of mercurial adolescent behavior; sweet one moment and staring at me nearly eye-to-eye with fierce, challenging, ice-blue eyes the next. I watch with pride and trepidation as he becomes more independent and more adventurous—crowd surfing at punk concerts and navigating public buses to friends' houses around town. I drive him to soccer practices and the skateboard park, pick him up from snowboarding, and attend his parent-teacher conferences, catching glimpses of his inner life while ferrying him and his friends to the movies and listening to their banter.

Kolya and Zoe are each somehow making sense of what has happened to all of us. They see Rebecca only sporadically but talk to her regularly. They are alternately nonchalant, angry, frustrated, and sad that their mother is so far away. I worry about how they have internalized or rationalized their mother's departure, but they appear generally reconciled to their lot. At bedtime the other day, Zoe casually calculated that for nearly a third of her life, she has lived virtually full-time with me.

These days, the kids and I don't do that much as a trio. Kolya and Zoe seem to think that the fact that we spent five months traveling together "24/7" means they have satisfied a lifetime supply of family togetherness. We share sporadic moments together at school-night pork-roast dinners, during an occasional ski day, on a spontaneous foray to the ice-cream parlor, or while taking a trip to our Thanksgiving gathering at Grandma and Grandpa's. The two of them are getting along much better, as I predicted they would; Kolya even sought Zoe's fashion advice before the freshman homecoming dance.

I've concluded that I'm a good enough Dad. It will have to do.

I still struggle with the awkward balance between leading my own life and showing up for the kids. As I was completing the book, Tory and I came to the conclusion that we couldn't figure out a way to continue our relationship dance. It would be easy to say that the rebound relationship was bound to failure, that I had started seeing Tory at a time when I wasn't emotionally capable of having a meaningful relationship with anyone, even a pet. But it's not that simple. I know I have hidden behind the kids to some extent, cloaking my own emotional needs under the blanket of fatherhood's demands. Like many single parents I've met, I have learned the painful lesson that starting a new relationship is a perilous high-wire act that involves balancing old loves with a new one. As I become more comfortable with my role as single father, I think I will be more open than I was able to be with Tory. Zoe, at least, does not have to worry imminently about the strange and wonderful twist her life would take if both her parents remarried. "If you marry Tory and Momma marries her girlfriend," she told me on the trip, "I'll have a dad, a mom, and two stepmoms."

I digest our trip in small bites: through an image from a dream that I recall when I awaken in the middle of the night or a story I hear Zoe telling a friend's mother about Borneo. I replay the cascade of events that led to the trip in snippets of nighttime reveries and in long gazes out of my car window toward the receding horizons of memory: Rebecca's departure, Bob's cancer, years of emotional floundering.

This much is clear: The trials of these past few years have brought with them an unparalleled and transformative time in my life. I feel more complete, less judgmental, more approachable. After Bob died, it surprised me to learn how many of my acquaintances had lost siblings to accidents, to childhood diseases, to cancer. Bob's story evoked their stories, hidden from plain view but obviously still resonating. Those friends offered touching condolences with the quaver that comes with hard-won compassion. Only now do I feel as if I am able to return the favor as a full-fledged member of the human race.

Our 'round-the-world journey, as journeys are wont to do, served the anticipated purposes of allowing me to both hide and seek—from my pain and into uncharted lands. Although I physically reemerged at the same spot where I started, my metaphorical journey has taken me, as kindly drivers did when I hitchhiked through Europe, "somewhere else." I am certain that the emotional challenges of the past few years rendered me a fuller human being, and I can honestly say that I am glad to have experienced such vulnerability and awakened more fully to my humanity. After such a long and intense period of disequilibrium, I feel, finally, as if I am reclaiming my life.

I often think about our experiences on the trip, and some of the events have gained meaning for me as I have reflected upon them. One memory that stands out is the time, back in Nepal, after our elephant-back extravaganza near Chitwan National Park, when I wandered into a little shop to telephone my friend Keith in Kathmandu. The phone lines were iffy and it took awhile to get through, so I struck up a conversation with the owner, who appeared to be about my age. He told me he split his time between Kathmandu and Chitwan and said he was divorced, which was interesting not only because of its relative rarity in Nepal but also because sharing that information with a stranger was equally uncharacteristic. He said that his daughter lived with him, which was rarer still. I told him my story, how I was visiting his country with my two kids after their mom and I had divorced.

He said the past few years had been hard for him, because in addition to the divorce, his father had recently died of cancer. I offered my condolences and, fearful of matching him tragic revelation for tragic revelation, told him about Bob. He expressed his condolences and we shook our heads. Ke garne, what to do?

We sat in silence, the pair of us, two men born and raised halfway across the world from each other. He could no more imagine taking his daughter on a trip around the world than I could imagine raising my children on the subcontinent. But here we were, sipping tea, sharing our sadness and our stories and an occasional comfortable silence as if it were the most natural thing in the world.

Grief and loss, I've come to believe, provide the glue that binds humanity together. Our grief helps us feel compassion for others who grieve. Our losses send us wading into the vast ocean of collective memory to remember dead children, parents, siblings, friends, landscapes, animals, and even our lost dreams. We cast and recast into that pounding memory surf until we have caught something of meaning. Out of those morsels of meaning we create, and recreate, our lives.

I wear a black onyx earring in my left ear that was Bob's, a gift from Renda after he died. I also inherited his tuxedo, a pair of silver-tipped cowboy boots, and many of his other clothes. Sometimes I dress up like him, even though I'm not much of a silver-tipped cowboy boot kind of guy. I live with Bob's death as if it were an old war wound or a sports injury that acts up from time to time when the weather changes or it's damp or cold. It is as much a part of me as the color of my eyes or the birthmark on my stomach. I finger the onyx on my left ear regularly, a somber and reassuring touchstone that links me to my lost brother.

I feel my breast regularly as well, as I imagine women do who have had sisters or mothers who have had breast cancer.

I call my parents and my brother solely to tell them that I love them.

I hug my children extravagantly, and often.

Once upon a time, Nature held forth in inscrutable fashion over all that creepeth and crawleth and flieth. Ice ages came and went, forcing plants and animals to migrate northward or southward, dooming some to extinction and forcing others into clever adaptations. Floods, hurricanes, earthquakes, fires, meteors, and cosmic events have helped to shape our planet and its life forms over the past four billion years or so.

Then something remarkable happened. At the dawn of the industrial revolution, when the human population was 1.5 billion, one species began manifesting as something almost unimaginable: *Homo sapiens* became a force of nature unto themselves, capable of altering the planet's basic mechanisms, ecosystems, and life forms.

More than 6.2 billion people now inhabit the planet. These days, virtually every reputable atmospheric scientist believes that humans, through their industrial effluent, are contributing to the transformation of our planet's womb. Every ecologist, wildlife biologist, botanist, zoologist, and researcher from any branch of science that studies the earth's natural systems would agree: Humans are proceeding with an uncontrolled experiment on our planet and are accelerating the rate at which its plants and animals are disappearing.

Wherever Kolya, Zoe, and I went on our journey, we witnessed evidence of looming environmental crises. After our return, a global environmental conference in Johannesburg, South Africa, urgently warned of increasing environmental degradation— brought on by desperate poverty in much of the developing world and obsessive consumerism in the West. As humans debate the severity of the planet's symptoms and the feasibility of various cures, the list of threatened and endangered plants and animals continues to lengthen.

We humans are destroying so much of our natural world, and it infuriates me that we are so reckless and heedless despite over-whelming evidence of the damage. Our political system, however, especially in its current incarnation, is hopelessly tilted toward a status quo that, by any objective measure, will not stop or even slow the destruction.

Why, I want to know, do we ignore the voices of our modern-day prophets, who warn of what is happening to the planet's health and our human psyche? Former Catholic monk and eco-philosopher Thomas Berry, in an interview published in the May 2002 issue of *The Sun,* suggested that nurturing the relationship between human and nonhuman communities is as fundamental to our survival as air or food or water: "There is only one community, and it lives and dies as a unit. Any harm done to the natural world diminishes the human world—and not only for the physical resources but also for psychic development and fulfillment."

Scientists, theologians, philosophers, writers, artists, and a few rare politicians are all eloquently and persuasively warning against eating our seed corn. I want to ask the whole world the question I asked Kolya: How do you feel, knowing that the orangutan and the Javan rhino and the Bengal tiger may soon be gone forever?

In certain Native American traditions, it is customary at the beginning of important rituals to invoke the importance of the web of life by saying, "All my relations." In the Lakota language, it's *Mitakuye oyasin,* an invitation and acknowledgment not just to our blood kin, living and dead, but to all the connections that make it possible for us to survive: our relations to the elk that we kill to feed our children; to the lichen that feed the elk; to the rock that hosts the lichen; to the forces that heated that rock and cooled it so the lichen might live. The invocation encompasses generations long passed to the spirit world and includes generations that will follow our footsteps on this earth.

Just about every major world religion, and many of the minor ones, subscribes to a creation myth that describes a male figure and a female figure, the primordial progenitors. In some myths they are two forces of nature. Sometimes they are two gods. Sometimes a god mates with a human. And sometimes a god, or the gods, creates two humans. Adam and Eve. Zeus and Athena. Izanagi and Izanami. In one way or another, the First Couple begets and begats the rest of the world.

The dominant scientific explanation for the evolution of life on earth shares a similar reductive theme. Physical anthropologists believe that *Homo sapiens* were preceded by several generations of *Homo erectus, Homo habilis,* and the first homonid, *Australopithecus.* Beyond that, humans derived from primates and before that from an unfathomably long period of mutation and natural adaptation.

In this evolutionary worldview, the begetting and begatting dates back to a few supercharged amino acids that are, in effect, everybody's great-great-great-grandfather and grandmother.

What it comes down to is this: Whether you subscribe to Darwinist, Christian, or Lakota theology, humans all effectively share a common ancestry. The common ground we all share, in effect, is the common ground—and all life that bursts forth from it. Indigenous cultures, from the Aborigines in Australia to the Inuit in Alaska, recognize their tribe's interdependence with the land and the life that grows from it. Modern civilizations have done their best to ignore this simple fact, with potentially disastrous consequences.

We are mixing and merging globally in unprecedented ways, like my friends Keith and Shakun who begat the world's first *Jewkalis*. The world has been getting smaller, and its inhabitants more connected. In 1963, after the Berlin Blockade and the erection of the Berlin Wall, and six months before he was assassinated, President John F. Kennedy made his famous *Ich bin ein Berliner* ("I am a Berliner") speech, invoking the Western world's solidarity with the plight of East Berlin's residents, imprisoned in their city by stone walls and concertina wire.

On September 11, 2001, millions of people around the world felt a similar solidarity with the United States. After the first plane crashed into the north World Trade Center building at just before 9 A.M., people all over the world called each other and said, "Turn on the television!" When the second plane crashed into the south tower, and then when the building collapsed at around 10 A.M., millions upon millions watched it live. The moment represented the first truly contemporaneous global experience of shared loss. Even the notoriously disdainful French press responded with a headline in *Le Monde* echoing JFK: *Nous sommes tous américains*, "We are all Americans."

So, here's my one big idea I learned from our trip. If, as I've suggested, September 11, 2001, provided the world with its first live, universal image of loss, that horrific day also bound much of humanity together in its glue. That sense of loss created infinite possibility for healing, possibility that has so far gone unrealized. If grief and loss are transformative, we are still waiting to learn our lessons—especially in this moment when so much of the world seems lost in hostility and in multiple threats of war.

I find optimism in the nearly universal theme of death and rebirth that is essential to so many cultures' mythologies and theologies. Thomas Berry has argued that people in many cultures readily accept the idea that they can be "reborn" in a given lifetime. "If such deep transformation is a normal human process," he said, "then it is feasible for it to occur on a cultural level as well."

I've also come to understand a simple truth in all my wanderings: The fundamental principle of conservation biology—that every organism in an ecological system is interconnected—applies not just to nature but to humans as well. As the nineteenth-century Scottish-born conservationist John Muir put it, "When we try to pick out anything by itself, we find it hitched to everything else in the Universe."

I don't pretend to understand the details of this Universal Theory of terrestrial relations. But I do believe that we are all inextricably hitched together as never before—by the warming waters of our seas, the melting glaciers of our poles, the diminishing canopy of our rainforests, and the disappearing marine life in our coral reefs. At this time of multiple crises, from the personal to the political to the humanitarian to the ecological, we need to realize a simple and profound fact that goes beyond JFK's exhortation and the headline in *Le Monde*:

We are all Earthlings.

Today, my view from the western edge of the Great Plains tells me that we were extremely fortunate to take our trip when we did.

World events conspire to make the world more frightening and incomprehensible each day. In Kuta beach on most lovely Bali, a bomb exploded in October 2002, killing nearly 200 people. News from Nepal brings worrisome reports that Maoist insurgents continue to kill and be killed. The unfolding aftermath of September 11 has led international authorities to uncover Al Qaeda cells in many places where we traveled, including Indonesia, Singapore, France, and Belgium. The volatile situation across the Muslim and Middle Eastern world, from Baghdad to Jerusalem, from Jakarta to Tehran, threatens all of us like the specter of an uncontrolled nuclear reaction. My heart goes out to all those whose lives are racked by violence, poverty, and the insanity of inhumanity.

I take some solace that, throughout the millennia of war and insurrection and famine and death, we humans have proven to be a resilient lot. We see hope in our children's eyes, foster hope for them in our own hearts. A few months after our return, the kids and I fell into a three-way embrace, pressing our noses up against each other and snuffling, snorting, reveling in our monkey kisses, our monkey selves. Every now and then, I am reminded that in a world of loss and wonder, the most appropriate response at times is a spirited hug—and a wild, exhilarating monkey dance.

ACKNOWLEDGMENTS

Travelers (and we're all travelers) always rely on the kindness of strangers. The patron saint who protects wayfarers has appeared to me in many forms over the years, bearing assorted gifts—a warm bed for the night, a home-cooked meal, a piece of ripe fruit, or the weary wanderer's greatest gift: a stranger's smile. During our trip, Kolya, Zoe, and I were oft visited by that patron saint—who appeared as a woman bearing directions to a secret swimming hole in Queensland, a Balinese shopkeeper who tied Zoe's sarong, a Nepali airline reservation agent who creatively finagled us tickets from Kathmandu to Zurich. We will do our best to pass those many kind gestures along the karmic chain.

I'd like to thank the following people especially, though this is an incomplete list of the generous and wonderful souls who helped us out or took us in: David and Laurie, for our send-off in Berkeley; Robin, Dean, and Shakti in Queensland; Lyndon and Catherine on Magnetic Island; "Darren Pearlman" and friends near Brisbane; Leonie, "Poor Dave," and Alice in Sydney; the folks at Orangutan Foundation International, especially Zaqie Al-Ichlas, Cristina Lebre, and the gang at Nam Cat Tien National Park in Vietnam; Scott and Sochua in Phnom Penh; Keith and Shakun in Kathmandu; K. C. and Kathleen, Daniel and Bénédicte, Jim and Véronique, Corrie and Thea, Milty, Jenny, and the Glucks of greater New York.

Thanks to the bus drivers, taxi drivers, waiters, waitresses, shop-keepers, guides, porters, hotel managers, park rangers, biologists, conservationists, and others who helped guide us along the way. A hoisted stubbie to Bill Pearce for helping to retrieve my cameras, and another heartfelt toast in honor of the couple from southern Australia who found my gear, whose names I wrote down but lost before I could properly thank them. I love Australians.

Grateful acknowledgment to Susan Cohen, Bill Drummond, David Littlejohn, and Bernard Taper from the University of California at Berkeley Graduate School of Journalism, for teaching me to get it right and to pay attention to detail.

To Martine Brechbuhl of Lausanne, Switzerland, who gave me my first typewriter—even though the "z" and the "y" were reversed.

Thanks to *Monkey Dancing*'s first readers, who helped me with blind spots and whose comments and insights I appreciated beyond words: Dorian Benkoil, Susan Booker, Bryan and Axson Morgan, Meg Lukens Noonan, and Wendy Redal. Special thanks to Jeannie Patton, who earned two gold stars for her sharp pencil and sharper eye.

To Lisa Kaufman, my patient and insightful editor, for showing the way to make this a far better book than I could have dreamed of by myself: Your words were wisdom, indeed.

To my agent, Scott Waxman, for doing everything an agent should do and more.

To my copyeditor, Kathy Streckfus, who gracefully reminded me how much I still have to learn about my native tongue.

To my friends and neighbors at Nyland CoHousing Community. Ten years and going strong. Thanks for being so stubbornly icono-clastic.

I'd like to thank Casey Sheahan at Kelty, whose friendship over the years supplied me with so much more than gear. The gear is great, though. To Kitty Graham at Cascade Designs, for her enthusiasm as well as assorted nifty camping stuff. You are the best at what you do. Thanks also to Janine Robertson at ExOfficio for the travel threads.

To our visionaries and prophets, who never tire of showing us there is a better way to think and to behave.

To all those who know loss, and grief, and smiles through tears.

To my family, all of them, for providing the strongest and most immediate strands of my web.

To my brother Steve. We are still here. I love you.

To my sister Renda. To love and remembrance.

To Tory, for opening my heart again.

To my parents, Ruth and Gene, for imparting to me an adventurous spirit and letting me follow it. You done good.

Lastly, to Kolya and Zoe: *ta, terima kasih, cám ón, ar kun, khap kuhn khrap, dhanyabaad, danke, merci, dank je wel, gracias,* and thanks, in order of countries we visited. The two of you contributed so much more than your characters and journal entries to this book. You also provided inspiration, the biggest challenges, and the funniest lines. I thank you both for your spirit of adventure, your (occasional) forbearance with my imperfections, and your implacable professorial styles. You continue to teach me more than I could ever teach you. Thanks for going along with Dad's crazy idea.

To all my relations.

PublicAffairs is a publishing house founded in 1997. It is a tribute to the standards, values, and flair of three persons who have served as mentors to countless reporters, writers, editors, and book people of all kinds, including me.

I. F. STONE, proprietor of *I. F. Stone's Weekly*, combined a commitment to the First Amendment with entrepreneurial zeal and reporting skill and became one of the great independent journalists in American history. At the age of eighty, Izzy published *The Trial of Socrates*, which was a national bestseller. He wrote the book after he taught himself ancient Greek.

BENJAMIN C. BRADLEE was for nearly thirty years the charismatic editorial leader of *The Washington Post*. It was Ben who gave the *Post* the range and courage to pursue such historic issues as Watergate. He supported his reporters with a tenacity that made them fearless and it is no accident that so many became authors of influential, best-selling books.

ROBERT L. BERNSTEIN, the chief executive of Random House for more than a quarter century, guided one of the nation's premier publishing houses. Bob was personally responsible for many books of political dissent and argument that challenged tyranny around the globe. He is also the founder and longtime chair of Human Rights Watch, one of the most respected human rights organizations in the world.

For fifty years, the banner of Public Affairs Press was carried by its owner, Morris B. Schnapper, who published Gandhi, Nasser, Toynbee, Truman, and about 1,500 other authors. In 1983, Schnapper was described by *The Washington Post* as "a redoubtable gadfly." His legacy will endure in the books to come.

Peter Osnos, *Publisher*

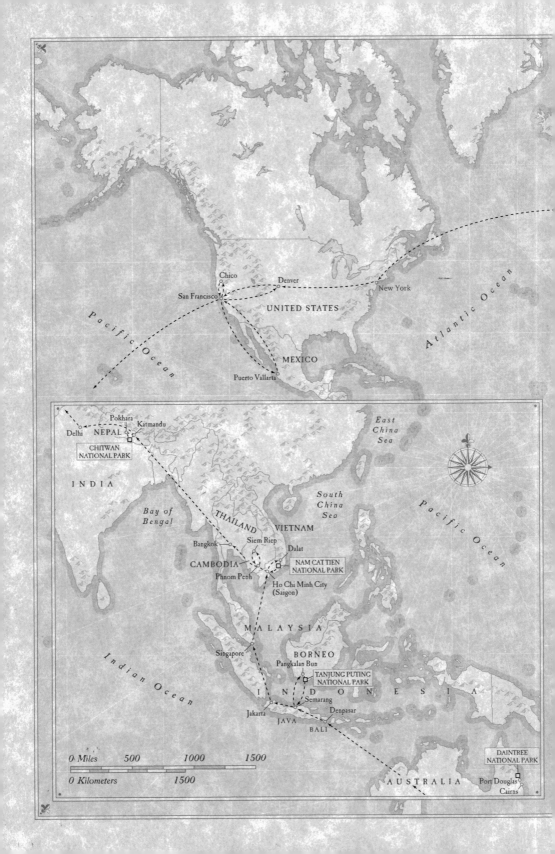